CW01018901

Implementing IPsec: Making Security Work on VPNs, Intranets, and Extranets

Implementing IPsec: Making Security Work on VPNs, Intranets, and Extranets

Elizabeth Kaufman

Andrew Newman

Wiley Computer Publishing

John Wiley & Sons, Inc.

NEW YORK · CHICHESTER · WEINHEIM · BRISBANE · SINGAPORE · TORONTO

Publisher: Robert Ipsen
Editor: Carol Long
Assistant Editor: Margaret Hendrey
Managing Editor: Frank Grazioli
Text Design & Composition: Benchmark Productions, Inc.

Designations used by companies to distinguish their products are often claimed as trademarks. In all instances where John Wiley & Sons, Inc., is aware of a claim, the product names appear in initial capital or ALL CAPITAL LETTERS. Readers, however, should contact the appropriate companies for more complete information regarding trademarks and registration.

This book is printed on acid-free paper. ∞

This publication is designed to provide accurate and authoritative information in regard to the subject matter covered. It is sold with the understanding that the publisher is not engaged in professional services. If professional advice or other expert assistance is required, the services of a competent professional person should be sought.

Authors' Disclaimer: Neither of our employers (Cisco Systems, Inc. and Yale University) had anything to do with this book or its contents. The opinions expressed are our own.

Library of Congress Cataloging-in-Publication Data:

ISBN 0-471-34467-2

Printed in the United States of America.

10 9 8 7 6 5 4 3 2 1

*To Angie and Nick, who had
the grace to pretend this project was
worth putting everything else on hold,
and the patience to wait it out.*

Contents

Acknowledgments

We take full responsibility for anything wrong or stupid in this book. We are, however, very grateful to several people for their generous assistance. Rob Adams, Dan Harkins, and Van Jacobsen all contributed valuable technical insight. Mary Emerson and Roszel Thomsen kindly reviewed and commented on the legal chapter.

We want to thank our patient reviewers, Steve Kent and Ed Kozel, for their restraint, their assistance, and their comments. Last, we thank our editors, Carol Long and Margaret Hendrey, for their fearlessness, their focus, and a lot of heavy lifting.

Foreword

The Networking Council Series was created in 1998 within Wiley's Computer Publishing group to fill an important gap in networking literature. Many current technical books are long on details but short on understanding. They do not give the reader a sense of where, in the universe of practical and theoretical knowledge, the technology might be useful for a particular organization. The Networking Council Series is concerned more with how to think clearly about networking issues than with promoting the virtues of a particular technology. It strives to relate new information to what readers already know and need, so they can develop customized strategies for vendor and product selection, outsourcing, and design.

In *Implementing IPsec: Making Security Work on VPNs, Intranets, and Extranets,* by Elizabeth Kaufman and Andrew Newman, you'll see the hallmarks of Networking Council books: examination of the advantages, disadvantages, strengths, and weaknesses of market-ready technology, useful ways to think about options pragmatically, and direct links to business practices and needs. The book also investigates pertinent background issues needed to understand who supports each technology and how it was developed—another goal of all Networking Council books.

The Networking Council Series is aimed at satisfying the need for perspective in an evolving data and telecommunications world filled with hyperbole, speculation, and unearned optimism. In *Implementing*

IPsec: Making Security Work on VPNs, Intranets, and Extranets, you'll get clear information from experienced practitioners.

We hope you enjoy this book. Let us know what you think. To contact us or get more information, visit the Networking Council Web site at www.wiley.com/networkingcouncil.

—Scott Bradner
Senior Technical Consultant, Harvard University

—Vinton Cerf
Senior Vice President, MCIWorldCom

—Lyman Chapin
Chief Scientist, BBN/GTE

—Ed Kozel
Senior VP Corporate Development, Cisco Systems

Introduction

The days of carefree networking are over. Today's IP networks carry billions of dollars worth of commercial transactions, intellectual property, and other data. Few network managers can afford to believe that their data will be able to sneak past the increasingly sophisticated cracking tools of their enemies, their competitors, or even the average bored adolescent. Several new security technologies are emerging to support this transition. Of these, the new IP security protocol (IPsec) has raised by far the most hope and, less auspiciously, hype as a possible cure for the widespread security problems of networks and networked applications.

   An overwhelming need for secure communications is driving many businesses to deploy first-generation IPsec products throughout their mission-critical infrastructures. People who would hesitate to buy a new brand of potato chip are now betting their business operations on this very green, very complex technology. Unfortunately, IPsec products can wreak havoc on critical applications and other enhanced network services. Interoperability problems between vendors, limitations in the base protocols, and failures to plan around known operational conflicts can cause difficulties that range from annoying to disastrous. Problems with IPsec could thus potentially outscore bored hackers as a new cause of catastrophic failures.

The IPsec protocols were designed to clear the hit list of well-known security flaws in the current Internet Protocol version 4 (IPv4) and to provide a preemptive strike against these same flaws in its possible replacement, the Internet Protocol version 6 (IPv6). They provide standard, highly generalized, cryptographic security mechanisms for authentication, access control, confidentiality, data integrity, replay protection, and protection against traffic flow analysis. They are also the only viable standards for secure network-layer transmission on IP. IPsec products can be valuable additions to an overall secure infrastructure.

Nevertheless, these same IPsec products can also create serious problems for critical applications and other enhanced network services. Ironically, network professionals have less time than ever before to study the details of protocol design and interaction that might enable them to avoid many problems specific to IPsec. As a result, configurations that looked fine in a lab are now having a "Godzilla Meets Network" impact on many large IP infrastructures. This book is a guide to surviving IPsec. It tries to answer the question "What do I need to know to deploy IPsec without breaking my network?"

You do not need to be an expert in IPsec protocol design to deploy IPsec products successfully. You do, however, need to understand its potential legal and operational impact on your network and your business. Many books will cover IPsec internals. This one is devoted primarily to its externals: how it interacts with the law and with other technologies, and how you can select products that will meet your needs.

How This Book Is Organized

We organized this book into four sections that map roughly onto a chronological planning and design process. Our objective is to provide an analytical and operational methodology that will help you to predict and avoid problems long after the details of this book are out of date. We encourage you, therefore, to go through the book more or less in order. It's tempting to skip ahead to the gory parts (the Martian invasion is always more interesting than the opening scenes in suburbia), but we urge you to read the background material first. Many of the technologies and regulations we discuss were still evolving as this book went to print. We urge you to double-check the details and to focus on understanding *why* things may not work rather than which specific things did not work at the moment we wrote about them.

Part One: Before You Start

Part One steps through the planning process for deploying any security technology and ends with a legal discussion specific to encryption technology. Chapter 2, "Laying the Groundwork for Security," describes how to document your network topology. Chapter 3, "Security Principles and Practices," discusses some of the issues surrounding security policies and practices. Chapter 4, "Encrypting within the Law," analyzes current worldwide regulatory trends for encryption technologies and examines how existing laws will impact your ability to legally purchase and install IPsec products.

Part Two: Technology Essentials

Part Two is a primer on the basic technological components of IPsec. Chapter 5, "The Risks of IP Networking," reviews the architectural characteristics of IPv4 that make it inherently insecure. Chapter 6, "Cryptographic Protocols and Techniques," is an overview of the cryptographic technologies fundamental to the current IPsec standards. Chapter 7, "The Basics of IPsec and Public Key Infrastructures," is an introduction to the IPsec protocols and key management techniques and also covers X.509 digital certificates and public key infrastructures (PKIs).

Part Three: Making It Work

In Part Three, we analyze how and why the IPsec protocols can break existing IP networks, and we discuss popular IPsec design scenarios. Chapter 8, "What Won't Work with IPsec," describes the root causes of IPsec performance problems and protocol conflicts and reviews the operational impact of combining various IPsec protocols with many common network services and technologies. Chapter 9, "IPsec and PKI Rollout Considerations," discusses gateway-to-gateway, end host-to-gateway, and end host-to-end host configuration options and explains some of the policy elements of a PKI.

Part Four: Going Shopping

Part Four provides some criteria for evaluating vendors and products. Chapter 10, "Evaluating Vendors," is a brief discussion of what to look for in an IPsec product supplier, and Chapter 11, "What to Ask Your Vendors," is a sample request for information (RFI) that you can use to compare IPsec product offerings and to evaluate their features in an operational context.

Finally, we give you some reference material, including an appendix, the IPsec RFC (2401), "Security Architecture for the Internet Protocol," plus a glossary and a bibliography of sources and further reading.

Who Should Read This Book

This book is for network managers and for network security professionals who can't afford a trial-and-error approach to deploying IPsec products on their production networks. It is not a guide for coders or for people who want a detailed anatomy of IPsec internals. We recommend that you refer to the published standards for IPsec (see RFC 2401) for protocol specifics. Security experts may want to skim Part One and Part Two, since they review basics of network security, policy, and cryptographic techniques. Network managers may want to skip the network mapping section in Chapter 2, "Laying the Groundwork for Security."

Conclusion

This book focuses on problems in order to help you avoid them. We do not hate IPsec, and we do not believe that any other comprehensive IP security technology could have avoided most of the operational pitfalls we describe here. It will probably never be possible just to sprinkle magic security dust over a large IP network and walk away. We do expect that IPsec products will become more interoperable, more functional, and easier to use as they mature. Do not wait, however, to enhance the security of your network. The people who want to steal or tamper with your data don't need that much of a head start. We hope this book helps you avoid some war stories (or gives you time to invent them instead of living through them). Good luck, and safe networking.

Before You Start

To deploy any new security technology effectively, you need a comprehensive knowledge of your IP topology, as well as a plan of action. Chapters 2 and 3 provide some basic guidelines for mapping an IP network and creating a security policy or, when that proves unfeasible, a set of principles and a prioritized plan of action. Experienced network managers and security professionals may want to skim these chapters or skip them altogether. Chapter 4 discusses the worldwide legal restrictions on the import, export, and domestic use of encryption technologies, and explains how those restrictions will affect your own use of IPsec products.

Laying the Groundwork
for Security

This chapter and the next discuss some basic prerequisites for adding security technology to a running IP network. This chapter emphasizes network and application mapping, which provides the analytical basis for Chapter 8, "What Won't Work with IPsec," and Chapter 9, "IPsec and PKI Rollout Considerations," in which we evaluate specific IPsec operations and design. Chapter 3, "Security Principles and Practices," outlines some basics of network security methodology. If you are already proficient in networking and security, we encourage you to scan the mapping section in this chapter, then skip directly to Chapter 4, "Encrypting within the Law."

Beyond Links and Perimeters

Traditional TCP/IP security commonly includes perimeter firewalls, bulk link encryptors, or, more recently, application-specific technologies such as *Secure Sockets Layer* (SSL). None of these mechanisms is as sensitive to the logical (network-layer) topology as IPsec. While it is sometimes possible to deploy traditional security products without thorough planning, it is impossible to wing it at any scale with IPsec. While it may be tempting to step straight into experimenting with or even deploying IPsec products on your network, resist the urge to jump straight to operation. A rushed approach will almost certainly have unexpected results and will not improve your overall network security.

The Tedium of Good Planning

Effective operational security is about 80 percent legwork and 20 percent technology. Whether you were drawn to investigate network security as an extension of your existing job or just because you love the technology, you have probably already discovered that most of the legwork is painstaking and tedious. Security work almost never involves tracking down the Hanover Hacker. Even if you do eventually confront an intruder, he will almost invariably prove to be an unlikable 12-year-old twerp with no life, a modem, and at least one parent who is a lawyer. The pursuit is often more interesting than the capture. The bulk of network security is (hopefully proactive) research, operations planning, and the cascading detail of best-effort prevention. The overwhelmingly nitpicking nature of good operational security explains why most long-time security professionals eventually beat a retreat to the relatively bigger-picture occupations of designing security products, farming llamas, or writing books.

Many of the tasks outlined in this chapter are both demanding and uninteresting. Small oversights can have significant consequences, however. Think carefully before you decide to skip the planning process and go straight into designing your security plan or deploying a new IPsec product. Good security relies on a sound knowledge of technical and organizational minutiae that vary from network to network. Blind spots will weaken or even break your overall solution.

Security Manager or Network Manager?

In many large organizations, network management and network security live in two (or more) distinct parts of the company with different budgets and reporting structures. If you are a security professional, you will find that your job is increasingly entangled with that of the network management staff, for the three major reasons that follow.

Dynamic Addresses, Mobile Users

First, network security is increasingly granular and dynamic. As Dynamic Host Configuration Protocol (DHCP) becomes prevalent and people need access to data from more locations inside and outside your company, your security solutions will need to adapt to a dynamic IP network in order to authenticate users and enforce security principles. In the past, both users and IP addresses tended to be static. The average person might have had one address for his PC or workstation on the corporate LAN and another for his home SLIP or PPP connection. Today, corporate users often drag their laptops around with them and obtain new addresses every time they restart their machines. They expect to work on business trips from airports, from hotels, or even from networks at other companies. Security perimeters can no longer work from static rules that associate a person with one or two IP addresses. Instead, they must rely on various user authentication technologies to identify users and their privileges, while also taking into account any additional constraints associated with a given user's current physical location. For example, you may want to make a sensitive database accessible to administrative staff when those employees are on the corporate network or connected via ISDN, but not when they attempt to connect across the Internet firewall. Security technology must be increasingly tuned to the activities of the IP infrastructure in order to apply meaningful restrictions and exceptions.

The Integration of Security with the Infrastructure

The second factor driving security professionals into networking organizations is the evolution of technology: Over time, security technologies are becoming increasingly integrated with the IP routing and switching infrastructure. Virtual private network (VPN) appliances, for example, displaced standalone encryption boxes. Now they, in turn, are sharing the market with VPN-enhanced routers. Standalone firewalls also seem to be evolving toward embedded software and/or hardware firewall components.

The technological evolution is a reasonable one. Most current standalone security technologies address fundamental design issues with the Internet Protocol. As a security technology matures, it is most transparent as an integrated network function, enabling secure deployment of other enhanced network and application services. Network vendors will force integration for other reasons as well. Security technology helps maintain high margins on IP networking equipment, for which the market is becoming increasingly price-competitive. Additional value helps vendors counteract the rapid commoditization of the core IP equipment business. Standalone firewall or VPN management consoles will probably migrate into classical network management applications, for the same reasons. Of course, overlaying security features on a general-purpose device can result in a lower level of security, even as it permits greater network functionality.

The Need to Avoid Downtime

The third, most practical factor is the fact that the new generation of security technology is capable of crippling more network functions than any of its predecessors. While the first wave of firewall installations caused many spectacular failures, these failures were straightforward (connections did not work) and easy to diagnose. IPsec can cause more subtle effects (see Chapter 8 for details) and often requires more sophisticated troubleshooting. The golden days of hours-long outages that no one seems to notice are past as well. Most organizations are so dependent on the robust operation of their IP networks that they try to avoid any downtime at all, even late at night and on holidays.

As security functionality drives deeper into the network, more network managers will need to learn the basics of security planning and deployment. As they plan for IPsec, security professionals will have to understand and plan for their corporate network and applications infrastructure—often for the first time. IP networks and security technology will become increasingly integrated over the next several years. Regardless of organizational or philosophical barriers, network and security managers should plan on being bunkmates and close collaborators for the long term.

Who Should Keep Reading

The rest of this chapter applies equally to network managers and security professionals, but may be more intuitively obvious to someone with a strong background in networking. It describes a layered approach to finding and documenting the network. While it might be possible to manage a couple of firewalls without reference to a detailed network map, you cannot deploy IPsec in the same way, even if you intend to manage thousands of end-host implementations in an exclusively end-to-end IPsec environment (see Chapter 9).

Mapping Your Network

Unless you are among the rare few who have designed and built a brand-new network from scratch, you will need to spend a large chunk of time researching your existing infrastructure before you can deploy IPsec effectively. This research is particularly important if you intend to deploy IPsec gateways in addition to (or instead of) relying on end-host products. In the world of network security, the unknown or undocumented is fundamentally insecure. Regardless of existing plans and policies, the truth is always and only on the wire: You need to know what's out there before you do anything else. To secure your network, you must find it first. You must identify every way into and out of it. You must document its current users, services, and access mechanisms, as well as plans for new connections and services. A detailed network map is your blueprint for success with IPsec, so that you not only know what to protect, but also can avoid breaking something critical.

Most Networks Have Hearts of Darkness

Maps of large networks tend to resemble the old Psalter world map (c. 1250 A.D.): a familiar spiritual center surrounded by sketchy masses, with dragons and supernatural figures at the edge (see http://portico.bl.uk/exhibitions/maps/psalter.html). Even if what's there is accurate, a lot of important information is missing. Most networks are collages of undocumented internal and external connections, with overlays of managed, well-understood backbone, access, and perimeter devices.

Building a complete, accurate map of your physical and logical network may be a task on the order of counting fleas in a kennel. In some cases, parts of your network will be so remote or inscrutable that they defy documentation. You must at least get a complete understanding of the areas that house or transport sensitive data, as well as locations that support important resources and users. If you choose to ignore or bypass parts of your network, you must indeed treat them as the fiery edges of the known world: Here there be dragons.

The Physical Infrastructure

The most straightforward, most powerful, and most difficult way to map a network is to start at the physical layer and move up the protocol stack. Your first task is to find the wires. An accurate physical topology is the only way to get three important pieces of information about your network: where data enters, where it exits, and how it travels. Figure 2.1 shows a typical network diagram.

While you probably already know how the major parts of your network hang together, you probably do not have a comparable grasp of all the external connections that terminate somewhere inside your network perimeter. These connections may include lines leased to other organizations, departmental remote access servers and Internet connections, and analog or digital dial-up devices on individual network-connected PCs. Finding these sorts of links is notoriously difficult. Network discovery tools are not sufficient, as they rarely reveal intermittent connections and can't find modems at all. Do not panic. You most likely will not need to scour every hall and ceiling of your multinational business to get a good idea of what's out there.

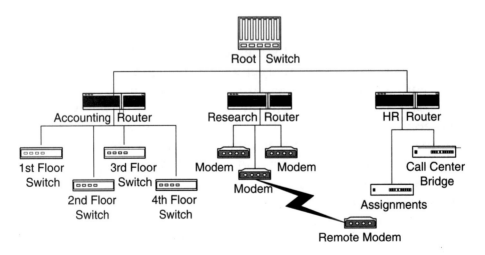

Figure 2.1   Logical diagram of a network core.

Three Ways to Find a Network

To get a decent map of your true connectivity in a reasonably nonintrusive way, you need to think like a detective, an accountant, and a hacker. Each approach will yield different information, depending on your business and what you are looking for. Of course, you can also pay a consulting firm to find your network. Outside consultants will save you time and stress, but they don't have the network equivalent of a divining rod. A consulting firm will generally charge a hefty fee for results that will be similar to, but much prettier than, what you would produce on your own.

The Sherlock Method

The detective method begins with a street-map-level view of your business. Identify buildings or parts of buildings that house organizational resources. Create a matrix for each building that identifies the types of connections you are looking for: analog modems, leased lines, dial-on-demand ISDN, and so on. Call the people in charge of the facilities in each area and ask what kinds of network connections they have. Talk to the local network administrator and ask for current maps. Ask if the local staff collaborates electronically with partners or contractors, and how that collaboration works (file transfer, email, shared server, etc.). It may seem like an onerous task, but phone calls take longer to think about than to make. Whoever helps out with local PC and printer problems may also know something about local connectivity. The Sherlock method is most likely to find active departmental Internet and partner connections, as well as a few modems. You may want to document each local segment of your network graphically, as shown in Figure 2.2.

Following the Phone Bills

When you have exhausted the useful information you can get over the phone or by email, start thinking like an accountant. Sometimes the best way to map layer 1 (the physical layer) is to start at layer 9 (the bureaucratic layer). The Bean Counter's Corollary states that for every external connection (except some homegrown or wireless connections) there is also a phone bill. Find a current organizational chart for your business, and locate the people who see the actual phone bills for your areas of interest. Phone bills often go to a central IS organization, which rolls them up and bills them back against a departmental budget. You

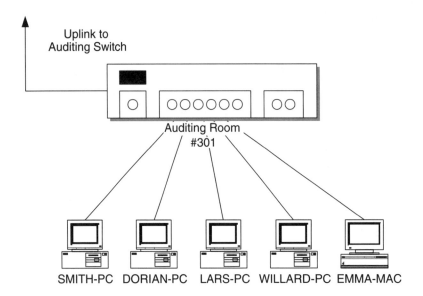

Uplink to
Auditing Switch

Auditing Room
#301

SMITH-PC DORIAN-PC LARS-PC WILLARD-PC EMMA-MAC

Figure 2.2 Detail of a local segment.

need to find someone who spot-checks the actual bills. You are looking for ISDN charges, analog lines (if your business has a digital Private Branch Exchange [PBX]), and leased line or frame relay charges. If you work for a large company with a small number of network and telephone service providers, ask your providers to give you a list of all your active connections, organized by location and type. If they're sending you bills, they should be able to tell you why. The accountant approach, where feasible, is best for locating expensive or toll-based dial-out connections. It may not find all of your analog modems, especially if they're used primarily for inbound access.

Seeing What Answers

The last investigative approach is to put on a hacker hat and see what answers the phone on your company's phone numbers. The Internet has many free versions of so-called war dialers, software that will automatically dial through a range of phone numbers and record which numbers answer with some kind of handshake tones.

CAUTION Be aware that it may be illegal to run a war dialer against numbers that do not belong to you.

Any search engine can find you several Internet Web sites that offer war dialers. You want to locate one that can differentiate among modem, fax, and PBX tones and can log which numbers answer with what tones. One common war dialer is called Tone Loc. Most freeware packages cannot perform detailed exploits against whatever answers the phone—if you are curious to see how bad the exposure is, you need to do some poking about by hand. Be very careful downloading and operating software from any site you do not know and trust. Test any package you plan to use on a standalone, guinea-pig PC against an iso-lated modem. Remember that the person who writes and posts a war dialer may have a personal passion for breaking into hosts and net-works just like your own.

The IP and Applications Infrastructure

The physical topology identifies the entry, exit, and transit paths for all data; in a rough way, it delineates potentially exposed access points to your network. The IP topology identifies important hosts and services and their major user groups; it describes the communications you need to protect, as well as their access methods.

Documenting your IP network should be easier than finding the wires it runs on. You do not need a complete inventory of IP entities. Such inventories are virtually impossible to build, especially since most large networks use dynamic addresses for end-user machines. Many public-domain and commercial software packages will find IP hosts and services (see Figure 2.3). Be careful about running them during

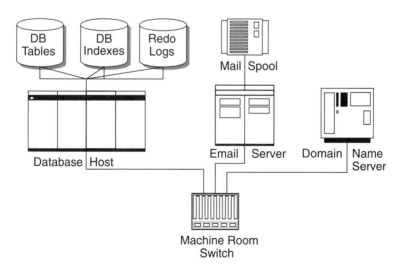

Figure 2.3 Network services.

business or high-use hours, and make sure you understand how they work. Some tools simply ping (send ICMP echo requests) through an entire network range, logging which hosts respond, but potentially clogging your network in the process. Other tools rely on router ARP caches (dynamic maps of the physical layer to IP addresses built by the Address Resolution Protocol) and then sequentially probe each IP entity to discover its active services. Like the security scanning tools described in Chapter 3, IP discovery tools can be intrusive to busy hosts and networks. Do not run any kind of scanning or probing tool during peak use hours.

Work around Existing Perimeters

If you already have firewalls, IP tunneling devices, or network address translation (NAT) boxes installed on your network, you need to run your IP discovery tools on the internal interface or interfaces of these devices in order to locate end systems. Your priority is to find major services, such as internal Web servers, and the rough logical location of their users. For example, your internal Human Resources Web server may be at 10.0.0.2, while the Human Resources staff LAN gets dynamic addresses from the 10.30.32.0 subnet. Users tend to move around inside and outside the company. Try to ascertain what the access requirements are for remote connectivity to any given service. Do the HR employees need to access their Web server from the corporate dial-up servers? Do contractors need access across the Internet from other companies? Bear in mind that if an important resource needs to be accessible to everyone from anywhere, it will be exceptionally difficult to secure. In Chapter 3, we'll lay out a tactical approach to developing a matrix of security priorities and principles that will allow you to evaluate the sensitivity of each key service and recommend specific changes.

Keep in mind that IP routing topologies are generally dynamic, and they can have a major impact on IPsec planning. Keep an eye on the normal traffic flow and on any fallback configurations. Look for and document any dial-on-demand backup links inside your network that might route traffic past a potential security perimeter.

Network Properties of Important Applications

Some advanced network applications rely on enhanced IP services such as multicast or QoS. Video and multimedia applications, for example, almost always require network protocol support beyond vanilla IP. Other applications are sensitive to delay or packet loss. Many backup software packages are highly intolerant of packet loss. IBM mainframe Systems Network Architecture (SNA) applications tend to be sensitive to delay, especially if encapsulated for wide area transmission in data-link switching (DLSw) packets.

As you document your network, make a note of any application or protocol that relies on special network support or encapsulation or that may be especially impaired by delays. IPsec, as we will explain in depth in Chapter 8, can wreak havoc on enhanced IP services. Dynamic multicast applications introduce distinct topology challenges, and the periodic pause in IPsec packet forwarding during Diffie-Hellman key generation can introduce time-outs and connection failures for delay-sensitive applications that persist long enough to require rekeying.

Finding these applications and services tells you what hole to punch where in your IPsec configuration. It provides the only accurate forecast of what you may be about to break.

Planned Services

Many large corporate networks are in the early days of a profound two-stage transformation. They are transitioning from an ad-hoc medium for internal information exchange to an organized foundation for internal communications (an *intranet*) and, at the same time, a critical staging ground for corporate business with partners and customers (an *extranet*). These transitions mean new applications and connections to your network, as well as new uses and users for old applications. The network is bound to change rapidly to support the new requirements that accompany these new uses. Ideally, these changes would be planned in advance and managed carefully. Often the best you can hope for, however, is that they are not totally unexpected. Find out what major changes are budgeted for the next year— major upgrades to current applications, new service offerings, and new applications. Even if your company does not currently depend on encapsulation or special IP protocols, someone somewhere has plans to change that.

To secure a network is fundamentally a composting problem: People never throw anything away, but continually layer new elements onto the existing base. The more you know about what's out there, the simpler it will be to identify your priorities and deploy effective solutions. In the case of IPsec, detailed knowledge of your network infrastructure is important to help you avoid mangling mission-critical services and applications.

CHAPTER 3

Security Principles and Practices

This chapter presents some ins and outs of taking on network security in a large and potentially indifferent organization. All of our recommendations are relevant to deploying IPsec, but few of them are particular to it. The advice that follows applies to network security in general, rather than to specific IPsec protocols.

   If you are a security professional with significant operational expertise, our suggestions may seem oversimplified, or may seem to neglect some basic principles of data security. If at all possible, we encourage you to take the tried-and-true policy-driven approach to designing, deploying, and operating a security infrastructure. Sometimes, however, the traditional discipline of security analysis and implementation does not integrate well with a given business or organizational culture. Resource constraints, organizational politics, and the imperative to show quick results may all undermine the success of a lengthy, comprehensive, policy-driven security effort. If such an initiative is impossible in your particular situation, we urge you to avoid paralysis and take action. If your company already has an organized, well-supported security initiative, you may want to scan or skip this chapter and move on to our discussion of legal issues in the next chapter.

Do You Need a Security Policy?

Many security experts argue that a comprehensive written policy is the cornerstone of a secure infrastructure, and that you cannot achieve any lasting results without one. In a business where the senior management is security-aware, such a policy is an invaluable tool. Unfortunately, however, some network professionals find that creating—let alone implementing or enforcing—a complete corporate data security policy is an impossible dream. If they attempt to push through a monolithic plan that would directly constrain business processes or behaviors, they encounter intractable bureaucracy and internal politics.

In an ideal world, you would be evaluating IPsec as part of a mature, comprehensive corporate security strategy, with the full support of your colleagues and senior executives. In an indifferent or resistant environment, however, such strategies may consume months or years of debate. In the meantime, the live network continues to run as insecurely as ever. In some companies, a single-threaded commitment to develop a uniform corporate security policy does more to delay useful action than to raise awareness or modify daily operations. If your organization resists a policy, we encourage you to try something different.

If Policy Is Not Possible

A simpler, albeit scruffier and less pure alternative to the monolithic policy is to develop a matrix of device-specific, service-oriented security practices designed to protect your company's operations and preserve its data and intellectual property. For example, instead of pushing a policy that all remote corporate network users must use smart cards, digital certificates, and IPsec ESP for authenticated, confidential entry, you could start by recommending that anyone who needs remote access to a particular database must have a reasonable password and use IPsec. The former approach seeks global behavior modification to support an abstract principle, while the latter attempts to establish local standards to protect a specific, valuable resource.

Your practices matrix should have a consistent logic, but it ought to be as tactical as possible. Do not propose a blueprint to build the Death Star. Your security guidelines must be specific, compelling, and enforceable. Focus on achieving incremental improvements in areas of critical need while building the experience, credibility, and momentum to take on more difficult or complex issues. Reality wins, and the reality is that few businesses will stop in mid-quarter to don a suit of plate armor. Most, however, will pause to zip their flies. As much as possible, translate your grand security schemes into a series of choreographed fly zips, and your chances of success will improve tremendously.

From Practices to Policy

If our practices-over-policy approach seems somewhat disingenuous to you, you are correct. We believe that if you can build significant momentum behind tactical initiatives to protect certain key resources, you will eventually be in a strong position to argue for the rationalization of those efforts in order to improve efficiency and lower costs. The operational result should be a consistent set of security practices that protect your company's most valuable assets. If you are careful to avoid a domino effect from other internal vulnerabilities, the results of your efforts may be practically indistinguishable from those of a much larger, much longer, monolithic policy effort. People who might contest an up-front security policy initiative may have more difficulty disputing the value of reducing the costs of existing installations.

Some businesses, primarily banks, are legally required to maintain a written policy. Yet even in these situations, when it comes to implementation, you may still find that an immediate practical focus will get you better security sooner than trying for the mass religious conversion implicit in many security policies.

Common Nontechnical Errors

This section may seem insulting, silly, or beside the point, depending on your background and social skills. However, it is rare to succeed at implementing network security without first gaining a certain level of organizational credibility. How you achieve that influence depends on you and your organization, but there are some approaches that have proven to fail time after time. We describe several of them in the following sections. Most of these annoying behaviors are nothing more than bad habits that most of us at one time or another have had to break. It's worth the effort to avoid putting off people who will be important to your long-term success.

Network security professionals rarely win corporate popularity contests. Security-oriented people tend to care deeply about issues that their colleagues would prefer to ignore. Their technologies of choice also tend to be complex, low performing, and difficult to use. In addition to these fundamental problems, many security professionals bring trouble on themselves by repeating a few basic mistakes. Consider living by the following *nevers*:

- Never perform unscheduled scans or intrusive analyses. (See "You Won't Even Know They're There [Until Your Web Server Explodes]," later in this chapter.)

- Never restrict access to a resource without explicit permission from its owner and (if appropriate) users.

- Never install or upgrade equipment unless you have tested it in-house in a configuration similar to that in which you plan to deploy it.

- Never install, upgrade, or reconfigure equipment unless you have a current backup and a solid fallback plan.

- Never make pronouncements that begin with the words "I don't care if."

- Never hesitate to take extra precautions, even if they cause delays.

Stay Away from Silly Jargon

As a general rule, avoid being melodramatic or using overtly military terminology—such as the United States Department of Defense Terrorist Threat Condition (THREATCON) ratings—unless that terminology is in common internal use. Talking about your bad root passwords as a *THREATCON Alpha* (implying a general threat of possible terrorist activity, the nature and extent of which are unpredictable) may entertain your colleagues, but it will not inspire them to take you seriously. Obscure language may also make your colleagues feel stupid and make them less willing to assist or support you.

Diplomacy Beats Drama

Do not escalate security concerns unless and until you have given your colleagues a fair opportunity to take ownership of a problem themselves, and you have a set of practical, achievable plans that do not require halting the operation of your organization. Your work, like everyone else's, must support your company's primary business.

If your efforts are technically or organizationally destructive, regardless of your intentions, the good guys and the bad guys will see you coming from miles away, and both will take evasive action. No matter how daft and oblivious your colleagues may seem, they are your best allies. Many security professionals fail not because they are technically inexpert, but because they never achieve credibility and influence within their own organizations. Don't fall into the role of "that security dork." You'll spend years trying to get out of it.

Assessing Current Vulnerabilities

Your detailed network topology is a map to your critical resources, their users, and their access infrastructures. If you want to take a quantitative approach, use the factors outlined below to evaluate the overall sensitivity of individual network elements. Assigning a rating from 1 to 10 on each of the seven factors will yield a total score between 7 and 70 for every resource you consider. Rate each resource as follows:

- On a scale of 1 to 10, rate the value of the resource (a) to your company, (b) to your company's enemies, and (c) to its competitors.
- On a scale of 1 to 10, rate the potential business impact of an authorized person's (a) reviewing, (b) revising, (c) seizing control of, and (d) destroying the resource.

Remember, the infrastructure that provides access to a resource is probably almost as vital as the resource itself. An operational but inaccessible key-card entry system has dubious value. It may also be worthwhile to identify the relative time-sensitivity of any data (minutes for stock data, decades for health records and weapons control systems), so you can guess what kinds of attacks you should anticipate. Brute-force cryptanalysis, for example, is only suited to stealing data with long-term value. Real-time capture of unencrypted data is ideal for an attacker seeking very time-sensitive information.

Name That (Potential) Attacker

Successful attacks are, by definition, rarely detected or traced back to the attacker. Even when companies discover a problem, they rarely rush to announce it to the world. As a result, no comprehensive research exists that identifies how many undetected (or detected but hushed-up) attacks are perpetrated by internal versus external attackers. What studies there are suggest that internal people are responsible for a high proportion of problems. Nevertheless, it is easier to motivate most companies to spend money to keep outsiders out than to keep insiders down.

The common definition of a *threat* is a capable, motivated adversary. Think carefully about people and organizations that might have the means and motive to go after your company's data or its network. If, for example, you work for a bank, your attackers could include some people who want to steal money or customer information and others who want to cripple your operations for competitive or political reasons. The most visible but often least damaging attackers are the trophy hunters. These include the various code-named hacker fronts that perform multiple high-profile attacks on Web sites or other visible corporate or government resources. Such attacks can be embarrassing, but they are likely to be unfocused and low-tech compared to the determined infiltration of a professional data thief who does not want newspaper coverage. Remember that the most successful cracker is the one whose activity is invisible—not the obnoxious, high-profile stunt man who posts JPEGs of Twinkie the Hamster to your home page.

Vulnerability Analysis

Security vulnerabilities result both from accidental processes and from deliberate planning. A simple focus on goals other than security can leave a technology open to exploitation. Some vulnerabilities result from complexity that increases over time or from unforeseen new uses of a technology.

A good vulnerability assessment is likely to uncover an almost shocking fragility. IP networks have problems built right into their base protocols. Your assessment should describe and, hopefully, distinguish among security holes that result from design (as with IP), from implementation (as with unwise choices of root passwords), from configuration (as with a firewall that is too permissive), and from operation (as with the human factors example discussed later in this chapter).

Scans and Security Posture Assessments

There are two common ways to assess the current vulnerability of a network element or infrastructure: scanning and *security posture assessment*

(SPA), also called tiger teaming. A *scan* is an automated mechanism used to probe network entities for known exploitable services. A SPA is a consultative service that includes a scan, as well as other analyses.

Numerous commercial and public-domain scanning packages can check systems and network elements for a large set of known configuration errors and vulnerabilities. These packages find by doing: They typically scan an IP address or range of IP addresses and then attempt multiple known attacks against the different services available on each device that responds to a probe. For example, most scanning software will check for default user accounts and passwords, as well as vulnerability to various IP-based attacks such as teardrop or odd packet fragmentation. Proper scans may also find some devices that you missed during your exhaustive topology-building exercise.

Public-Domain or Commercial Software

Be wary of downloading public-domain scanning software to run against your network. You may be dropping a hungry cheetah into a herd of slow, fat wildebeests. Handing out a free security scanner is an excellent way for an unscrupulous individual to insert back doors into a vulnerable network. Do not assume that everyone who posts public-domain software is an altruist (though many are). Unless you are literally singing for quarters on your security budget, it is worth investing in a commercial package. Even very good public-domain packages may not get updated often. Make sure that you run the most current version of whatever software you choose. Software vendors routinely update their packages to include new attacks.

Outsourcing

If you prefer to outsource your vulnerability assessment, you can hire an external agency to do it for you. You can choose among systems integration companies or firms that specialize in security and more general-purpose consulting. These firms vary tremendously in their expertise. The firm that is re-engineering your IS systems may or may not be the best choice to audit your network security. Be sure to do the following:

- Interview multiple candidates.
- Get and check references.
- Verify that the individuals who will assess your network are experienced and trustworthy.

- Ask your candidate companies if they bond their employees, and if not, why not. This would also be a good moment to ask about any criminal records on staff.

- Review a sample report. You are looking for observations and recommendations beyond a catalog of scan results with the associated fixes. For example, if the sample report is only a list of problems (every root password is the same dumb word), each accompanied by the self-evident correction (create unique, hard-to-guess root passwords), you probably want to look for a different partner who can reach past the obvious. If the sample report describes a real company's network by name, that indiscretion should raise a huge red flag. You are relying not only on the skill but also on the discretion of your outsource partner.

- Do not be overimpressed by fancy layouts or power ties.

- Choose the candidate whose expertise and employees are best suited to your network.

You Won't Even Know They're There (Until Your Web Server Explodes)

No matter what your consultants or product literature may say, security assessments are almost always intrusive. Hosts frequently crash or enter odd dysfunctional states in response to determined attacks. Many systems rely on one or two central servers that they access via NFS or some other online mechanism. Those hosts may fail in unexpected ways if a core resource becomes unreliable or unavailable. Anticipate a domino effect. Again, remember: Never run an unplanned security audit; never touch any system without an available, current backup and the permission of its owner.

Promiscuous Mode Devices

Promiscuous mode devices include *sniffers* and *remote sniffers*. These devices or software packages capture all data that transits their local wire, no matter what the destination address. Sniffers are often jumping-off points for network-based data theft (known as *passive attacks*), but the same technology is also the basis for other network technologies. Remote monitoring (RMON) probes, described in Chapter 8, "What Won't Work with IPsec," are common monitoring tools and also function as sniffers. As you check your network for vulnerabilities, don't forget to identify any sniffer-type technology, and make sure it can be used only for its correct purpose.

Other Data Perimeters

Remember that any organization, however small, has a large, dynamic mesh of data perimeters. Vital information enters your business over networks, in the mail, by phone and fax, on paper, and in employees', partners', and customers' brains. Vital information exits your business in the same ways. While many organizations become preoccupied with their network perimeter, a highly security-conscious company will want to assess and secure each perimeter consistently. Even if your job is focused on the network aspects of data security, remember that one barred window will not secure a whole house.

Human Factors

Even when a remote attacker targets an online resource, human judgment and behavior, not weak technology, often provide the access points. Several years ago, a large company invested a lot of money to test and install a top-rated firewall. Very early one weekend morning, when the firewall had been online for a couple of weeks, a junior operations technician got paged awake with a critical alert. He returned the call, and an authoritative voice that identified itself as belonging to an Executive Vice President began to berate him: "If you don't give me access through that firewall immediately, you are fired." The technician panicked and instructed the voice on how to bypass the firewall (in this case, a dial-in back door). Millions of dollars worth of corporate intellectual property and confidential data were gone before anyone even heard about the incident. Of course the technician made a mistake, but it was not exactly a shocking mistake, under the circumstances. Most companies are full of untrained or half-trained individuals who could, in an instant of panic or poor judgment, inadvertently compromise valuable assets.

Some very advanced (and expensive) SPAs analyze potential human operational vulnerabilities, in addition to the normal technical poking and prodding. While they probably cannot subject every employee to a polygraph test and are unlikely to find out what key network personnel are possible blackmail targets, such analyses can pinpoint weak spots in normal escalation and support plans.

Filling Out the Matrix

Take the time to review your audit results carefully. Prepare to be unpleasantly surprised. Most organizations have at least one or two glaring holes in important systems, even when they have substantial investments in security technology. Share the report with trustworthy colleagues who can help you plan your technical and organizational approach. Many security professionals treat security assessments as top-secret documents. Although you may want or need to keep portions of the report to yourself, do not alienate potential supporters by treating them as if they are planning to publish your dirty laundry in the *International Herald Tribune* or are about to hire a hacker to trash the network. Any bad eggs in your company will have performed their own research.

In your matrix, summarize the *types* of vulnerabilities you have discovered for each resource. For example, bad root passwords are administrative vulnerabilities, while most IP attacks take advantage of operating system flaws or normal but undesirable characteristics of IP (see Chapter 5, "The Risks of IP Networking"). For the latter, identify the specific missing component: authentication, authorization, access control, confidentiality, audit trails, or nonrepudiation. Assign an overall vulnerability rating to the resource based on the number and severity of specific issues in the matrix. Use your gut instinct—there's no real formula to tell you how to prioritize, for example, one big problem against four smaller ones.

An Implementation Strategy

The chapters that follow will walk you through the steps of planning your security implementation. Although they focus on selecting and deploying appropriate IPsec products, the methodology they identify should help you with other security technologies as well. As you gear up to evaluate, purchase, and install new products, take some time to think through your overall approach, as follows:

- Plan your interventions carefully.
- Be especially careful to ensure that your first few steps are successful. While it may be tempting to focus on your mission-critical resources first, you might be wiser to start with something that

can stand up to a couple of inevitable new-product and first-try glitches.

- Don't experiment on your source code servers, your customer databases, or the software that monitors the pressure, temperature, and water level in the uranium core.

- Above all, do not escalate concerns about your audit results or security matrix unless and until you have a set of practical, achievable plans that do not require halting the operation of your organization. Of course, there are exceptions to this rule: If your audit revealed ongoing attacks or extreme vulnerabilities that place your company, human lives, or the planet in immediate jeopardy, you need to react quickly.

- Make sure that other people share your sense of urgency before you start pulling cords out of walls.

In general, it's a good idea to work with the immediate owners and operators of your vulnerable resources, rather than going immediately to their management. If they are intractable, you may need to go over their heads, but it's usually better to start with a direct approach. No one likes to be squashed from above by a lead piano. Even sensible people become uncooperative if they get thrashed from on high without reasonable notice. Remember that these folks will eventually inherit some amount of responsibility for maintaining the solutions you install. Your life will be simpler and your work more successful if they aren't nursing a grudge.

Finally, bear in mind that network security is a marathon, not a sprint. Plan in terms of months and years, and focus on incremental improvements.

Encrypting within the Law

In almost every country, a working knowledge of encryption regulations is a detestable *must*. Because the laws are complex, the paperwork cycles are long, and the potential penalties are severe, we suggest that you start your legal planning at least five months before you intend to deploy IPsec. If you are already far along in your implementation and are thinking something like "Laws? You mean, there are restrictions on crypto?" we recommend that you immediately halt deployment until you ascertain your legal status and obtain any necessary licenses.

This chapter is a guide to interpreting regulations and their possible impact on your security plans. It is not a country-by-country guide to encryption law. As this book went to press, international regulations and licensing procedures were changing so frequently that any specific details would have gone quickly out of date. The last section, "Where to Get More Information," points you to some online sources that are usually current. Government licensing agencies are always the most authoritative sources for regulatory information. Note that encryption licenses are not like other technology licenses that you negotiate with a vendor or an inventor. They are more similar to a firearms or driver's license, which you request from your government but may not always receive. Encryption licenses must be renewed; they may also expire or be revoked.

Overview

Most governments restrict the import, export, or local use of encryption. These restrictions range from red tape to near-bans, depending on the country, the technology, the user, and the intended use. Unless you deploy only in countries that do not restrict domestic encryption for your particular business and you purchase only locally developed technology, the laws of one or more countries will limit your use of IPsec. Encryption controls can be more frustrating than any technology problem: They are often obscure, and their impact is difficult to predict. Most network professionals would prefer being plucked bald hair by hair to wading through licensing paperwork. Governments tend to enforce the laws on a case-by-case, product-by-product basis, and they show significant variation in their decisions. Even if you only plan to use IPsec Authentication Header (AH) for data integrity, you still must find out what laws exist for every country where you plan to purchase or install an IPsec product or to route IPsec traffic.

It can be tempting to ignore encryption controls in order to focus on the more appealing challenge of building your secure infrastructure. Encryption regulations are not formalities, however, and violating them is *not* the legal equivalent of tearing the "Do Not Remove" tag off a mattress. Always adhere to the following guidelines:

- Do not ignore the laws or try to evade them.
- Design your network so that you can build, operate, upgrade, and repair it legally.
- Do not wait until the last minute to figure out what constraints may apply to your network or to your preferred vendors: Licensing paperwork can take months.
- Plan ahead for a legal network. It will save you a lot of trouble.

Disclaimer

We are not lawyers, and this chapter does not offer legal advice (other than advising you not to break the law). Terms of this chapter are not legal terms of art. We have done our best to be accurate, but we cannot guarantee that the information here is useful, complete, or correct. Even if it were perfect when we went to print, truth is time's roadkill in the world of encryption controls. Your mileage will vary.

Terminology

An additional disclaimer: The terms we use here are not legal definitions, nor do they reflect the content of any single country's regulations. We included these descriptions to give you a sense of what may be restricted by any given country. In general, encryption regulations are very granular, restricting not only algorithms and key lengths, but also their modes of transfer, who can use them, and how they can be used.

What Is an Import?

An *import* involves the transfer of cryptographic products or data from a foreign entity to a domestic entity. Cryptographic data can include the specification of an *application programming interface* (API) designed to enable a third party to add cryptographic functions (*crypto with a hole*); it need not contain actual cryptographic algorithms. The transfer may be physical (in a box or on paper), electronic (from a Web site), or verbal. Purchasing a product from a foreign country for delivery to your home office is probably an import. Downloading cryptographic software from a foreign Web site to your personal computer may be an import. Having a foreigner whisper the RSA algorithm in your ear as you wait for the bus anywhere in the world may also be an import. Research your local laws to determine what is and is not okay to transfer.

What Is an Export?

An *export* involves the transfer of cryptographic products or data from a domestic entity to a foreign entity. Again, cryptographic data can include the specification of an API designed to enable a third party to add cryptographic functions (crypto with a hole); it need not contain actual cryptographic algorithms. This transfer may be physical (in a box or on paper), electronic (via publication on a Web site), or verbal. Sending a product from your home office to a foreign country is probably an export. Posting cryptographic software on your globally accessible Web site may be an export. Whispering the RSA algorithm into a foreigner's ear as she waits for a bus anywhere in the world (including outside your home office) may also be an export. No product needs to clear customs to break the law. Some countries assign equal weight to tangible (product) and intangible (data) exports. Research your local laws to determine what transfers are illegal or require a license.

What Is an End User?

Many licensing schemes include the concepts of an *end user* and an *end use*. The term "end user" generally refers to the local organizational entity that will control the encrypting platform and can respond to a warrant for data interception. The end user usually needs to be an administrative individual or group located with or near the installed device. It is generally not acceptable to claim the corporate headquarters in London as the legal end user for an encryption platform installed in a Japanese field office. A multinational IPsec network may have multiple end users for licensing purposes. Where these restrictions apply, approval for one end user does not imply approval for another. If you want to expand your IPsec infrastructure to include other locations, you may need to obtain additional licenses.

What Is an End Use?

An *end use* is the intended function of an encrypting platform. The description of an end use outlines what data is to be encrypted and for what purpose. End use can be a moving target for IPsec, as people often deploy it in place of an application-layer solution for the same traffic. For example, a bank might use IPsec technology for secure bulk transmission of customer financial data, while a consulting firm might deploy it to transmit accounting data and email over a WAN (instead of deploying an actual encrypting database or email program). The end use is a crucial decision point for most licensing processes. In some cases, for instance, end users might get approval to use 3DES to encrypt financial information but not email or voice traffic. You must be specific about your end-use intentions for many license applications. If you are approved for one end use, that does not mean you are implicitly approved for another. If you are operating under end-use restrictions, when you deploy an IPsec VPN to encrypt one kind of data, you may not expand it to encrypt other kinds of data without an additional license.

Encryption for U.S. Businesses with U.S.-Only Networks

The United States does not currently restrict the import or domestic use of encryption, except in the case of third-party encryption services, managed VPN services that encrypt other people's data (see the section entitled "The Regulations Don't Favor IPsec"). If you are building an IPsec network to support your own business, and the encrypting platforms and encrypted traffic will remain exclusively within the United States, you can purchase and deploy whatever you want. Domestic use restrictions periodically show up in Congress (generally attached to some other legislation), so it's a good idea to verify your legal status anyhow. See the last section, "Where to Get More Information," for links to the current regulations.

Encryption for Everyone Else: Cracking Open the Door to Hell

Restricting access to IPsec may seem about as reasonable as restricting the distribution of dental floss. If many encryption policies seem arbitrary, complex, or absurd, it is because they attempt to reconcile the irreconcilable. They aim to allow certain classes of users to protect certain types of data and transactions while simultaneously prohibiting other classes of users from doing exactly the same thing. Cryptographic technologies enable anonymity as well as data secrecy and integrity, and they do not discriminate against unsavory users or rebel at politically unpopular uses. Like commercial fertilizer, they have legal, extralegal, and criminal applications.

Broad Availability Does Not Imply Deregulation

Strong encryption products are available from a range of vendors worldwide, and equally strong (algorithmically speaking) public-domain encryption is available all over the Internet. Because encryption is so ubiquitous, people tend to forget that it is regulated, or they assume that existing regulations are somehow unenforceable. Remember that encryption obstructs covert data interception and retrieval—activities that are fundamental to the domestic and international intelligence activities of most governments. The goal of most correctly configured IPsec networks is to provide an authenticated, impenetrable channel for data communications—the stuff of sweaty nightmares for law-enforcement and intelligence agencies. Some countries still treat encryption as a munitions item. Do not underestimate the seriousness of encryption regulations. The laws are not strange anachronisms that your government has forgotten to repeal. As encryption products enter mainstream markets, governments are increasingly alert to the challenge of enforcing regulations and procedures that were not designed to scale well. We caution you against putting yourself in a position where a government agency has the legal leverage to make an example of you or your company.

Because encryption laws change frequently, this chapter does not attempt an exhaustive, country-by-country survey of what is legal for export, import, or use. Instead, it presents an overview of general restrictions and regulatory trends, and suggests an approach to ensure that your security plans remain well within the relevant laws and limitations.

The Politics of Cryptography

Government restrictions on the technologies of personal and commercial privacy (mostly but not exclusively cryptography) are very controversial in almost every country that currently has or is considering strong controls. The political dispute is often reduced to a caricature—those opposed to cryptography regulations call for individual privacy protection against Big Brother, while those in favor of strong controls use the tried-and-true argument that women and children will die from terrorist acts assisted by cryptography. However, there are more than two sides to the cryptography issue; the situation is actually fairly complicated. Each participant is serving a private agenda that extends beyond the issues that may be raised publicly. The following sections discuss the positions and motivations of several of these participants.

Industry, Experts, and Lobbyists

We will not analyze any specific instances in detail, but elements common to international cryptography debates are worth identifying. One interesting factor is how few regular citizens are vocal about encryption controls, although so-called public interests are constantly touted in public forums. Parties who claim to advocate decontrol on behalf of the general population are commonly high-tech businesses, technical experts, or professional lobbyists. The high-tech business stands to gain financial rewards from unfettered market access to the common man's pocket. For technical experts, the debate provides a public forum to air strongly held personal beliefs. Professional lobbyists may want to keep the debate raging to ensure their own professional stature. These different groups may not deliberately misrepresent the interests of their fellow citizens, but they often fail to back claims with any real research, and they have shown little willingness to modify their positions based on direct market feedback.

Law-Enforcement Agencies

Law-enforcement agencies also invoke so-called public opinion to support their interests. Some have tried to use the encryption debate indirectly to expand their own domestic surveillance capabilities, while claiming to address the common person's overwhelming concern about public safety. Of course, as we discuss in the section "Alternatives to Third-Party Key Access," any law-enforcement agency that must present a warrant or court order to commence legal surveillance probably does not need a key escrow or key recovery system. Some law-enforcement agencies advocate key escrow as a mechanism to preserve their ability to serve a warrant without acknowledging that it is equally valuable for performing surveillance *without* a warrant.

Intelligence Agencies

Intelligence agencies, whose operations are probably most at risk from widespread strong cryptography, tend to wave the flag for public safety as well as national security. Practically speaking, however, their pressing concern is gaining a technological leg up for their own foreign surveillance apparatus by pressuring product manufacturers for visibility into, if not direct modifications to, their commercial encryption packages. These agencies tend to support almost any regulatory process that requires case-by-case licensing and detailed reporting systems. These procedures allow them to track international purchases and to deal with and exert pressure on individual encryption vendors for licensing purposes.

Most active parties in the encryption debate, regardless of how loudly they invoke the common interest, are pursuing their own personal, political, or business objectives. If you care about individual or corporate access to strong cryptographic systems, it is probably worthwhile to read up on the issue in your own country (see the section "Where to Get More Information" for a starting point). Do not assume that anyone is already representing your interests, whatever they are, in this controversy.

Important International Bodies

Several international bodies have published statements on recommended cryptographic controls for their member states. The two most significant of these are the Wassenaar Arrangement on Export Controls for Conventional Arms and Dual-Use Goods and Technologies (commonly referred to as The Wassenaar Arrangement, or simply Wassenaar) and the Organization for Economic Co-operation and Development (OECD).

These recommendations identify collective priorities and set some important precedents, but they are nonbinding. Member states are responsible for their own policies, and they require neither approval nor review of those policies from other members. These international efforts are political rather than regulatory in nature. They establish the baseline for international discussion and often create pressure among member countries with different positions in the policy debate. Participants in Wassenaar include countries such as Finland, France, and the United States that have diverse encryption policies— evidence that a wide range of positions is possible among subscribers to the same organization.

The Wassenaar Arrangement

The Wassenaar Arrangement is a 33-member organization that sets standards for the export of conventional arms and dual-use goods (technologies with both military and civilian uses). It succeeded the Coordinating Committee for Multilateral Export Controls (COCOM), which set baseline controls for 17 countries prior to March 1994. The Wassenaar Arrangement has a broad scope, addressing items that range from traditional arms to fluorocarbon electronic cooling fluids, off-highway tractors, and cryptographic technologies. Its primary goal

**PARTICIPATING STATES OF THE WASSENAAR ARRANGEMENT
(AS OF DECEMBER 1998)**

Argentina, Australia, Austria, Belgium, Bulgaria, Canada, Czech Republic, Denmark,
Finland, France, Germany, Greece, Hungary, Ireland, Italy, Japan, Luxembourg,
Netherlands, New Zealand, Norway, Poland, Portugal, Republic of Korea, Romania,
Russian Federation, Slovak Republic, Spain, Sweden, Switzerland, Turkey, Ukraine, United
Kingdom, United States.

is to prevent the transfer or diversion of sensitive technologies to certain countries and entities. Its emphasis, therefore, is on export controls and reporting requirements.

Although Wassenaar does not specifically dictate policy, it has been influential in establishing the lowest-common-denominator characteristics for the export of software and hardware cryptographic platforms. It has also helped to propagate some common exemptions through a clause called the General Software Note in the original arrangement and replaced in December 1998 by the Cryptography Note. The Cryptography Note explicitly decontrols 56-bit cryptographic hardware and software, as well as 64-bit software and hardware that is *mass market* in nature. The term "mass market" indicates software of a specified maximum cryptographic strength (presently 64-bit keys for a symmetric algorithm) that is available via retail, mail-order, electronic, or telephone sale and does not require substantial user configuration or vendor support. Wassenaar also decontrols some specialized cryptographic applications, including the following:

- Personalized smart cards for decontrolled functions (such as subway fares)
- Point-of-sale terminals
- Automated teller machines (ATMs)
- Financial transactions and credit-card settlements
- Software and/or hardware used exclusively for authentication

The first version of the Wassenaar encryption controls was more liberal for software than for hardware, but the two are now at parity. See "Where to Get More Information" at the end of this chapter for pointers to current information on the Wassenaar Arrangement (Wassenaar 1998).

The Organization for Economic Co-operation and Development

The OECD is a 29-member organization that provides a forum to discuss and formulate recommendations for member states' social and economic policies. Although the OECD is not a closed organization, candidate members must affirm support for the Articles of the OECD Convention and must demonstrate some form of commitment to a market economy, "democratic pluralism," and human rights. In 1998, the OECD also created an umbrella organization called the Centre for Co-operation with Non-Members to expand its policy and regional influence, primarily with China and Russia.

The OECD sponsors working groups and produces reports on many different issues. In 1996, it formed the Ad hoc Group of Experts on Cryptography Policy Guidelines to study issues of cryptography use and regulation and to produce a set of guidelines for its member countries. In March 1997, the OECD approved two publications: "Guidelines for Cryptography Policy" and "The Report on Background and Issues of Cryptography Policy." The policy guidelines established eight principles (see the sidebar entitled "The Eight OECD Principles on Cryptography") and stated a number of goals for the expanding international use of cryptography. Some critics have argued that these principles are essentially indecisive distillations of the obvious and provide little substantive guidance. They point out, for example, that the principles of trust in cryptographic method (#1) and protection of privacy (#5) are generally in conflict with the principle of lawful access (#6). It seems a little unrealistic, however, to knock the OECD for failing to resolve a controversy that few of its member states have been able to settle for themselves. In its inability to ignore the claims of either privacy or public safety advocates, the OECD provides one more example of the difficulty of establishing a principled framework specifically designed to encourage only legitimate uses of cryptography (OECD 1997).

OECD MEMBER COUNTRIES (AS OF DECEMBER 1998)

Australia, Austria, Belgium, Canada, Czech Republic, Denmark, Finland, France, Germany, Greece, Hungary, Iceland, Ireland, Italy, Japan, Korea, Luxembourg, Mexico, The Netherlands, New Zealand, Norway, Poland, Portugal, Spain, Sweden, Switzerland, Turkey, United Kingdom, United States.

THE EIGHT OECD PRINCIPLES ON CRYPTOGRAPHY

1. **Trust in cryptographic methods.**
   Cryptographic methods should be trustworthy in order to generate confidence in the use of information and communications systems.

2. **Choice of cryptographic methods.**
   Users should have a right to choose any cryptographic method, subject to applicable law.

3. **Market-driven development of cryptographic methods.**
   Cryptographic methods should be developed in response to the needs, demands, and responsibilities of individuals, businesses, and governments.

4. **Standards for cryptographic methods.**
   Technical standards, criteria, and protocols for cryptographic methods should be developed and promulgated at the national and international level.

5. **Protection of privacy and personal data.**
   The fundamental rights of individuals to privacy, including secrecy of communications and protection of personal data, should be respected in national cryptography policies and in the implementation and use of cryptographic methods.

6. **Lawful access.**
   National cryptography policies may allow lawful access to plaintext, or cryptographic keys, of encrypted data. These policies must respect the other principles contained in the guidelines to the greatest extent possible.

7. **Liability.**
   Whether established by contract or legislation, the liability of individuals and entities that offer cryptographic services or hold or access cryptographic keys should be clearly stated.

8. **International Co-operation.**
   Governments should co-operate to co-ordinate cryptography policies. As part of this effort, governments should remove, or avoid creating in the name of cryptography policy, unjustified obstacles to trade. (OECD 1997) [1]

[1] "The Eight OECD Principles on Cryptography," from Recommendation of the Council Concerning Guidelines for Cryptographic Policy. Copyright © OECD 1997. 62/Final. Material available on OECD Web site at www.oecd.org/dsti/sti/it/secur/index.htm.

International Overview

Cryptographic technologies offer a unique set of benefits for networks and networked applications. They can provide strong proof of identity, ensure data integrity, and enable highly confidential communications. IPsec is one of the first general-purpose mechanisms to apply cryptographic technology to bulk data, rather than point transactions. With the increasing strength and availability of tools that encrypt stored data and electronic transmissions, however, existing surveillance mechanisms that enable third-party interception and/or recovery of data are generally rendered obsolete. Many governments have stated that the proliferation of inexpensive, virtually unbreakable encryption may endanger public safety and national security by preventing government law-enforcement and intelligence agencies from identifying and interpreting data and electronic data transmissions. Of course, as observed previously, the governments' approach tends to be somewhat contradictory. Most governments would prefer a mechanism for recovering and intercepting data that offers their own agencies exclusive surveillance privileges on private communications.

Types of Controls

Encryption restrictions vary according to both the use and the user. They come in three basic flavors: import, export, and domestic use. An increasing number of countries limit not only what you can buy or sell across their borders, but also what you can build and use for yourself or for your business.

Governments typically restrict security platforms based on multiple technical criteria, including algorithm, key length, key strength, key generation, key management, and overall product design. For IPsec products, you may encounter limits on what AH and *Encapsulating Security Payload* (ESP) transforms you can deploy, what key lengths and strengths you can use, and whether you can enable IKE or must rely solely on preshared keys of a certain length or strength. Some governments restrict how many bits of randomness can be part of a bulk encryption key; longer keys are padded with known text or zeroes. As described previously, governments may also restrict the transfer of APIs that enable third-party encryption, as well as the transmission of intangible data (such as verbal descriptions of unpublished encryption algorithms) or specifics of cryptographic product design. Whether they provide authentication or confidentiality services, most encryption products must navigate a bewildering array of recommendations and restrictions before their green lights can flash legally in your wiring closet.

The Regulations Don't Favor IPsec

Although encryption laws change frequently, do not assume that they will soon evolve to enable simple global deployment of IPsec. As the world evolves toward broader crypto use, many governments are moving toward broader crypto controls. And while regulations increasingly share terminology such as "key escrow" and "key management infrastructure," the meanings of those terms tend to vary by country. International regulations are terrible hairballs, and as more countries struggle to establish their own policies, they will almost certainly get hairier.

Do not expect any given country's laws to be symmetric or to have an obvious-to-the-casual-Ph.D. logic. In the United States, for example, there are tight restrictions on cryptographic export, but none on cryptographic import. Domestic use restrictions in the United States vary by industry and use. Most individuals and businesses may encrypt data with any algorithm and any key length they choose. Financial institutions are required to encrypt many of their external communications. In contrast, U.S. telecommunications carriers that provide encryption services are required by The Communications Assistance for Law Enforcement Act (CALEA) of 1994 to provide law-enforcement officials with on-demand source and recipient information, as well as plaintext message content, in near real-time (CALEA 1994).

Basic Regulatory Categories

This section provides some very general information on typical import, export, and domestic use controls. Again, we have not attempted to describe the current policies of any specific country.

Authentication

Cryptography, as we discuss in Chapter 6, "Cryptographic Protocols and Techniques," can authenticate individual identities and can establish the integrity, origin, and recipient of a message or transaction. Cryptographic platforms designed exclusively to support authentication do perform some data encryption, but only of information that is fundamental to the authentication process. Most authentication-oriented encryption products rely on public key cryptography. In the current world of IPsec, you are most likely to use this type of technology in the form of a *certification authority* (CA) or smart card.

Controls for Certification Authorities

The laws that restrict import, export, and use of authentication-oriented encryption products such as CAs are currently more permissive than those that control bulk data encryption products. It is almost always easier to get a license for strong authentication than for similarly strong data encryption. This situation may change as digital signatures attain more certain legal status around the world. Many governments are considering a combination of *implicit* requirements, which would direct private CAs to meet a minimum technical standard, and *explicit* requirements, licensing or accreditation processes for CAs that would have some kind of formal legal standing. As always, you should not assume that your preferred authentication product is legal for use without checking with your government or your vendor.

Controls for CAs may restrict the algorithm and public key length for certificates. They may require that the CA maintain (escrow) a copy of the private key associated with each public key that it signs either locally or with a third party. Controls may also specify how the CA generates and stores its own private key, in addition to other operational integrity and security features unrelated to cryptography.

Bulk Data Encryption

IPsec ESP transforms use bulk data encryption, generally but not exclusively symmetric algorithms, to encrypt data. Many countries control almost every aspect of these algorithms for export, import, or domestic use. They specify what algorithm or algorithms are legal for which users and what specific uses. Most at least limit key length. Additional regulations may control the effective strength of keys by limiting how many bits are actually random or by restricting other elements—such as key lifetime—that affect the strength of the key management system. In some cases, IPsec with preshared keys may be legal, while IPsec with IKE quick mode is not. Some countries permit one mode of DES (EBC) and deny another (CBC). A number of governments certify products on a case-by-case basis, regardless of their design. France is among those countries that currently require a one-time source code review of cryptographic products for import and/or domestic use. Based on a detailed review, these countries certify a specific version of a product for select customer types (such as banks) and particular uses (such as encrypting financial transactions).

Voice over IPsec

In Chapter 8, "What Won't Work with IPsec," we recommend against combining voice over IP (VoIP) and IPsec for operational reasons. In many network topologies, due to SA negotiation and key generation, IPsec may introduce delays or periodic latency for some real-time voice applications. In some circumstances, you may also face additional regulations that specifically restrict voice encryption. Following both legislation and convention, voice-transmission facilities generally provide intercept capabilities that enable real-time monitoring. Most commercial phone switches have an intercept port for diagnostic and law-enforcement purposes as part of their standard configuration. Of course, the traditional circuit-switched nature of voice networks greatly simplifies call interception. On a circuit-switched network, an entire voice call follows a single path through the network, with all content delivered in sequence. Packet-switched IP networks use a *many pieces, many paths* model. Data is transmitted over multiple routes and may travel in fragments and out of order. Even plaintext IP traffic is difficult to intercept on a WAN unless the interception point is right at a single point of entry into the WAN cloud—and even then, the packets may be out of order or fragmented. Encrypted or not, VoIP presents a new challenge for call-interception technology.

As this book went to press, there were no strong precedents for licensing of voice encryption in cases where the voice component is just another type of data payload in an IP packet. Platforms that combine VoIP and IPsec may or may not be more difficult to license for import, export, or domestic use in different countries. The regulatory status of encrypted VoIP is sure to be contentious and may well result in additional paperwork for or even restrictions on your preferred network encryption technology.

Key Escrow and Key Recovery

Recently, many governments have begun to add *key escrow* and/or *key recovery* requirements to their encryption regulations. The terms "key escrow" and "key recovery" (jointly, *third-party key access*) refer to sets of requirements, rather than specific technologies. Many security experts and privacy advocates believe that third-party key access (also referred to as *government access to keys* [GAK]) is the security equivalent of a boat with no bottom. Although they vary in many operational respects, these regulations all require a technical hook for the replication of private keys, the plaintext recovery of stored ciphertext, and the interception and decryption of real-time ciphertext.

Regardless of your personal beliefs about the rights and wrongs of data recovery or third-party data interception, remember that both mechanisms are designed to expose plaintext that would otherwise not be available, and that most vendors currently implement them in unique, noninteroperable ways.

Wiretaps and Warrants

The legal terminology and requirements surrounding data interception and recovery vary from country to country and from instance to instance, but they boil down to the ability to capture and review data as it transits a network and to retrieve and review stored data. On an IP network, real-time data interception requires the data equivalent of a wiretap (traditionally associated with voice calls). Recovery of data generally relies on some kind of a search warrant. Encryption confounds data interception and data recovery by making the interesting bits difficult to identify and, once located, illegible. Suppose, for example, that a law-enforcement agency wanted to monitor all encrypted telnet transactions between Spot the Dog and the host red.hydrant.com. Without some mechanism to expose the encrypted contents of each IP packet, it would be difficult to identify which specific sessions belonged to Spot, and the content of those sessions (if the agency were able to single them out) would be unintelligible.

Real-time versus Retroactive

A real-time monitoring mechanism is designed to capture data as it is created or exchanged. A retroactive one enables retrieval after the fact. In most cases, a wiretap is a real-time mechanism; it targets an ephemeral exchange whose content exists only for the lifetime of that session. The data exists on the wire for some period, but is not assumed to persist after the fact (on a hard drive, for example). A wiretap is thus better suited to monitor an online chat session than an e-mail exchange. Wiretaps are usually not retroactive—that is, they are not used to capture bulk data that may later prove interesting—although there are some exceptions to this principle. Data-recovery mechanisms are almost always retroactive. They identify and retrieve specific data from a persistent store such as a hard drive or backup tape. Complex evasions aside, wiretaps have a better chance at locating data intact than do warrants, for which a target may well discard sensitive information as it arrives, rather than risk later discovery.

Basics of Crypto-Busting

The only way to decipher an encrypted message is to obtain (get or guess) the decryption key or keys or to locate a copy of the original plaintext. Since encryption systems rarely leave plaintext lying around, third-party decryption generally relies on access to keys. Finding encryption keys is part of the larger science of *cryptanalysis,* solving cryptograms or cryptographic systems. It can involve *brute force*—trying every possible key to decrypt a given lump of ciphertext. It can also use the introduction of *known plaintext* to an encryption engine so that the third party has before and after lumps of data to work from in guessing keys. IPsec gateways, depending on their design and configuration, are relatively vulnerable to known plaintext attacks, since it is not difficult to manufacture traffic and redirect it around IP networks. If an IPsec gateway is encrypting SMTP traffic across a WAN, for example, it's very simple for a third party to *bounce* email off the mail host (perhaps by mailing a nonexistent user a copy of the Encyclopedia Britannica) in order to send known plaintext through the gateway. IP source routing, if permitted, can allow a third party to route a continuous stream of traffic into and out of an IP gateway. A well-configured IPsec end host is marginally less vulnerable to a known plaintext attack via IP, since it (usually) supports fewer general-purpose network functions.

The U.S. Example

Although a lot of research focuses on how to decrypt a message without access to the decryption keys, most governments are interested in a regulatory mechanism to guarantee simple and speedy availability of those keys. In November 1996, for example, the United States issued an Executive Order requiring that *strong* (stronger than 40-bit DES) U.S. encryption products integrate a *key management infrastructure* (KMI) in order to receive more favorable export licensing. This order and its related regulations mandated that vendors of strong encryption products develop application-layer and network-layer KMI systems or an equivalent plaintext access mechanism to enable third-party access to encrypted data either on disk or, in the case of IPsec, in transit. Without KMI support or some equivalent (see the section "Alternatives to Third-Party Key Access"), strong U.S. encryption products are generally not exportable, except to U.S. subsidiaries, financial institutions, online merchants, and healthcare companies.

Which Keys Matter?

Most commercial encryption systems, such as encrypting email (S/MIME, PGP, PEM), SSL, and so on, rely on a persistent key or keys to encrypt and decrypt data. The encrypt/decrypt keys are usually a private/public key pair. Older link-layer encryption products mostly rely on a long-lived symmetric key to encrypt and decrypt data. Third-party key access systems have evolved to address the design problem of securely acquiring and storing persistent keys. As businesses and governments have become more aware of the power and associated sensitivity of keys used to assert identity, they have taken an increased interest in storing (escrowing) the private keys associated with individual identities and applications. If the objective is to decrypt a message, the escrow must store the necessary decryption keys; if the objective is to provide a backup identity mechanism, the escrow must maintain a copy of the identity key or keys.

The Special Case of IPsec

Third-party key access raises a special set of problems for IPsec. Because it uses ephemeral Diffie-Hellman (DH) keys instead of one persistent key to encrypt data, IPsec requires substantially different mechanisms to support any key recovery scheme intended to enable wiretapping. IPsec uses persistent keys for authentication only, relying on secret key algorithms such as DES and RC4, with a series of ephemeral, localized encryption keys to perform bulk data encryption. Simple escrow for the end host or gateway public keys would not enable a third party to decrypt the encrypted data. Disclosure of one session key (or multiple session keys) would not simplify discovery of other session keys or of the original master keys. A third-party key access mechanism for IPsec (assuming IKE) would require the capture and disclosure of every ephemeral session key, with some type of reasonably well synchronized time stamping for all keys and all encrypted datagrams, in order to identify which key was used to encrypt what data.

IPsec and Third-Party Key Access

Not only does the Internet Engineering Task Force (IETF) strongly resist any standards activity that acknowledges or appears to legitimize third-party key access regulations; it is also generally recognized that most key escrow and key recovery mechanisms would fundamentally weaken the assurance provided by a correctly implemented IPsec product.

The IPsec standards do not include any option to support key escrow or key recovery, and it seems unlikely that they will anytime soon. In August 1996, the Internet Architecture Board (IAB) and the Internet Engineering Steering Group (IESG) issued RFC 1984, strongly opposing both of these mechanisms.

Deploying IPsec with Escrow or KMI

If you elect or are compelled to deploy IPsec platforms with proprietary escrow or KMI capabilities, you must plan carefully to ensure that your third-party key access mechanisms function correctly without compromising the security of your IPsec infrastructure. If you try to build a multivendor, escrowed IPsec network, you may also encounter intractable problems with multivendor noninteroperability.

Feasibility Considerations

As discussed previously, most key escrow systems retain a copy of a persistent encryption key (often but not always the same key used for authentication). In the context of IPsec, such a system is not particularly useful, as it would contain only the host or gateway's private key. It would allow a third party to spoof the identity of an IPsec end host or gateway, but would not provide access to plaintext or simplify decryption of intercepted ciphertext. A third-party key access system that enabled data interception for IPsec ESP traffic would need to retain or escrow a copy of each session key. Because ESP packets do not contain timestamps, the escrowed session keys only reduce the search space to decrypt a given bit of ciphertext. If you understand the transit path of a given packet, can identify which IPsec end host or gateway encrypted it, and have relatively long key lifetimes, it may not be exceptionally difficult to guess which keys to try first. Nevertheless, there is no rigorous way to associate a particular session key with a single intercepted datagram.

No Standard, Even outside the Standards

In 1996, the U.S. Government Department of Commerce chartered a by-invitation-only committee of industry, government, and subject-area experts to address the overall feasibility of a U.S. Federal Information

Processing Standard (FIPS) for KMI. That committee, the Technical Advisory Committee to Develop a Federal Information Processing Standard for the Federal Key Management Infrastructure (TACDFIPSFKMI), met from December 1996 through November 1998. It disbanded without producing a FIPS (or being able to remember the committee acronym, we assume). Its final report does describe many requirements for and characteristics of a *key recovery system* (KRS) in the abstract. These requirements, however, preclude the possibility of a FIPS-compliant KRS for IPsec, at least if one goes by the spirit of the standards. The committee states:

> (Req. 24) A vendor of a cryptographic end system that makes use of a standard communication encryption protocol shall provide documentation demonstrating that the product transports KRI [Key Recovery Information] in a fashion consistent with the specification developed and adopted by the cognizant standards body for the protocol in question. (TACDFIPSFKMI 1998)

Since the IAB and IESG, the supervisory bodies of the IETF (the "cognizant standards body"), have explicitly rejected the possibility of an IETF-standard KRS, it seems unlikely that a vendor could defensibly claim a KRS implementation to be consistent with the IPsec standards. People have, however, proposed several different mechanisms for a KRS that are logical technical extensions of the standards.

Interoperability

Given that third-party key access mechanisms for IPsec fall outside the published standards, it follows that any such mechanism will almost certainly be vendor-proprietary. Many vendors have filed patents for their own key recovery mechanisms, and there has been very little cross-licensing to date. Time-to-market and competitive pressures will probably support the push toward proprietary schemes. The implications of proprietary third-party key access will vary depending on whether you need a single instance in one location or your entire IPsec network must support it. If you need only one or two platforms to support key access, you may still be able to build a multivendor infrastructure, provided that your key access systems interoperate in a standard way with other IPsec systems. If every IPsec device (or the majority of them) must support third-party key access, you will almost certainly become dependent on a single vendor for all of your IPsec products. That dependency could be particularly problematic if your network spans countries with different key escrow requirements. We recommend that you do your best to avoid a single vendor dependency, if possible, but you may have no choice.

Scalability

If you have a large fully or partially meshed IPsec infrastructure, you need to assess the scalability of your third-party key access mechanism. If it is collocated with the IPsec platform, find out how quickly it can add keys and what happens if the repository (probably a hard disk) gets full. Will the device overwrite existing keys? In what order? Or, worse, will it enter a strange failure mode, possibly failing to generate new keys and dropping its IPsec connections as the keys expire? Distributed key repositories can make your life extremely difficult in the event that you actually need to get a key out of one of them. Imagine that you have a thousand IPsec gateways with local session key storage, and a law-enforcement agency appears with a lump of ciphertext and a (presumably retroactive) warrant for its decryption. Which gateways do you approach? This problem is especially nasty if you're using *network address translation* (NAT), since it may take longer to identify the candidate gateways and associated keys.

A centralized key repository, either self-managed or third-party managed, raises other scaling challenges. How many keys can the repository receive at one time? In a remote dial scenario, in which IPsec clients are terminating ESP sessions on a dial gateway, you may see extraordinary key turnover, especially as new sessions start. Some dial service providers estimate a turnover of 1 percent of subscriptions per minute. Thus, for example, a dial service with 1 million users will see 10,000 new connections per minute, on average. For a key repository, that means 10,000 new session keys to store per minute, not including any additional keys for existing connections. Ask your vendor how many keys the platform stores per minute and what it does if it becomes overwhelmed or runs out of storage capacity. Which keys will it overwrite first?

Security

Both centralized and distributed key repositories pose significant security challenges, both in design and in operation. Stolen keys mean stolen data. If it's worth encrypting the data, it's worth ensuring that the key storage device is very secure. Both local and centralized repositories may face the problem of needing to allow remote, in-band access to stored keys. If a repository does not allow remote access, make sure that a human being can get to it fast enough to satisfy a warrant. If it does allow remote access, it had better be an extremely secure mechanism, with strong authentication, confidentiality, and audit capabilities. Any system that allows remote access is an obvious target for the active or potential human threat that inspired you to deploy IPsec in the first place.

Local key storage systems also inherit the security problems of their host platforms. Most commercial IPsec gateways and end host implementations are based on commercial or proprietary operating systems that are not hardened from a security perspective. Commercial networking software and hardware are usually designed for low cost, feature richness, or time-to-market, not security. Centralized systems should be designed to be highly secure, but good design does not automatically translate to good implementation. It's worth finding or commissioning a third-party audit of any key access implementation to ensure that it can withstand a range of determined attacks.

Alternatives to Third-Party Key Access

Some cryptographic experts claim that cryptographic systems designed to enable an unauthenticated party to make real-time or retroactive use of private or bulk data encryption keys are weaker than systems that do not. Architects of third-party key access enabled systems counter that a well-implemented key recovery or key escrow product is often more secure, practically speaking, than a poorly implemented system intended to provide *perfect forward secrecy* (PFS). This point is valid in an off-topic sort of way: The fact that a good implementation of a weak design concept is more secure than a bad implementation of a strong design concept does not make an obvious case for the weak design concept. Religion aside, many individuals and businesses that routinely provide data access to authorized third parties resist third-party key access mechanisms because they believe that they are inherently vulnerable to unauthorized exploitation. They contend that such technologies really enable two things: back-door recovery of stored encrypted data (useful for disaster recovery) and third-party monitoring of encrypted data in transit. For a user who is already willing to cooperate with law enforcement or other authorized third parties to provide plaintext when necessary, third-party key access products seem like an unnecessary risk.

Private Doorbell

Some vendors have used security concerns, as well as their own interest in selling unmodified cryptographic products, to argue that certain encryption platforms—including most (if not all) IPsec software and hardware—inherently offer authorized data access similar to that of a key recovery or key escrow product. This capability has been referred to somewhat indiscriminately as *clear zone, private doorbell*, or *operator action*. These are fancy names for a common, noncryptographic characteristic of many gateways and applications: the ability to allow their managers to provide access to plaintext either prior to encryption or after decryption, rather than relying on a built-in mechanism to identify, capture, and decrypt ciphertext. For an IPsec gateway, the basis for operator action is the packet filtering capability specified in RFC 2401. The access point would generally (but not exclusively) be on the incoming LAN interface of the encrypting platform, and the access mechanism would be a network sniffer (as described in Chapter 3). Private doorbell is a natural fit for gateway products, but has also been applied successfully to applications and some IPsec end host products.

The private doorbell approach takes advantage of procedural regulations that, in some countries, require law-enforcement agencies to obtain a written order to perform legal interception of a business's or private party's data, and to present that order to the person who operates the communications facility that will serve as the interception point. Private doorbell proponents argue that any mechanism that supports legal fulfillment of a warrant ought to be as good as third-party key access in the eyes of law enforcement. Since this approach never exposes cryptographic keys, it is not vulnerable to the same kinds of third-party exploits that are possible with third-party key access products, though it is vulnerable to properly placed passive attacks (Kaufman 1998).

Standards Status

Although private doorbell is a regulatory analysis that requires no modification to IPsec, the IAB and IESG have opposed it. Their rejection appears to be a principled extension of RFC 1984, in which they argue against any approach—even those that simply interpret the regulations as favorable to IPsec—that might undermine a user's confidence in cryptographic systems.

U.S. Export Status of Private Doorbell Products

In the United States, private doorbell products, including many IPsec gateways, have been classified as *recoverable* technology. They enjoy broader exportability than nonrecoverable products, but do not have the full permissions of third-party key access products. A few products support both third-party key access and operator action. No other national government has ruled to date on any special import, export, or domestic use status for private doorbell products. At least 15 U.S. companies export products in this new licensing category.

Product Selection and Licensing

If you are building a multinational network, your first priority will be to identify where you need to install encrypting products and/or route encrypted traffic. Overlay your network topology on a map of the world, and make a list of where everything lands. You will need to identify the restrictions on product import and domestic use in every country where you plan to install your product. You will also need to identify any domestic use restrictions wherever you plan to transit encrypted traffic. The restrictions will vary according to your company's primary business, as well as what types of data you plan to sign and/or encrypt.

Vendor Licensing

Once you have identified where you need to deploy IPsec devices, you need to figure out what vendor or set of vendors can legally sell you a product in those countries. Ask each company where it is permitted to sell encryption products and what restrictions it has on algorithm, key length and strength, key management, customer types, and customer use.

If you have a site in the U.K. and one in the Sudan, and your vendor cannot export products directly to Sudan, it is against the law for you to receive the product in London and re-export it to Sudan yourself. If you plan to return your equipment for upgrades or repair, you need to verify that each country's export laws enable you to send the product back to its original source or to a specific repair location. Most countries make an exception in their re-export restrictions to permit hardware and/or software *return material authorizations* (RMAs), but don't take that for granted without checking.

Back-door Deals

Be aware that almost every company individually negotiates its import and export privileges with agencies inside its own government and foreign governments. The international grapevine hums with stories of eye-for-an-eye, back-door-for-a-back-door deals between certain companies and certain governments. If you find a company with privileges that are dramatically better than those of its local competitors, take the time to ask why. The answer ought at least to pass the laugh test. ("Our technology was so much better that our government felt it should be available to the world" is an example of an answer that does *not* pass the laugh test.) Remember that even if you aren't concerned about some intelligence agency taking a look at your network, a built-in back door will create an exploit opportunity for whomever it is that you are protecting your data against in the first place.

As you learn about various restrictions, overlay them on your topology, paying particular attention to potential interoperability problems among regulatory domains. Verify that your preferred products can negotiate different algorithms and transforms with different peers, in the event that you'll be running DES on some parts of your network, but 3DES and IDEA on others. Your completed topology should have a list of products and geographical locations with their required algorithms and keying mechanisms for optimal, legal interoperability.

The Licensing Process

Before you can install encryption products, your final step is to ask your preferred vendors to assist you in obtaining any licenses necessary for providing a copy of the product to each location on your planned network. You may need to provide detailed address and contact information for each license. In some instances, you will not need any additional licensing beyond the permissions that the vendor has negotiated for its products in advance. If your vendor has a blanket licensing agreement, find out what products it covers and when the license expires. You may need to negotiate additional licenses for major upgrades of IPsec platforms, and you may be unable to buy more products if your vendor fails to obtain full license renewal.

If you do need individual licenses, your vendors should help manage the arrangements competently. They should not charge you anything additional for licensing, even if they need to hire a lawyer to handle the process. Some vendors try to push foreign certification processes onto their customers. Such an approach is perverse: Why should you have to pay or invest hours of your own effort in order to buy their products? The self-service method is also likely to fail. Certification processes will almost certainly require information that the average customer cannot provide, such as platform functional specifications, design documents, or source code.

Prepare to Wait

Product licensing can take anywhere from several days to several months, depending on which countries need to process the licenses and whether there is anything unusual about your request. Ask your vendors what to expect, and double each answer. Above all, do not start this process 48 hours before you need to order your first IPsec product. If you do decide to hire a lawyer to help you with encryption licensing, confirm that she has prior experience working with cryptographic controls in the countries where you need licenses. Encryption law is a relatively small specialty, but an increasing number of people are taking work in the area. Don't spend your money training someone. Make sure that your candidate has already handled other licenses successfully.

Where to Get More Information

The following table lists sources of further information related to issues discussed in this chapter. Remember that any Web resource or book may be incomplete, inaccurate, or out-of-date. Always check directly with each government's relevant regulatory agencies or with qualified legal counsel before importing, exporting, deploying, or discussing proprietary details of any cryptographic system.

SOURCE	AUTHOR/HOST	DESCRIPTION
http://cwis.kub.nl/~frw/ people/koops/lawsurvy.htm	Bert-Jaap Koops	Crypto Law Survey. A very useful online source for country-specific encryption control information.
www.gilc.org/crypto/ crypto-survey.html	The Global Internet Liberty Campaign	"Cryptography and Liberty: an International Survey of Encryption Policy." An electronic document with country-by-country information.

SOURCE	AUTHOR/HOST	DESCRIPTION
http://cwis.kub.nl/~frw/people/hof/DS-lawsu.htm	Simon van der Hof	Digital Signature Law Survey. Modeled on Bert-Jaap Koops' work.
www.wassenaar.org	The Wassenaar Arrangement	Provides links to each member state's cryptography control pages online, where available. The Wassenaar details specific to cryptography are in the General Software Note and in the Dual-Use List, Category 5, Part 2, "Information Security."
www.oecd.org	Organization for Economic Co-operation and Development	The main OECD Web page.
www.oecd.org/dsti/sti/it/secur/index.htm	Organization for Economic Co-operation and Development	The two OECD reports on cryptography.
The Limits of Trust: Cryptography, Governments, and Electronic Commerce	Stewart A. Baker and Paul R. Hurst	An interesting, if slightly U.S.-centric analysis of international cryptography issues and regulations. See the bibliography for more information.
www.steptoe.com/WebDoc.nsf/Law+&+The+Net-All/All	Steptoe and Johnson, LLP	The Washington, D.C.-based law firm that employs both Stewart Baker and Paul Hurst. Tracks legal issues online and provides an interesting but patchy collection of resources. (You can also browse the company's archives.)
www.t-b.com/export.htm	Thomsen & Burke, LLP	A Baltimore, Maryland-based law firm with substantial international encryption expertise. Provides some useful background information.

Two

Technology Essentials

This book is about working with (and surviving) IPsec products. It is not a detailed examination of the IPsec protocols or other networking technologies. However, we do introduce some technical and architectural concepts that are fundamental to any long-term success with IPsec. The three chapters that follow provide brief overviews of IP network security issues, public and private key cryptography, the IPsec protocols, and public key infrastructures. We do not give a complete description in each area, but rather focus on the concepts that are most central to a strong operating comprehension of IPsec networking.

The Risks of IP Networking

The same technology that has enabled the mad growth of the global Internet has also left its users vulnerable to a range of serious threats. IPsec was born to solve the security problems created by version 4 of the Internet Protocol (IPv4) and to provide a secure architecture for the next generation, Internet Protocol version 6 (IPv6). Prior to IPsec, the architectural attributes of TCP/IP forced many network managers to rely on application-by-application security or point products such as firewalls to protect IP networks and hosts. Although these technologies can be very useful, they require constant modification to support new internal applications, and they do not provide a generic mechanism to secure traffic end to end. In this chapter, as an introduction to our discussion of IPsec in Chapter 7, "The Basics of IPsec and Public Key Infrastructures," we describe some of the security risks inherent in TCP/IP design.

IP Functional Overview

IP is like a Disney (albeit a somewhat X-rated Disney) version of Frankenstein's monster. It is a beast that escaped from a United States government research project to spread enlightenment, frivolity, and commercialism worldwide. Almost 20 years before anyone thought to use silly terms like "information superhighway," the Defense Advanced Research Projects Agency (DARPA) funded a project that eventually brought us the Internet Protocol suite. The DARPA initiative had two main objectives:

- To establish a foundation for a flexible communications protocol
- To provide a mechanism for successful open collaboration among government, academic, and private-sector researchers

It's important to recognize that IP was *not* designed to support a global commercial marketplace or to optimize anonymous, real-time distribution of pornography: Those uses came later. The main goal of IP was to provide an inexpensive, versatile, scalable data infrastructure that could be bombed nearly out of existence and still function.

Basic Design Characteristics

There are three key attributes of IP that are relevant to the need for and operation of IPsec:

- Protocol- and media-independence
- Stateless data transport
- Fault tolerance

Protocol- and Media-Independence

IP is independent of any lower-layer protocol (see Figure 5.1); that is, it can traverse nearly any transmission medium. There are even joke standards for sending IP packets by bird. (See RFCs 1149 and 2549.) IP uses its own addressing scheme to enable identification of senders and receivers of datagrams, no matter where or how they are connected. Because IP also allows local management of the network and routing infrastructure, the addressing scheme provides almost no assurance that the sender and recipient addresses are authentic. In

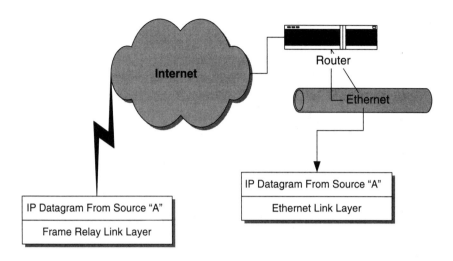

Figure 5.1   IP datagrams are lower-layer independent.

other words, an IP packet, no matter what it looks like, may come from almost anywhere.

Note that IP is as vulnerable as any other protocol to *eavesdropping* attacks, in which a device (often called a *sniffer*; see Chapter 3 for details) copies all traffic from its connected network segment, even if it is bound for somewhere or someone else. The eavesdropping attack is one of the most common techniques for stealing data. We discuss how IPsec interacts with sniffers in Chapter 8, "What Won't Work with IPsec."

Fragmentation and Reassembly

Because different lower-layer protocols impose different limitations on packet size, IP allows datagrams to be broken or *fragmented* into smaller pieces and *reassembled* at the destination. (Note that IPv4 and IPv6 handle fragmentation and reassembly differently. IPv4 allows any intermediate gateway to fragment a packet, while IPv6 allows only the originating host to perform fragmentation [really sending a packet of the lowest common size for the path]). Some IPsec implementations have had problems handling fragmentation and reassembly correctly. We describe this problem in slightly more detail in Chapter 7.

IP Is Stateless

IP is a *stateless* protocol. There are no setup or bandwidth requirements governing how one IP device can send data to another. Statelessness also means that each packet is handled on its own, without reference to preceding packets. Certain protocols and applications that run over IP require both connection setup and the timely delivery of data. The concept of state is indirectly important for IPsec because some of these higher-layer services conflict with IPsec when both are applied to the same traffic flows. We discuss these conflicts in Chapter 8.

Fault Tolerance

The IP protocol is also *unreliable*. That is, intervening gateways perform no integrity check on the payload of an IP datagram, and they are not bound to ensure that any given datagram is delivered at all. See Figure 5.2, which shows the loss-tolerant nature of IP. Applications or higher-layer protocols, principally the *Transmission Control Protocol* (TCP), are responsible for discovering the data loss or corruption. TCP supports an efficient packet acknowledgment system that identifies lost data, although it does not have any strong way to verify the source or authenticity of data.

Because neither IP nor TCP keeps close track of traffic, it is relatively trivial to disrupt, redirect, or inject packets in flight.

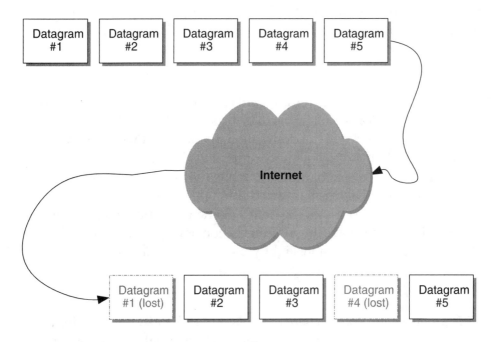

Figure 5.2 The IP protocol tolerates datagram loss in transmission.

Summary of IP Security Risks

Security risks specific to IP networks fall into two broad categories:

- Data theft
- Data tampering

Generally speaking, data on a vanilla IP network is visible to anyone, could come from anywhere, and might be modified to say anything, unless there are intentional and proactive safeguards in place.

People and businesses who use IP networks tend to do so with the assumption that they can trust the origin and content of the data they work with, and that their transactions, if not secret, are reasonably private. On IP networks, that expectation is similar to an expectation to win the lottery. In other words, it's based on hope rather than on any reasonable calculation of probability. The designers of IPsec intended to change those odds. In the next chapter, we review the cryptographic building blocks that underlie the IPsec protocols.

Cryptographic Protocols and Techniques

Cryptography is the foundation of IPsec and of many other security technologies. It is also a wildly complex field that can boggle the brain and drive fine minds to madness. You do not need to understand cryptography to implement IPsec, just as you do not need to understand the internal combustion engine to drive a car. It does help, however, to have a good appreciation of its uses, so that you can make reasonable, legal purchasing decisions and can analyze tradeoffs between product performance and cryptographic strength.

This chapter is not an exhaustive guide to cryptography; it focuses on the aspects of cryptography that are most relevant to deploying IPsec and provides an overview of some common, complementary authentication technologies. If you do find yourself fevered for details, though, you're in luck—our publisher just happens to print a very comprehensive guide by Bruce Schneier called *Applied Cryptography*. It makes a fine gift, and will impress your friends at home and your colleagues in the office.

Cryptography Basics

In this section we briefly discuss symmetric encryption, public key (or asymmetric) encryption, and hashing functions. In the context of IPsec, symmetric encryption provides data confidentiality (with some ancillary data integrity services), public key encryption enables strong device and data authentication, and hash signatures provide high-speed data integrity checks.

Brute Force and Known Plaintext Attacks

If data is worth encrypting, it's usually worth stealing. *Cryptanalysis* is the science of analyzing cryptographic algorithms, generally with an eye toward figuring out how to reveal the original *plaintext* (unencrypted data). Bad encryption algorithms simplify cryptanalysis by providing some clue to the plaintext or encryption key in the *ciphertext* (encrypted data) or by exposing some mechanism (usually unintentionally) that can degrade the overall encryption strength. Good encryption algorithms can be vulnerable to *brute force* and *known plaintext* attacks (there are other forms of attack we do not discuss here). A brute force attack requires trying all possible keys for a given lump of ciphertext until you get the right one and can decrypt the data. A known plaintext attack entails injecting a lump of known plaintext into the encryption engine to produce a *before* and *after* pair of plaintext and ciphertext to aid in deducing the encryption key. IPsec gateways, depending on their configuration, can be very vulnerable to known plaintext attacks, since it is not difficult to redirect traffic unobtrusively across an IP network. See the section "Basics of Crypto-Busting" in Chapter 4, "Encrypting within the Law," for some additional comments on cryptanalysis.

Symmetric Encryption

Encryption algorithms are *symmetric* when the same key is used both to encrypt and to decrypt. Symmetric key algorithms are often called *bulk* encryption algorithms because their relative speed suits them to the encryption of large amounts of data.

Common Symmetric Algorithms

The most common symmetric key algorithm is the *Data Encryption Standard* (DES). DES is in broad commercial use and has been favored by the U.S. government for 20 years. Unfortunately, it is not optimized to run on a general-purpose CPU, and it has a fixed 56-bit key that is increasingly vulnerable to brute force attacks. The so-called *3DES* (triple DES) mechanism ameliorates the relative weakness of the 56-bit key by applying DES to the same data three times, with three different 56-bit keys. Unfortunately (but not surprisingly), 3DES takes three times as long to execute as single DES, so it's not a screamingly fast performer.

Another symmetric key algorithm is IDEA, a 128-bit symmetric algorithm popular with Swiss banks and many other financial institutions. Other common algorithms include a collection of algorithms created at RSA Data Security: RC2, RC4, and RC5 (note that Security Dynamics Technology, Inc. is the current patent holder for RC2 and RC4). See Figure 6.1 for an example of symmetric bulk encryption in action.

One-way Hash Functions

One-way hash functions operate over an arbitrarily long message and produce a fixed-length *hash signature* (output value). They essentially create a unique electronic fingerprint for a given message. Hash

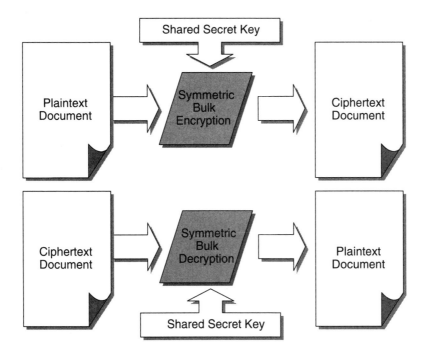

Figure 6.1   Symmetric bulk encryption at work.

functions are one-way because the signature cannot be reverse-engineered to retrieve the original data, just as a common thug's thumbprint can uniquely identify him but cannot be manipulated (at least not yet) to produce another identical thug. One valuable way to use a hash function is to apply it to the same lump of data before and after transmission. If the results match, the data passes the integrity check.

Cryptographically Secure Hash Functions

Some one-way hash functions are *cryptographically secure* and have several additional attributes:

- They are designed to run quickly on a general-purpose CPU.
- It is very difficult to retrieve the original message from the hash signature (see the preceding thug example).
- For any given message, it is very difficult to produce a second message that will generate the same hash signature (as it would be difficult to create another common thug with the same thumbprint as the first). The unique association of a hash signature with a particular lump of data makes it a powerful tool for confirming that data's integrity.

Keyed Hash Functions

Keyed hash functions are one-way hash functions that share a key between the sender and recipient(s) of a message. They provide a mechanism for confirming both the integrity of the data and the sender and recipient's possession of the same shared key. The *Hashed Message Authentication Codes* (HMAC) mechanism (RFC 2104) is a standard component of IPsec.

The primary limit of a hash function's strength is the size of the hash signature (all other things being equal). Currently, the two most popular hash functions are Message Digest #5 (MD5) and Secure Hash Algorithm #1 (SHA-1). MD5 produces a 128-bit signature. It is fast and in common use, but some recurring patterns in its output may indicate a weakness in the algorithm. The SHA-1 algorithm is somewhat slower and produces a 160-bit hash output. It too is in increasingly common use with IPsec.

Public Key Cryptography

Public key—also known as *asymmetric key*—cryptography uses a pair of separate, related keys. The two keys are generated together, and each key can decrypt what the other encrypts. One, the *private* key, must remain secret, while the other, the *public* key, must be available to any party who needs to interact securely with the holder of the private key. If the holder of a unique private key encrypts a message, only someone with a copy of the associated public key can decrypt it. That operation provides strong proof that only the holder of the unique private key could have encrypted the original message, securing both privacy and proof of origin for the message.

The two most common public key algorithms are the *Rivest, Shamir, and Adelman* (RSA) algorithm and the *Digital Signature Algorithm* (DSA). (See Chapter 11, "What to Ask Your Vendors," for a discussion of the patent status of the RSA algorithm.) Diffie-Hellman (DH) is a key exchange protocol that uses public key mechanisms to establish a shared secret key, and is a common complement to both RSA and DSA in IPsec implementations.

Digital Signatures

Public key cryptography can operate in conjunction with a one-way hash function to provide data attribution as well as privacy and integrity services by generating a *digital signature*. Figure 6.2 shows an encrypted and signed document. The holder of a private key can calculate the hash signature of a message and then encrypt it with her public key. Any holder of the public key can then recalculate the hash signature on the message, decrypt the original hash signature, and compare the two. If they match, the recipient has proof of both the author and the authenticity of the message.

Pretty Good Privacy (PGP)

Public key cryptography has been around for well over 20 years, but the difficulty of building a *public key infrastructure* (PKI)—among other factors—has slowed its deployment. A related technology, Phil Zimmerman's *Pretty Good Privacy* (PGP), is one of the most broadly deployed cryptographic systems. PGP enables a *web of trust* model, instead of relying on a strict trust hierarchy. Groups of individuals

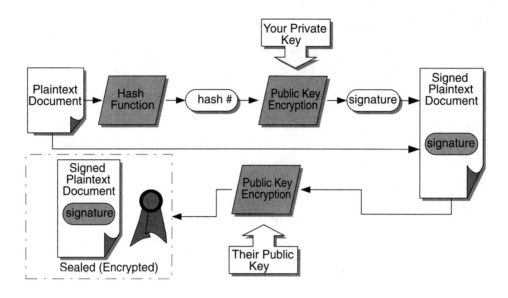

Figure 6.2 An encrypted and authenticated (signed) document.

share public keys face to face (usually in a bar). Each signs the others' keys, attesting to their authenticity. Additionally, each person decides whether to trust the others as *introducers*, individuals empowered to vouch for the authenticity of other unknown keys.

Over time, as overlapping concentric circles of people sign one another's keys, the web of trust grows. Many businesses deploy PGP with a *corporate signing key* (CSK) that enforces a one-level hierarchy. Users sign and trust this key by default, allowing the business essentially to compel trust of other keys, as appropriate. Existing PGP applications can digitally sign and encrypt email and other arbitrary data. PKI fans often criticize the scaling properties of the web of trust model, but no existing cryptographic trust model has yet been shown to scale better than PGP.

Steganography: The Data Vanishes

Given the grisly regulatory status of cryptography in many countries (see Chapter 4), we thought it worthwhile to point out that there are other ways to communicate secretly. *Steganography* is the science of concealing data, whether by hiding it in the heel of a boot, tattooing it (gently) to the belly of a pigeon, or encoding it pixel by pixel into a

JPEG image of King Henry VIII eating a plate of spaghetti. While cryptography makes a message unintelligible, steganography conceals its existence. Because steganographic techniques generally require a significant volume of nonsecret transmission (such as a boot, a pigeon, or a picture of King Henry VIII), they are not currently very efficient mechanisms for transmitting a lot of data securely across a network. For a virtual private network, for example, a steganographic approach would require much more data transmission than a cryptographic one. If, however, the bulk of the data traveling between two points is not sensitive, steganography might provide an interesting alternative to cryptography, especially for cases in which using strong encryption products is against the law. Very few commercial products support steganographic techniques today, but it's a trend to watch. Note also that some steganographic tools use cryptography to distribute the interesting bits of data randomly into the nonsensitive bits of data (Wayner 1996).

Cryptographic Authentication Mechanisms

Confidentiality isn't very useful if you aren't sure with whom you are communicating. Most cryptographic protocols (including IPsec) require some form of authentication prior to any data exchange. Many of these mechanisms also bootstrap or provide the keying material for the ensuing secure communication. The following are common cryptographic authentication mechanisms.

Preshared Secrets

In the *preshared secret* model, two or more entities securely *preshare* (exchange) a *secret* (key) in advance. IPsec devices may use a floppy disk or another manual distribution mechanism that is safe from eavesdropping. After sharing the key, the parties either negotiate or use a preconfigured symmetric algorithm to encrypt data between them. This mechanism establishes that each participating entity has the key, but it cannot distinguish between them as senders or recipients of data. Support for preshared secrets is mandatory for IPsec devices. Although they provide a quick and inexpensive way to bootstrap an IPsec implementation, preshared secrets are cumbersome to maintain and do not scale well.

Third Parties and Preshared Secrets

A more scalable model uses a third-party *key distribution center* (KDC) that shares a unique secret with each trusted participant. (In this context, the third party is a mediator in the cryptographic communication rather than a vendor add-on [as in "third-party product"].) The KDC must participate in each initial secure negotiation, because none of the other participants knows any secret but its own. Since the KDC has an established trust relationship with all participants, it can use each one's shared secret to generate an *introducer* that contains the identity of the communicating parties and a randomly generated piece of data. It encrypts every introducer with each participant's respective secret and delivers it to that party. (Note that this delivery can use an insecure channel, since the data is encrypted.) Each party can decrypt its introducer and use the shared random data as an initial shared secret with the other party. Although the KDC is most commonly associated with Kerberos (discussed later in this chapter), it's actually a general-purpose mechanism.

Third Parties and Public Key Cryptography

Public key cryptography can also use a trusted third-party method that does not require any active mediation for introductions. For example, one party could approach a third party for a copy of the second party's public key. It could then encrypt a proposed shared secret with that key and send it to the second party. The second party is the only entity that could decrypt that secret, since it is the exclusive holder of the associated private key. It may either accept the proposed secret and encrypt a response to prove receipt, or offer an alternate key, using the the same mechanism with the first party's public key.

The most common third-party solution for public key cryptography is a *certification authority* (CA), the foundation component of a public key infrastructure (PKI). A CA uses its own private key to sign the public keys of trusted individuals using a *digital certificate* format. The CA thus vouches for the authenticity of an entity's public key. Anyone who trusts the CA may by inference trust any party carrying a valid certificate with that CA's signature. We discuss PKI technology and related issues in Chapter 7, "The Basics of IPsec and Public Key Infrastructures."

Authentication and the Zero-Knowledge Proof

If a secret is your proof of identity, disclosing that secret to prove your identity is clearly a bad idea, since it allows any recipient to impersonate you. Disclosing a shared secret presents a similar risk, since you may inadvertently be sharing it with an unauthorized party. Proving that you know something without actually disclosing that something is called a *zero-* or *partial-knowledge* proof.

One partial-knowledge solution for authentication is the *challenge handshake* (Figure 6.3). This mechanism allows an individual to authenticate itself to another entity (such as a remote host or a *remote access server* [RAS]), and relies on the prior existence of a preshared secret between the two (often a password). The first party initiates the sequence by presenting the second party with a nonsecret credential, such as a user name. The second party generates and sends back a random string. The first party then combines the random string with the password, hashes it, and returns the result. The second party repeats the calculation using its own version of the shared secret. If the two parties' results match, the first party has proven that it knows the shared secret without ever disclosing it. Assuming that the parties use a new random string each time, a malevolent entity can't forge the process without somehow stealing a copy of the shared secret. (Note, however, that there are some other known ways to attack challenge handshake authentication sequences.)

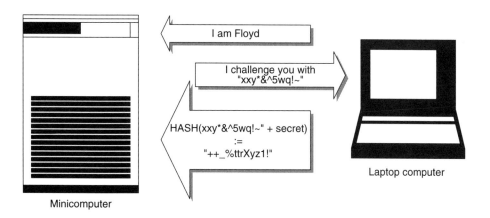

Figure 6.3 The challenge handshake—authenticating without disclosure.

Kerberos

Kerberos is a set of services that support a KDC-based authentication system. Born of MIT's Project Athena in the 1980s, Kerberos is very popular at many U.S. colleges and universities. It has been slow to catch on in the business world because it requires application-by-application customization. Kerberos V (RFC 1510) is likely to become more widespread, in part because it provides the new security model for Microsoft Windows 2000 (NT 5.0). In some instances, a Kerberos KDC can replace a PKI infrastructure as an authentication mechanism for IPsec. We discuss this option in the following chapter.

The Basics of IPsec and Public Key Infrastructures

As the designers of IPsec began their work, many Internet engineers shared a sense of impending doom about the viability of IPv4 and were deeply involved in the design and prototyping of IPv6. IPsec is thus a hybrid: It is both a retrofit to the many flaws in IPv4 and a preemptive strike against insecurity in IPv6. Like many hybrids, it has some unexpected quirks. (We discuss the impact of those quirks in Chapter 8, "What Won't Work with IPsec.") Even so, IPsec is the only broadly accepted standard for secure network-layer transport on IP. It is more versatile and less expensive than both application and link-layer encryption technologies.

IPsec is a very complex set of protocols and mechanisms. Although you do not need to be an expert to make it work, it is important to understand its fundamental components and the ways they relate to one another. This chapter is an introduction to IPsec components, with a focus on how they integrate into IPv4.

The Anatomy of IPsec

IPsec was designed to have an open, modular architecture. This modularity allows it to evolve to address new requirements, new cryptographic technologies, and newly identified problems with existing security mechanisms. The following sections discuss the elements of IPsec that were Internet standards as this book went to press.

Two Security Protocols

IPsec has two basic security protocols: the *Authentication Header* (AH) and the *Encapsulating Security Payload* (ESP). AH is an authenticating protocol that uses a hash signature in the packet header to validate the integrity of the packet data and the authenticity of the sender. ESP is an authenticating and encrypting protocol that uses cryptographic mechanisms to provide integrity, source authentication, and confidentiality services. We describe both protocols in some detail in the sections that follow (Kent 1998a, 1998b).

Two Modes of Operation

Each protocol can operate in one of two modes: *transport* mode, in which the protocol operates primarily on the payload of the original datagram, and *tunnel* mode, in which the protocol encapsulates the original datagram in a new one, treating the original as the data payload. In tunnel mode, the source and destination IP address are often, but not always, different from those in the header of the original datagram.

The Implementation Options

IPsec can operate on an *end host* (a single- or multiuser host or server) or in a *gateway* (a network element that is neither the originator nor the ultimate recipient of the IP traffic). End-host and gateway products come in several common flavors:

End Host

A *native stack.* Many OS vendors integrate tunnel- and transport-mode IPsec directly into their bundled IP stacks.

A *replacement stack.* A third-party vendor may write an entire drop-in replacement for the original stack. Although this approach may simplify the work of supporting IPsec, it is a nontrivial effort to reproduce the full functionality of the native IP stack and to evolve the new stack in parallel with the operating system.

A *bump in the stack.* Most third-party vendors try to insert their IPsec implementations into the native stack, either by writing to a known API or by reverse-engineering a released version of the stack. Tunnel mode is easier to implement in this way than transport mode, since the IPsec operation only needs to intervene before the *network interface card* (NIC) driver has inserted the datagram into a link-layer frame. For transport mode, the third party needs to go deeper into the guts of the stack.

Gateway

A *bump in the wire.* Many IPsec gateways are dual-interface boxes with no other integrated network functionality. Such devices are referred to as *bumps in the wire* because they are simple encrypting units that remain largely transparent to other network devices.

An *integrated gateway.* In other cases, the IPsec gateway is an enhancement to an IP router or firewall.

Security Associations

The *security association* (SA) is a critical component of the IPsec architecture. An SA is a record of the information an IPsec entity needs in order to support one direction (outbound traffic or inbound traffic) of an IPsec protocol connection. Its contents will vary for each connection, and can include authentication and encryption keys, specific algorithms and modes, key lifetimes, *initialization vectors* (IVs), and source IP addresses. The SA tells an IPsec device how to process incoming IPsec packets and how to generate outbound IPsec packets.

Multiple SAs will exist for any exchange. IPsec devices embed a value called the *security parameter index* (SPI) in the IPsec header to associate a given datagram with its appropriate SA on the receiving host. It is vital, of course, that each host or gateway apply the correct SA to each IPsec datagram. The standards define a rigorous mechanism for ensuring that each SA is unique. IPsec devices store these SAs in a *security association database* (SAD) (Kent 1998c).

The Authentication Header (AH)

The AH protocol can detect packet corruption or tampering and can authenticate the identity of a sender by end user or by source IP address. Currently, the IPsec *peers* (communicating parties) in AH may use either MD5 or SHA-1 to create a hash signature using a secret component of the SA, the packet data payload, and several parts of the packet header (Madson 1998a, 1998b).

The AH Packet Header

Figure 7.1 shows a typical authentication header. The AH header has five essential fields:

- The *next header,* which usually describes the layer 4 header (TCP/UDP/ICMP) for an IPv4 datagram
- The length of the hash signature (note that this value will be constant for each hashing algorithm, since each has a fixed-length output)
- The security parameter index (SPI)
- The anti-replay sequence number field (this prevents an attacker from *replaying* [resending] a packet as part of an attack)
- The hash signature itself

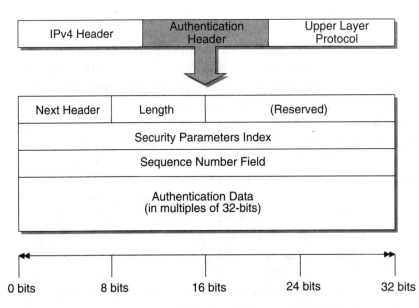

Figure 7.1 A typical authentication header (AH).

Sending an AH Packet

To transmit an AH packet, the IPsec host or gateway must do the following:

- Identify the appropriate SA, SPI, algorithm (MD5 or SHA-1), and secret key.

- Increment the anti-replay counter (anti-replay is on by default).

- Assemble the data to be hashed in a fashion appropriate to the specific standard in force.

- Set the *time to live* (TTL), *type of service* (ToS, now known as the *differentiated services* or DS byte), and header checksum fields to zero. This operation allows these fields to be modified in flight without altering the hash signature. (Note that for IPv6, you also need to zero out the hop limit field in the base header and all fields whose OPTION TYPE bit is set to indicate a mutable value.) Calculate the hash value and the other packet header fields.

- Insert the AH header directly between the IP header and the layer 4 header. In tunnel mode, the entire original datagram is the packet payload, so the AH header goes between the newly created outer IP header and the original datagram. (Note that for IPv6, the AH header belongs after all hop-by-hop headers.)

Receiving an AH Packet

A receiving host or gateway reverses the transmission process described in the previous section and discards any datagrams whose recalculated hash value doesn't match the original. If the relevant SA specifies anti-replay, the sequence number must fall within the proper *window* (range) of numbers, and must not be a duplicate of any prior packet. Figure 7.2 shows detail of an authentication header.

The Encapsulating Security Payload (ESP)

The ESP protocol can provide confidentiality, authenticity, and integrity services. Tunnel-mode ESP also offers traffic-flow confidentiality. Early drafts of the ESP protocol focused on confidentiality, but the final standard also includes a great deal of functionality from AH.

The ESP standards currently support two *transforms*, or operations: DES and 3DES (described in Chapter 6, "Cryptographic Protocols and

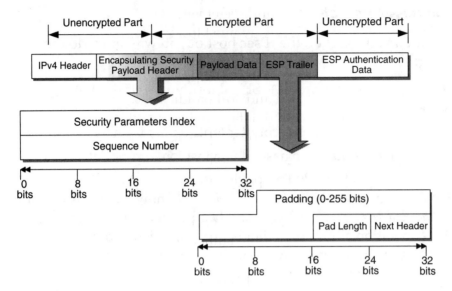

Figure 7.2 Authentication header (AH) detail.

Techniques"). The two transforms are very similar, and DES support is mandatory. Of course, the ESP standard will eventually support transforms for many other encryption algorithms (Madson 1998b).

The ESP Packet Header

Like AH, the ESP header contains the following:

- The security parameter index (SPI)
- The anti-replay sequence number field

Unlike AH, the ESP header also includes the *next header* field as part of the packet trailer. The packet payload may include padding to conform to the specific cryptographic transform and to ensure that the next header field ends on a 4-byte boundary. The trailer may also contain a variable amount of authentication data.

Sending an ESP Packet

To transmit an ESP packet, the sending host or gateway must do as follows:

- Identify the appropriate SA and associated SPI. If the SA indicates integrity/authenticity, the host or gateway must also locate the correct hash algorithm and secret key. If the SA indicates confidentiality, the host or gateway must locate the appropriate cryptographic transform and secret key.

- Increment the anti-replay counter (if appropriate).

- Assemble the ESP payload and add padding, if necessary. In tunnel mode, the entire original datagram becomes the ESP payload, and the sender creates a new outer IP header that precedes the original packet.

- If specified, encrypt the ESP payload with the appropriate cryptographic algorithm.

- If specified, calculate the integrity check value (ICV) over the headers and payload (minus the authentication data itself), using the correct hash algorithm.

- Insert the ESP header, payload, and trailer (plus authentication/ integrity data) directly after the IP header. (Note that in IPv6, the ESP data belongs after all of the hop-by-hop headers.)

Receiving an ESP Packet

A receiving host or gateway reverses the sending procedure described in the previous section. If the SA specifies authentication services, that check essentially mirrors the hash check for AH: The host or gateway must discard any packet that fails the integrity check. If the SA specifies the anti-replay option, the host or gateway must also discard any packets that are repeats or that fall outside the receiver's window. The last step is to decrypt the packet payload.

Figure 7.3 shows an ESP-transformed datagram. In this example the datagram contains an optional ICV that provides authenticity and integrity. If the ICV were not present, IPsec would not detect modification to the payload, but the decryption would probably produce gibberish. An ICV generally provides a more positive mechanism for discarding modified data with minimal overhead.

Why Bother with AH?

Since the final standard for ESP supports both authentication and integrity, you may be wondering why anyone would bother to implement AH. There are, however, both practical and historical reasons to use it for certain services.

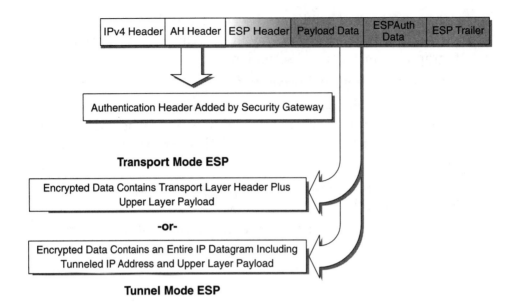

Figure 7.3   Encapsulating Security Payload detail.

- A standards-compliant ESP implementation *must* support DES encryption, even if the host or gateway never uses it. Under certain strict regulatory regimes, AH may be the only IPsec protocol legal to use, since cryptography for the purposes of authentication (as opposed to confidentiality) is usually acceptable. See Chapter 4, "Encrypting within the Law," for details on the regulatory issues for IPsec.

- AH also provides a higher assurance of authenticity and content integrity, since it operates on the IP payload *plus* all immutable (and all predictable) fields in the outer IP header.

Authentication Header (AH) and Encapsulating Security Payload (ESP)

AH and ESP can operate on the same datagram. Figure 7.4 shows AH and ESP headers together. Although it is possible for an end host or gateway to apply both protocols to the same connection, that scenario is not the most common. In a more typical combination, the end host generates transport-mode ESP datagrams, while an intermediate *security gateway* (SG) encapsulates those ESP packets into tunnel-mode

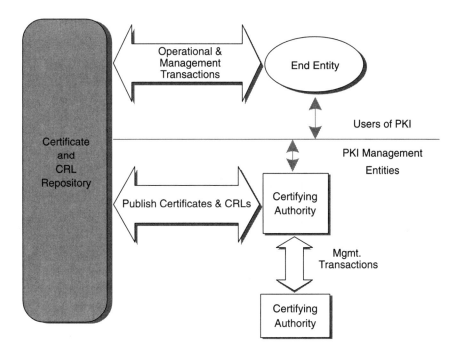

Figure 7.4   AH and ESP headers together.

AH. A mirror-image configuration at the other end of the connection (an SG de-encapsulates, and an end host decrypts) would provide end-to-end confidentiality and a strong defense against tampering across the WAN. The inverse configuration—in which the end host uses AH and the gateway tunnels ESP—would also make sense for many VPN topologies.

IPsec Authentication: Defining a PKI

As we discussed in Chapter 6, confidentiality is not generally useful without prior authentication. The AH and ESP standards do not require automated key management, and they do not mandate any *particular* authentication mechanism. Preshared secrets, however, can get you only so far before you're liable to fall to the floor with hash signatures frothing from your ears, nose, and mouth. Most large IPsec installations use a PKI for authentication. Windows 2000 users also have the option of authenticating with a Kerberos KDC (see Chapter 6 for a brief description of Kerberos).

A CA functions as a sort of electronic notary public: It is a trusted electronic entity that vouches for the authenticity and credibility of individuals, applications, entities, and (sometimes) data. A PKI is built around the concept of an embedded CA hierarchy that can establish potentially complex trust relationships among users, applications, hosts, and network elements.

Whose Key Is It?

The attributes of a public/private key pair are most powerful if those keys are strongly bound to the identity of the person or thing they purport to represent. There are two basic questions that confront anyone deploying a PKI:

- What other nonprivate information needs to be associated with any given public key to establish a unique, unambiguous credential? For example, if two James L. Smiths work in the same department, what is a meaningful way to distinguish them?
- What process is used to authenticate a person or object to the PKI before obtaining a credential? The strength of the PKI is highly dependent on the certainty of each initial authentication.

X.509 Certificates

The *International Organization for Standardization* (ISO) X.500 standards suite defines a complex basis for registering and retrieving information about people, places, and objects. This set of standards was designed to have a potentially unlimited scope, and its identifiers are hierarchical to simplify the unique characterization of objects. The X.509 standard provides a mechanism to associate a public key with a collection of subcomponents sufficient to uniquely authenticate the claimed owner of the object. These subcomponents are collectively known as a *distinguished name* (DN). The signed association of a DN with a public key is known as an X.509 *digital certificate*.

X.509 certificates are organized in a hierarchical structure in which a *certification authority* (CA) signs each certificate. The *root* or most trusted CA signs its own key and those of other CAs to form an inverted tree structure. Although this structure scales well, the root is very vulnerable. In addition, CA hierarchies are not optimized to support nonhierarchical trust models, such as introducer-based relationships.

The Public-Key Infrastructure (X.509) (PKIX) Initiative

For true IPsec interoperability, there must be a standard mechanism to establish trust relationships among arbitrary IPsec peers. Not only must those IPsec peers interoperate at a protocol level; they must also be able to authenticate one another in a reliable, standard way. The mission of the IETF *Public-Key Infrastructure (X.509)* (PKIX) working group is to create standards that enable a flexible, interoperable X.509 PKI optimized for Internet protocols, applications, and end users. Many applications, some of which predate IPsec, require an X.509 PKI to operate correctly; these include privacy enhanced mail (PEM), SSL, and Secure Multipurpose Internet Mail Extensions (S/MIME). Figure 7.5 shows some PKI entities.

PKIX Standards Focus

PKIX has a very broad charter. It has focused on several specific areas:

- Certificate and CRL profiles
- Management protocols
- Operational protocols
- Policy templates and guidelines

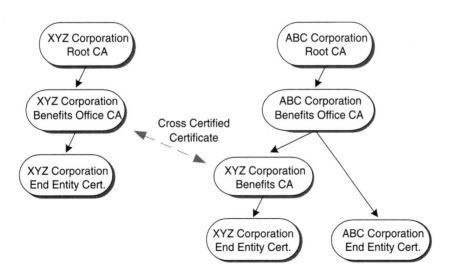

Figure 7.5   PKI entities.

PKIX X.509 v3 Certificate Profile

The PKIX working group has specified an Internet X.509 v3 certificate profile that is designed to provide flexible functionality and local control (see RFC 2459). The format permits two main conditions:

- A root can be either local or global. Several companies have built commercial service offerings that provide CA and certificate services to end users and corporations. Name constraints are not fixed by a global hierarchical model and subordinate to the CA tree above any given *end entity* (EE), as with prior standards. Any necessary naming constraints are identified in X.509 v3 name constraint extensions in the certificate itself.

- An extension field also identifies certificate policies and a related *certification practices statement* (CPS). Since the CPS is identified by reference, the base document can be updated as necessary. See Chapter 10, "Evaluating Vendors," for a discussion of the CPS.

Cross-Certification

The X.509 hierarchical model poses a major challenge for a world that depends on many nonhierarchical trust relationships. In its purest form, it presents a metaphysical conundrum: Either there are individuals never permitted to trust one another, or there must be a fixed, single root CA in the sky whose trust characteristics are uniform, universal, and absolute—an infallible and incorruptible root whose trust is implicit and fundamental to all.

One workaround has been to have individuals participate in multiple trust trees, since trust can exist only within a given hierarchy. PKIX outlines an alternative called *cross-certification,* which allows hierarchies (or pieces of them) to trust one another. (See Figure 7.6.) Essentially, a CA in one hierarchy signs another CA's public key (and other certificate request components) after validating the authenticity of the key/subject relationship. After this new certificate is created, a validation path in the signer's trust structure exists for all certificates signed by the subject of the certificate.

PKIX has also defined a policy-mapping extension for the X.509 v3 certificate that allows certificate policies from one trust structure to be mapped onto certificate policies in another at the time of cross-certification (see RFC 2459). This mechanism extends a simple trust relationship to potentially complex trust policy between organizations.

C	Country
SP	State or Province
L	Location
O	Organization
OU	Organizational Unit
CN	Common Name

Figure 7.6   Example of cross-certification.

Attributes of an X.509 Certificate

For IPsec, the most common credential is an X.509 digital certificate. These certificates can be dauntingly complex, but how you choose to use them can have significant implications for the long-term usefulness and flexibility of your PKI. The following sections discuss some critical elements of an X.509 certificate. See Figure 7.7 for a sample certificate.

The X.509 certificate contains several required attributes. How you assign these attributes will impact the value and functionality of your PKI.

What's in a Distinguished Name (DN)?

A public/private key pair is supposed to be mathematically unique. A DN is supposed to be both globally unique and socially meaningful. The contents of a DN are, according to the ISO standard, potentially open-ended. Needless to say, the effort to standardize the structure and content of a DN remains contentious. The issues may seem wildly overblown if you are simply trying to bootstrap a CA to support 10 VPN routers. Consider, however, that the X.509 certificate could become a ubiquitous authentication mechanism for employees, partners, customers, and even telephones. Given that once they're issued, certificates are difficult to take back, it makes sense to spend some time thinking through what your PKI must support over time and how you can ensure that the credentials it issues are particular and meaningful.

```
Certificate
    Data:
 Version: 0 (0x0)
        Serial Number:
            19:98:03:23:03
        Signature Algorithm: md5withRSAEncryption
        Issuer: C=US, SP=Connecticut, L=Woodside,
                O=Rodent University,
                OU=Mole Rat Services,
                CN=Rodent Certificate Authority,
                Email=rodentx509@rodent.edu
  Validity
            Not Before: Mar 23 14:58:00 1998 GMT
            Not After : Mar 23 14:58:00 1999 GMT
 Subject: C=US, SP=Connecticut, L=New Haven,
                O=Rodent University,
                OU=Mole Rat Services,
                CN=buckteeth.fang.rodent.edu,
                Email=pointy.teeth@rodent.edu
        Subject Public Key Info:
            Public Key Algorithm: rsaEncryption
            Modulus:
                00:c3:b3:08:17:fe:a0:57:d8:38:23:eb:3a:37:31:
                35:32:27:ab:be:e8:24:22:b5:52:d5:d5:17:02:fc:
                b1:d7:8b:07:15:d1:f7:d2:df:0f:71:20:3c:cd:c7:
                ea:8a:38:b7:7c:23:db:14:f0:44:43:78:d7:73:c4:
                de:b8:ba:e7:f7:8b:f3:f5:f8:0c:a4:22:13:7b:c8:
                a0:a7:3a:78:3b:2d:03:73:a1:c4:77:71:b0:d7:3c:
                7c:54:08:7a:75:3a:78:07:f7:73:db:5d:0c:f3:ee:
                f3:da:2e:3f:33:e5:e5:fc:83:7e:47:dc:ce:ce:38:
                7e:ed:17:cf:b2:47:4d:b1:c1
            Exponent: 35537 (0x10001)
    Signature Algorithm: md5withRSAEncryption
        35:b2:5f:38:0a:51:12:2f:25:72:12:3b:13:10:7e:04:df:5d:
        e7:af:d4:a2:13:b1:55:73:71:20:33:13:2a:3e:37:2b:0c:7c:
        7e:bb:87:21:71:2b:a0:d3:8c:d3:57:45:a8:ea:e0:8b:d3:ec:
        0e:cc:34:53:da:24:4e:c7:52:ed:ec:e5:13:c3:1a:3b:17:03:
        34:3f:d7:41:a7:a4:f3:cb:7c:8e:ff:77:42:bc:40:32:04:c7:
        7b:e7:a3:5d:b1:40:a3:ad:a0:a3:72:38:ca:c4:28:ee:8b:cb:
        0c:df:c7:0c:73:01:2c:4e:ea:d3:2c:d3:fe:3a:d3:03:7d:14:
        54:70
```

Figure 7.7   A sample X.509 certificate.

Structure of a DN

A DN consists of multiple hierarchical subcomponents. The early
X.509 definitions enumerated a small set of attributes that could be

assembled into globally unique identifiers. We describe those sub-components in the following sections. Note that not all DNs include all subcomponents. Depending on the required scope of the name, a country and organizational name might be sufficient to ensure uniqueness. The SP and L components add additional specificity. The OU component may be included if an internal organizational unit needs global visibility.

C, SP, and L: Geopolitical Location

The original X.509 hierarchy was structured along geopolitical bound-aries. The first set of subcomponents, therefore, identifies the country, state or province, and location. These might appear as follows:

```
C=US, SP=New York, L=New York City
```

O and OU: Organizational Entity

The O and OU fields describe an organization and a unit within that organization. In principle, the O field identifies the organization in some official way, such as the name under which it was incorporated. The organizational unit should be unique within the organization and should have a label that identifies it unambiguously. These might appear as in the following:

```
O=Wiley Computer Publishing, OU=Food Services
```

CN and SubjectAltName: Common and Alternate Names

A final and valuable subcomponent is the CN, or common name. The common name provides uniqueness within the organization or organizational unit. A common name should be the full name of the certificate owner, such as

```
CN=Gregory Efimovich Rasputin
```

Unfortunately, it has become common to use the CN field to identify the *fully qualified domain name* (fqdn) or alias of the machine or service that stores the certificate, as in the following:

```
CN=mailer.rodent.edu
```

This practice arose because earlier versions of the X.509 certificate format did not have separate fields for that purpose. PKIX has officially rejected this practice in favor of the *subject alternate name* (subjectAltName) field, which is a sequence of one or more of the following:

DNSName. The fqdn or alias.

IPaddress. The IP address.

rfc822Name. A name whose format resembles an Internet standard email form of *person@domain* (such as nobody@wiley.com).

URI. A *uniform resource identifier* (URI). Note that a World Wide Web *uniform resource locator* (URL) is one type of URI that identifies a resource available on a Web server. "URI" is a more generic identifier. The two are often used interchangeably, but "URI" is the specific tag name used by the PKIX subjectAltName sequence.

For *terminal* certificates (ones that will never belong to a CA), the subjectAltName field can take the place of a CN field. The preferred mechanism for identifying certificates belonging to Web servers, for example, is to omit the CN field and include a subjectAltName field containing only a dNSName element.

In some events (particularly when the CN is that of a device), the subjectAltName sequence includes an rfc822Name field that identifies the real human being responsible for the certificate (and the person presumed to have access to the private key).

The Issuer and the Subject

A DN identifies both the owner of the certificate and the signer of the certificate. These two fields are known respectively as the *subject* and the *issuer*. Since the issuer of a certificate will appear as the subject of his own certificate, it is appropriate that both of these fields be represented in DN form.

The Serial Number

Just as those who manufacture products often place unique serial numbers on a series of otherwise identical items, X.509 certificates are also distinguished by serial numbers. A certificate issuer must attach a unique number to each and every certificate that he produces. This mechanism enables a unique reference to any given certificate using the combination of issuer DN and serial number. This unique reference can be critical if, for example, a subject's status changes and the CA needs to revoke a certificate.

Validity Range

Two fields contain dates that bound the validity of the certificate. Outside this date range, the certificate is invalid. There are many reasons to place boundaries on the validity of a certificate. The subject's DN might become irrelevant over time (for example, if a person leaves the company), or the organization might not want too much sensitive data protected by a single public key pair. For a wide range of reasons, certificates eventually expire and must be renewed. The renewal process usually requires a new key pair, but it is possible to issue a new certificate with a new validity range that retains the old public (and thus private) key.

PKI Planning

Before beginning to issue certificates, it helps to make a few decisions:

- Which will be your root CA?
- How many other CAs will participate in your hierarchy, and which keys will they be authorized to sign?
- How will you authenticate people, applications, or devices before issuing a certificate?
- What will be the default validity period for your certificates?
- Will you reuse the public/private key pair when you renew a certificate?
- Which fields of the DN will be required, and how will you standardize their contents?

Certificate Revocation

Granting certificates raises some serious issues, and taking them away can also pose a major challenge. The original issuer of a certificate is the only entity that can revoke that certificate. The X.509 certificate mechanism allows a CA to issue a *certificate revocation list* (CRL) containing invalid certificate serial numbers. Each CRL also contains a NextUpdate field to announce the date or time for the next CRL.

In theory, devices or services that authenticate using certificates must retrieve a current CRL before enabling access or establishing communication. There is, however, a huge potential scaling problem if, for example, 10,000 IPsec end hosts must retrieve a CRL before establishing IPsec connections with one another. If the CRL lives on a CA inside the enterprise and the end host is connecting from outside the security perimeter, there may be a security challenge as well. Revoking a CA's certificate is even more difficult, and can pose huge operational challenges. Needless to say, different commercial CAs and IPsec products handle CRLs differently.

Key Escrow

See Chapter 4 for a discussion of IPsec and key escrow.

IPsec Encryption Key Management

Consistent with IPsec's open architecture, the IPsec security protocols (AH and ESP) are designed to be agnostic with regard to automated encryption key management. However, standards-compliant IPsec implementations must support both preshared keys and the automated key management mechanism called the *Internet Key Exchange* (IKE) protocol (see RFC 2401). IKE is a specific design instance of a larger design framework called the *Internet Security Association and Key Management Protocol* (ISAKMP; see RFC 2408). ISAKMP is an authentication and key exchange framework that is independent of any specific keying technology. IKE relies on another protocol, called OAKLEY, for secure keying within the ISAKMP model.

The OAKLEY Protocol

OAKLEY is a protocol that uses a Diffie-Hellman (DH) key exchange to establish a shared key securely between two peers (see RFC 2412). OAKLEY works within the ISAKMP framework to establish IPsec SAs.

The OAKLEY key determination standard establishes an initial ISAKMP SA, but allows a more lightweight mechanism to establish subsequent SAs.

The Internet Key Exchange Protocol

IKE is an implementation subset of ISAKMP and OAKLEY. It is a secure key management protocol designed to establish IPsec SAs and to enable fast rekeying of existing SAs. IKE operates in two phases. Phase 1 sets up the authenticated and encrypted channel. Since all key exchanges result in SAs, a successful phase 1 exchange will create an SA for each end of the communications channel, as well as the key required for phase 2. Phase 2 establishes one or more application SAs.

A phase 1 IKE exchange creates an SA for each communicating party that has the following:

- Identity information for the remote peer
- Proof of the validity of that identity
- A securely obtained key appropriate for AH and ESP

All phase 1 exchanges establish key material using a DH operation. The remote peer has three ways to prove its identity: preshared keys, a DSA digital signature, or RSA encryption.

Authentication with Preshared Keys

Standards dictate that IKE implementations must support preshared keys, but are agnostic as to the actual sharing mechanism. Due to the order of events in a phase 1 exchange, preshared keys enable IPsec peers to identify each other by IP address only. (See Chapter 6 for a more detailed discussion of preshared keys.)

Authentication with DSA

IKE implementations are also required to support DSA for a phase 1 exchange. DSA has the advantage of being in the public domain. In spite of its burdensome patents, however, RSA encryption has significant advantages over DSA. It is generally more appropriate for large IKE implementations.

Authentication with RSA

The RSA mechanism has several advantages over digital signature authentication for a phase 1 IKE exchange. The peers in RSA encrypt the DH key, so a third party would have to crack two cryptographic systems to steal the key. The IPsec peers also encrypt their identity information, preventing eavesdropping on the authentication exchange. One drawback of RSA authentication is that to protect privacy, the peers do not exchange certificates. The initiating peer must already have a known-good copy of the responder's public key.

Summary

IPsec is a suite of protocols that interface with each other in well-known ways. It has a modular architecture, and the current standard protocols are relatively agnostic with regard to specific cryptographic technologies. Although all IPsec products must support preshared keys, most IPsec installations require a PKI for scalability and management sanity. PKIs raise a number of issues with implications for an organization that extend far beyond IPsec-related concerns.

In the next chapter, "What Won't Work with IPsec," we examine how IPsec integrates with other common network technologies and enhanced services.

Three

Making It Work

The chapters that follow explore the specifics of deploying IPsec without breaking existing network technologies or preempting your ability to add new enhanced capabilities over time. Chapter 8, "What Won't Work with IPsec," evaluates the root causes of operational conflicts and performance problems with IPsec and analyzes how the various IPsec protocols interact with many common technologies. Chapter 9, "IPsec and PKI Rollout Considerations," describes several popular IPsec design scenarios, as well as some pitfalls you should work to avoid.

What Won't Work with IPsec: Other Network Services and Technologies

No one builds a network for the sole purpose of securing it, just as no one buys a goldfish for the sole purpose of flushing it down the toilet. Network security professionals have always had to remain mindful of two antithetical requirements: open connectivity and transparent data access. The most common network security product today is a firewall, which performs packet-by-packet analysis at the WAN perimeter. IPsec introduces a new level of complexity. By adding headers and signing or encrypting either the payload or the entire datagram, IPsec makes it difficult to layer additional services onto a secure traffic flow. In the world of enhanced IP networks, network managers must address a technical question with no easy answers: "How can I aggregate a collection of dissimilar higher-level protocols onto a wire, and into a datagram, without causing the protocols to eliminate the useful properties of one another or to break the higher-level applications?" Since traffic that demands high security is often a candidate for other special handling, IPsec makes that challenge even more acute.

This chapter discusses common technologies that often do not combine well with IPsec. We start by describing the root causes of conflict to provide an analytical basis for predicting problems in advance. In the second part of the chapter, we break IPsec performance claims into several measurable components. Next, we provide a hit list of protocols you should consider exempting from your IPsec policy configurations, and we briefly examine operational issues for a range of technologies. For the sake of convenience, we have arranged these technologies into several functional categories: bandwidth optimization, packet classification, network infrastructure, network monitoring, network management, and voice and video. In the next-to-last section, we provide an interoperability reference matrix. The wrap-up cautions against despair.

A Moving Target

This chapter is not a guide to evaluating or deploying any network services other than IPsec, but it is designed to point out the types of operational problems you may inadvertently create on your network as it interacts with other technologies. Bear in mind that many of the technologies we discuss here were still changing as this book went to print. We expect that both IPsec and other emerging technologies (such as voice over IP) will continue to evolve for the next several years, at least in part because of the challenges we describe in this chapter. It is probably more important, therefore, that you understand generally *why* things may not work well with IPsec than specifically *which* things did not work well when we wrote this book.

IPsec Design Objectives

As we discussed in Chapter 1, the designers of IPsec were motivated to provide a next-generation security infrastructure for IPv6 and to create a set of protocols to address the lack of security services in IPv4. It's a reasonable, if somewhat oversimplified claim that the current IPsec standards focus primarily on solving security problems that come from the physical, link, and network layers—rather than on offering security services up the network stack to other protocols or directly to applications.

The standardization of a general-purpose secure transmission mechanism for IP has several advantages. It is very consistent with the overall layered design of the Internet, where protocols are intended to integrate without overt reference to or dependencies on one another. IPsec also does not overly constrain the security choices available to application designers, security professionals, or *Information Systems* (IS) managers. The drawbacks to this design focus are most evident in cases where network managers want to preempt the generic effects of IP's layered, connectionless, stateless design to configure network functions differently for various individuals and applications. IPsec also faces significant scaling challenges and is not optimized to support multipoint, real-time applications and services.

Ugly Outcomes of IPsec Design

In complex environments, IPsec can be the wild child of network technologies. A functional IPsec infrastructure needs careful forethought and must respect the topological and operational characteristics of other deployed and planned services. Otherwise, it can swamp compressed WAN links, degrade delay-sensitive applications, and complicate certain uses of enhanced IP services such as *Quality of Service* (QoS). The better you understand the interplay between IPsec and other network technologies, the better you can plan to minimize or avoid problems. At best, you will need to plan carefully as you deploy IPsec, in order to avoid impeding or eliminating your ability to use other network technologies. At worst, you will need to identify and resolve areas of outright conflict for which you must choose between IPsec and other important capabilities. If you skipped the network mapping discussion in Chapter 2, "Laying the Groundwork for Security," you may need to go back to it. You must have a good understanding of your physical and logical topology to plan around the operational characteristics of IPsec.

Predicting Problems

There are two common underlying causes for most operational problems with IPsec: limited processing power of shared gateways (often at or near the WAN edge) or of end hosts, and order-of-operations conflicts with other technologies. Certain topologies, especially those that rely on shared gateways, may encounter both obstacles.

Order-of-operations problems arise when IPsec and other services or technologies are applied to the same traffic. Processor overload can occur even when you apply services to different traffic, if shared hosts or gateways cannot handle the incremental load. In general, it is easier to plan around difficulties with processing power than it is to resolve order-of-operation conflicts. The former is often, in the end, a matter of investment, while the latter may force a choice between technologies.

Symptoms

Network technologies can interact in subtle and not-so-subtle ways. A subtle interaction might cause periodic, imperceptible (to a human user) packet loss and retransmission, resulting in lower overall performance. A not-so-subtle interaction, on the other hand, could cause abrupt application failure or dramatically degraded connectivity. IPsec, when combined with other technologies, may cause either, both, or—if you plan carefully and aren't too adventurous—neither type of interaction.

Integration glitches are not, of course, the exclusive domain of IPsec or of security technologies. Network managers have always had to consider potential integration problems as they add new functionality. For example, many people experienced both subtle degradation and outright failures when they first began tunneling LAN protocols such as IPX over IP. IPX requires that packets be delivered in the exact order in which they were sent, but the IP datagrams carrying those packets routinely arrived out of order, causing the higher-layer applications to drop the packets. Tunneling technology needed to evolve to support the more fragile LAN protocols. Multiprotocol tunnels over IP still cannot take full advantage of the resilience of the underlying network.

Limits on Processing Power

Large IP networks tend to be complex entities supporting many types and generations of applications and operating systems. Even in organizations where Microsoft Windows is a de facto standard for new client stations, there may be hundreds of other devices that continue to run other software indefinitely. Although many of these end hosts have sufficient processing power and memory to support an IPsec client, the cost and effort to upgrade them can be prohibitive. A common strategy for an initial technology deployment, therefore, is to begin with an appliance or WAN gateway implementation (see Chapter 9, "IPsec and PKI Rollout Considerations," for more on design). This option does not enable end-host authentication or confidentiality, but it can provide these services for a network or subnet across the wide area. In this scenario, a network manager would enable IPsec AH or AH+ESP in tunnel mode either on a standalone (bump in the wire) device on the interior of the WAN edge router or on the edge router itself.

The Curse of the Edge Gateway

Ironically, the edge router is generally a low-end device with little excess processing power. IPsec functions such as SA negotiation, key generation, and bulk encryption are computation-intensive and can overwhelm a general-purpose CPU unless they have specialized hardware support. Even with hardware support, IPsec (usually IKE) still can cause delays. Transport-mode IPsec can also add latency, depending on the CPU power available in the end host. Generally speaking, however, the average PC has more cycles to spare for IPsec than the average edge gateway. Whether you elect to implement IPsec on a router, a standalone gateway, or your end hosts, you need to evaluate the relative performance capabilities of various products and platforms.

Evaluating IPsec Performance Claims

The discussion that follows may make you think that there is no such thing as an honest performance figure and that all IPsec vendors are evil, money-sucking entities that exist only to foist shoddy, ill-specified products on their unsuspecting customers. A more moderate response would be to ensure that you understand the test process that produced any given performance number, and to verify that comparisons among platforms are based on comparable measurements. Performance numbers for networking products have always been variable. IPsec introduces a couple of additional twists.

What Is Performance?

"Performance" is a catch-all term that encompasses several operating characteristics of an IPsec platform, including supported data rate, connection density, computation delay for SA negotiation or key generation, and data encryption speed. Most current commercial IPsec products are software implementations on a general-purpose CPU with some hardware components to accelerate cryptographic operations. Software products have the advantage of being relatively easy to modify, but they can encounter memory constraints, processor restrictions, and arbitrary-seeming configuration limitations.

What Does "Wire Speed" Mean?

Performance is generally a significant part of an IPsec purchase decision. It is one of the deciding factors in how well a given product will scale to meet the needs of your network and network users. It is not always straightforward, however, to convert a number from a marketing brochure into a real predictive measure of a platform's performance on your network. Most vendors, for example, will describe various media types as delivering *wire-speed* performance. Talk of wire-speed IPsec would seem to imply that a device is capable of encrypting and decrypting any packet size at the maximum data rate supported by its connected media (for example, 100 Megabits per second for a fast Ethernet device), but it rarely does mean that. Marketing numbers generally do not reflect operational expectations of a device. Performance testing of IPsec devices is also variable. Many factors may dramatically improve a marketing claim without reflecting how a platform will actually perform in your environment. A device advertised to run at Ethernet speeds may perform at less than half that rate on your network. It is important to ask for details if you need to predict actual performance.

Marketing Metrics

Typically, performance claims are made in *megabits per second* (Mbs) or an equivalent data rate, such as Fast Ethernet (100 Mbs) or *DS3* (also T3 or 48 Mbs). Even well-intentioned vendors may inadvertently mislead potential customers by not clarifying the details of their testing processes and results. The following sections should help you to understand what a given performance claim means for your environment.

Bits versus Bytes

If you are accustomed to evaluating applications or storage devices, make a mental note that network performance measurements are made in bits, not bytes. Since there are 8 bits in a byte, an 8-Mbs device can transmit 1 *megabyte per second* (MBs), ignoring protocol overhead. If you have a feel for how large your largest data transfers will be in bytes, remember to multiply that figure by 8 to estimate your minimum performance requirements.

Full Duplex or Half Duplex

If a vendor claims 100-Mbs performance for an IPsec device, it's critical to understand whether that figure is *full duplex* or *half duplex*. If the figure is full duplex, the device in question can sustain 100 Mbs both in and out (decrypting and encrypting simultaneously). Most data-rate claims are actually half duplex, meaning that you must divide by 2 to obtain a meaningful performance number for most network environments. For example, an encryption device rated at 100-Mbs half duplex can actually sustain 50 Mbs in and out, decrypting and encrypting simultaneously. Unfortunately, even the full duplex number does not give you a true sense of performance unless you know what packet sizes were used for testing.

Packet Size

The packet size, or range and distribution of packet sizes, will dramatically alter the outcome of an encryption performance test. All other factors being equal, sending bigger packets yields higher performance, but sending more *packets per second* (pps) yields lower performance. Encryption hardware is generally optimized for bulk data encryption with one or more algorithms. Processing overhead for an IP datagram also tends to be constant and relatively slow in a network-layer encryptor. IPsec performance therefore tends to improve with packet size; for example, the system spends relatively less time processing datagrams on 100 Mbs of 1500-byte packets than on 100 Mbs of 64-byte packets. On an Ethernet, the minimum packet size is 64 bytes, and the maximum is 1504 bytes. Thus, the two most useful performance numbers are the data rate for 64-byte packets (or the minimum packet size on any of the connected media types) and the rate for 1500-byte packets (or the maximum packet size for the connected media type). Depending on the packet-size mix on your network, which will vary based on your topology and your applications, your actual performance will fall somewhere between the high and the low performance numbers. Traffic statistics from your own network are the most valuable criteria, assuming you can filter them to profile the traffic you actually plan to encrypt. Some vendors base their performance numbers on pure encryption speed without accounting for any packet overhead at all, while others provide a straightforward overview of how their products function for different packet sizes. In order to compare performance figures, you must have data rates for the same packet sizes from every vendor you are considering.

Security Association (SA) Negotiation

SA negotiation, described in Chapter 7 ("The Basics of IPsec and Public Key Infrastructures"), precedes any IPsec transmission and includes several cryptographic functions. Every IPsec connection involves at least two SAs. An AH+ESP connection involves four. A shared gateway may have to calculate tens or hundreds or thousands of SAs per minute, depending on your particular design. On a real network, link congestion or other factors can delay SA negotiation, but most testing environments measure only the latency involved in the necessary protocol operations. If, for instance, a hardware platform can calculate SAs at a rate of one per second, 500 AH+ESP connections will take over 33 minutes for SA negotiation alone. That delay may not be fatal if it is spread out over a long period, but it can severely limit performance in an environment that must support a high volume of dynamic connections. Remember that data encryption does not begin until SA negotiation is complete.

Most hardware IPsec devices calculate SAs at a rate faster than one per second. Even at 25 per second, however, you may see a noticeable delay in a dynamic environment with many users. For example, if you create a telecommuting service for 10,000 employees based on IPsec, you are likely to see usage spikes at certain times of the day or in advance of project deadlines. If half of those employees try to terminate an AH+ESP tunnel on a single gateway device that can support an SA negotiation rate of 25 per second, constructing SAs alone will take more than 13 minutes. Commercial dial-up services are challenging as well. Many dial service providers estimate a turnover of 1 percent of subscriptions per minute. For example, a dial service with 1 million users could see an average of 10,000 new connections per minute. Using our formula above, that would mean 26 minutes worth of SA negotiation for every minute of dial service. Network operators often refer to such bottlenecks as *train wrecks*. If a single device were performing SA negotiation for a service of this size, in order to absorb even minimal service spikes, it would need to negotiate at a rate of approximately 1500 SAs per second—a speed one or two orders of magnitude faster than any hardware likely to be commercially available in 1999. Any high-volume tunnel termination will perform better if the computation-intensive cryptographic functions are distributed over *several* devices. See Chapter 7 for a technical description of SAs and SA negotiation.

Session Key Generation

If you intend to use Diffie-Hellman (DH) for session key generation, you need to be concerned about key generation speeds. DH calculations and round-trip protocol times are the primary performance inhibitors on a well-implemented version of IKE. Depending on your average key lifetime, a shared gateway may need to calculate many keys per hour. Numerous vendors provide performance figures for key generation, but as with data encryption, you need to know what they're really showing you. Key generation speeds are generally higher for shorter keys, but shortening key length decreases the relative strength of your data encryption. Using a shorter exponent also increases key generation speeds, but that too creates a weaker encryption key, which may not meet your needs.

Random number generation is another potentially computation-intensive aspect of key generation. For every key generation performance claim, ask the vendor what key length and how many bits of randomness were used for the test. Find out how a platform handles different exponent lengths and whether it can smooth out potential utilization spikes by pregenerating session keys. Key pregeneration has some security implications and is useful only on a device with spiky utilization. If a gateway is constantly busy, it will never have the opportunity to pregenerate keys. For a detailed description of IPsec key generation and management, see Chapter 7.

Combined Factors Affecting Performance

As you consider the discrete performance figures for encryption, SA negotiation, and key generation, remember that a busy IPsec gateway device or end-host implementation will be performing all three simultaneously. The specific product design will affect how a device performs real IPsec handling. Generally speaking, a product with specialized hardware for encryption, random number generation, and public key operations will outperform a software-only implementation in which every function is waiting for the same processor.

Order-of-Operation Conflicts

While it is possible to work around or throw money at a certain number of performance problems, *order-of-operation* conflicts are much more difficult to resolve. An order-of-operation conflict occurs when your requirements and network topology dictate that you apply technologies in a certain order, but that design produces an undesirable result. The result can be that one of the technologies doesn't function as expected or that unlucky target datagrams get mangled and dropped. Figure 8.1 shows the importance of order-of-operation. The basis for these conflicts is simple: Encrypted data is not machine-readable until it is decrypted. All IPsec protocols prevent modification of any header above IP for packets in flight, and AH places further restrictions on parts of the IP header itself. Any network technology that involves special step-by-step (*hop-by-hop*) handling as it transits the network is a candidate for conflict with IPsec, as it may need to analyze an encrypted portion of the packet or to make a change that violates the IPsec specification, causing the packet to be discarded. The following rule of success will help indicate whether and where you may encounter a problem: Encrypt last and lowest, decrypt first and lowest (with "lowest" meaning lower in the network stack than any analysis or modification required by an intermediate network service or technology). Unfortunately, as we discuss in the following section, this formula is not entirely consistent with common IP network topologies or with the design of other network technologies.

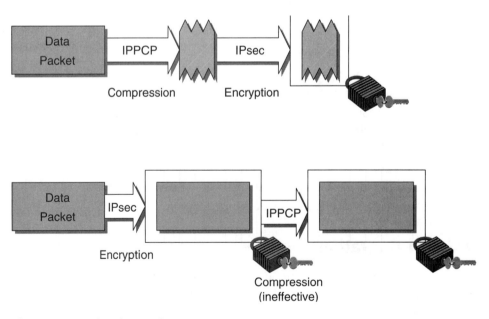

Figure 8.1   Order-of-operation matters.

Protocol Layering and Packet Policies

Layering is fundamental to the design of TCP/IP and IPsec. It means, among other things, that information is not supposed to flow *down* the network stack. In other words, the operation of IPsec is neither dependent on nor influenced by the application data content of IP packets. Although layering is sound technical design, it does work against some intuitively attractive network mechanisms. Many people want their networks to apply different lower-level packet handling techniques based on the application driving the data, the data payload, or even the user driving the application. A network manager might want, for example, to ensure that all of Simon's traffic is diverted into an IPsec tunnel, while all of Ralph's continues to flow in the clear. These policies violate the principle of layering if and when a gateway is expected to classify and act upon an incoming packet based on higher-layer data.

Note that layering is a principle, not a law of nature or the curse of the mummy's tomb. Network managers violate it all the time, invoking neither fire, nor famine, nor clouds of locusts. Still, IPsec was designed to adhere strictly to the principles of protocol layering, and thus is not optimized for mechanisms in which the data content of a packet affects whether and how IPsec (or any other lower-layer protocol) handles a given datagram. Many order-of-operation problems arise as a result of protocol layering issues, especially when multiple technologies (such as IPsec and Quality of Service) act on the same packets.

Proprietary Tweak Warning

Remember that protocol implementations—especially those that are not yet de facto or industry standards—tend to evolve and gain more options over time. In the meantime, every product vendor will approach order-of-operation problems differently. IPsec and other standards-based IP services will likely evolve to integrate more fully over time. Some network equipment manufacturers are already circumventing the lengthy evolution process by tweaking their IPsec implementations to integrate better with other technologies. Proprietary tweaking probably provides the shortest path to allowing IPsec to support some other emerging standards, but it has severe drawbacks. One of IPsec's major advantages over other IP encryption schemes is that it is an open standard. If your IPsec deployment relies on product-specific modifications, you will obviously lose vendor independence, a fundamental benefit of using standards-compliant technology.

The Predictive Power of Topology

To locate potential problems, begin with the network topology you built in Chapter 2. Identify where and to which kinds of IP traffic you plan to apply IPsec and other services. For data that will require more than IPsec, such as sensitive client-server database traffic, step through the actual transit path of a datagram as it travels each potential route through your network, and ask yourself if each required packet operation will succeed or fail. Locate the critical operational points on your topology where a device needs to either modify the datagram or handle it differently based on a level of transparency, such as the ability to identify the transport headers. Ask yourself whether the device will have sufficient power and visibility to perform the required function. Be sure to look at whether different routes through the network may alter the order in which IPsec and other technologies touch the datagram. Remember that any given intermediate device between end hosts may need to perform hundreds or thousands of similar transactions every minute, and will need to scale appropriately.

Your network topology, your choice to deploy IPsec on end hosts or in gateways, and the IPsec protocols and modes you use will all affect your ability to deploy other network services. Generally, an end-host implementation of ESP in transport mode is among the most flexible protocol instantiations of IPsec, although it is also one of the most administratively expensive. Gateway implementations of IPsec ESP and AH+ESP in tunnel mode, two of the more administratively straightforward ways to field an initial IPsec deployment, are among the least flexible in terms of supporting other enhanced IP services.

Meltdown Alert: Protocols to Watch

In the rest of this chapter, we discuss how various classes of network technology do or do not integrate with IPsec. This section is a reference for exceptions that you may need to make in your IPsec network to avoid disrupting services or segmenting (breaking) your IP infrastructure. In an IPsec gateway configuration, you need to be very careful that these protocols arrive at their destinations unencrypted. You must either apply IPsec consistently and symmetrically or, more likely, create explicit exceptions in your configuration to account for these protocols. The list focuses on protocols that can create a meltdown effect for end users, and it is not all-inclusive. It shows protocols and, when applicable, their destination ports.

Problem protocols are of three types:

- Protocols that may be destined for a variety of external gateways or end hosts, such as SMTP or HTTP

- Protocols that operate on intermediate hosts or gateways inside the IPsec network, such as SNMP

- Protocols that can be highly latency-intolerant, such as voice over IP or multicast

To anticipate potential problems with a protocol that does not appear on our list, ask yourself whether it fits into any of these three categories. Table 8.1 offers a list of protocols to watch.

Table 8.1 Protocols to Watch

PROTOCOL	PURPOSE	PROTOCOL/ DESTINATION PORT
AH	Authentication Header	IP protocol 51
BGP-4	Routing	TCP/179
DNS query	Name Service	UDP/53
DNS Zone XFER	Name Service	TCP/53
DVMRP	Multicast Routing	Uses IGMP
ESP	Encapsulating Security Payload	IP protocol 50
FTP	File Transfer Protocol	TCP/20, 21
H.323	Voice	TCP, UDP/1300, 1718–1720
HTTP	World Wide Web	TCP, UDP/80
HTTPS	World Wide Web (SSL)	TCP, UDP/443
IGRP	Routing	IP protocol 9
IGMP	Multicast Group	IP protocol 2
ISAKMP/IKE	IPsec Key Exchange	UDP 500
Kerberos	Authentication	TCP, UDP/88
MGCP	Voice Gateway (emerging)	Uses RTP
MOSPF	Multicast Routing	Uses OSPF
NTP	Network Time Protocol	TCP, UDP/123

Continues

Table 8.1   Protocols to Watch *(Continued)*

PROTOCOL	PURPOSE	PROTOCOL/ DESTINATION PORT
OSPF	Routing	IP protocol 89
PIM	Multicast Routing	TCP, UDP/496
PING (ICMP echo)	Network Management	IP protocol 1
POP3	Email Client	TCP, UDP/110
RADIUS	User Authentication	TCP, UDP/1812
RIP	Routing	UDP/520
RTCP	Voice	Uses RTP
RTP	Voice	Uses Multicast
SGCP	Voice Gateway (legacy)	UDP/440
SNMP	Network Management	TCP, UDP/161, 162
SMTP	Email	TCP/25
SS7	Voice Signaling	TCP, UDP/14001
Syslog	Device Logging	TCP, UDP/514
Telnet	Network Management	TCP/23
TFTP	Device Update	UDP/69

Configuring Exceptions

A proper gateway configuration may need to account for bidirectional traffic for client-server protocols, and to read logically as follows (the example uses Telnet):

```
No IPsec from <IP client range/TCP random high port> to <IP server
range/TCP port 23>
```

AND
```
No IPsec from <IP server range/TCP port 23> to <IP client range/TCP
random high port>
```

Of course, the actual configuration will vary from vendor to vendor.

Bandwidth Optimization

IP networks provide a stateless, best-effort delivery service for all IP packets. When traffic demand exceeds the available bandwidth, network elements drop packets without notification. In this context, the higher-level protocol is responsible for noticing whether packets reach their destination and for retransmitting those that do not. IP is thus an *unreliable* protocol; that is, it is not responsible for ensuring that every datagram successfully reaches its destination.

This packet-go-lucky egalitarianism works extremely well until the traffic load exceeds the available transmission facilities and the network becomes congested. IP is designed to degrade network availability more or less equitably among the various active applications. Well-designed TCP-based applications avoid congestion by backing off or slowing their transmission rates as the network begins dropping datagrams (Stevens 1997).

Some Packets Are More Equal than Others

In cases where the available network capacity cannot provide robust delivery for all packets, network managers may apply some form of bandwidth optimization technology. For the purposes of this chapter, we have grouped into this category two families of technologies: those that reduce overall traffic volume by compressing it and those that improve network availability to high-priority traffic through a quality of service (QoS) or class of service (CoS) mechanism. This section summarizes potential problems of using IPsec with these types of technologies.

A solid understanding of your physical and logical network topology will help you to plan ahead and to avoid "smoking network" problem diagnosis. Again, due to rapid changes in some network technologies, the information here may not be current by the time you read it. It's more important to be able to predict a technology's potential interaction with IPsec than to memorize the specific issues we cover here.

Link-Layer Compression

One obvious way to optimize network bandwidth is to reduce the volume of traffic. You can achieve traffic reduction either by removing applications and users from the network or, more realistically, by applying compression to the congested links.

Compression versus Encryption

Compression and encryption have fundamentally different goals. Compression products generally operate by identifying repeating patterns in data and then replacing each repetitive sequence with a token or a reference to an earlier instance of that sequence. Essentially, compression is designed to reduce data to its most basic elements for efficient transmission and/or storage.

Encryption, on the other hand, eliminates predictable patterns from a data stream by replacing them with random-seeming characters in order to obscure the original content. It's a truism in the security industry that encrypted data ought not to be compressible. (In fact, some compression schemes actually expand encrypted data, due to system overhead.) The practical implication of this situation is that any compression on a data stream must be performed prior to any encryption. From a topological and network-layering perspective, it is vital to compress first and higher, encrypt last and lower. Decryption must obviously precede decompression in this model, in order not to corrupt the data payload.

Compression and IPsec

In the IPsec context, compression must be performed at the network or application layer prior to any actual data encryption; decompression must be performed after decryption. If the compression is performed after encryption, only the unencrypted elements of the datagram (such as the IP headers) will compress, which will not yield a significant size reduction. If compression is performed first but at layer 2, the IP layer will be obscured from any IPsec operation until after the data has been decompressed.

Because of this vital order of operations, layer 2 or *link-layer compression*—in which the entire datagram except for its layer 2 headers is compressed for transmission across a point-to-point link—does not integrate well with IPsec ESP, whether in tunnel or in transport mode. This conflict can become critical on low-speed network links that rely on layer 2 compression to reduce link utilization. Many networks have layer 2 compression products deployed at the edges of their point-to-point WAN links in order to reduce congestion. Layer 2 compressors significantly reduce the volume of data that transits a link (except, of course, when that data is already compressed, as with GIF or JPEG images). If portions of that traffic are already encrypted before they reach the compression device, they cannot be compressed. In fact, not only does IPsec ESP preempt compression of the payload; in tunnel mode it actually expands the data by adding additional headers.

If you plan to encrypt only a tiny percentage of your traffic, the increased load on your compressed WAN links may be negligible. If you plan to encrypt the bulk of your traffic and you depend on effective link-layer compression, you may face a serious congestion problem.

IP Payload Compression Protocol (IPComp)

Of course, people have known for years that an effective network compression and encryption scheme must compress the packet first and at a higher layer than it encrypts, and must provide a symmetric decryption and decompression capability. One working group in the IETF has specified a mechanism to compress the data payload of IP datagrams without preempting the operation of IPsec and many other packet manipulation processes. RFC 2393 is a standards-track document that describes the *IP Payload Compression Protocol* (IPComp), also referred to as the *Internet Protocol Payload Compression Protocol* (IPPCP). IPComp supports a range of compression algorithms and offers hope for interoperable, multivendor end host and gateway combinations that can apply compression and IPsec to the same traffic.

IPComp does come with certain performance tradeoffs that may affect network operation. Payload compression is often less effective at reducing overall traffic volume than an equivalent compression algorithm applied at the link layer, because flow-by-flow compression can reduce the available number of repeating patterns. Also, compression, like encryption, is computation-intensive. On a low-end WAN edge device, IPComp may simply allow you to trade an order-of-operation conflict for a problem with processing power. When necessary, however, the processing limitation can often be resolved by upgrading hardware or by separating the two functions onto different platforms.

Is Compression a Reasonable Substitute for Encryption?

Occasionally some wingnut individuals will assert that compression is nearly as effective for data confidentiality as encryption. These technology quacks are almost always selling compression products. Although it is true that compressed data is not instantly human-readable, it is absolutely *not* true that compressed data is significantly more confidential than plaintext. Because compression devices must periodically communicate to exchange up-to-date decompression dictionaries, real-time expansion of compressed data is trivial to achieve. Anyone who proposes compression as a viable alternative to encryption is either a little naive or more than a little unethical.

Quality of Service

"Quality of service" (QoS) is a generic term that covers a large collection of mostly proprietary mechanisms for prioritizing network access. This section gives a very basic overview of generic QoS technologies. It is not a detailed guide to these technologies, and it does not cover many important issues specific to QoS implementation and administration. It aims to give you a general understanding of how the different flavors of QoS work and how their configuration and operation may interact with IPsec.

Inbound Queues and Outbound Prioritization

In order to evaluate QoS technologies, it's important to recognize that they fall into two basic paradigms:

1. Queue management mechanisms that determine how packets may be discarded as they enter a gateway

2. Scheduling and prioritization mechanisms that determine which packets are forwarded first as they exit a gateway

Scheduling mechanisms divide into better-best-effort and preemptive access categories, and preemptive access technologies can be further differentiated into packet prioritization and proactive reservation methods. Although QoS implementations vary from platform to platform, with varying degrees of complexity and configurability, they tend to function in similar ways.

Queuing Basics

As IP packets transit a network, they enter and exit many intermediate switching and routing devices that parse each datagram enough to forward it on along the appropriate network link toward the packet's ultimate destination. Every datagram enters the router or switch from a particular network interface. Each such interface is associated with a queue, where the forwarding device stores packets waiting to be examined and sent on. When the switch or router copies a packet from that inbound queue, it classifies the packet according to some portion of its packet header information and copies it to the outbound queue associated with the correct next hop in that datagram's journey across the network. This generic model offers two decision points for applying a QoS mechanism: the inbound queue and the outbound queue.

Inbound Queue Management

An inbound queue management mechanism provides an algorithm for managing the inbound queue length on a packet forwarding device (a switch or router). Crude queue management techniques simply shorten the queue on a last-come-first-dropped basis; others can discriminate somewhat among packets. A simple implementation will do nothing until a queue is full, and then will drop a packet from the queue (generally the last, the first, or a random pick). A more advanced, more effective approach is to perform active queue management. Active management of inbound packet queues is designed to enhance overall network performance by dropping packets before the inbound queues are full. Dropping packets before absolutely necessary may seem like a counterintuitive way to improve performance, but this system allows TCP-based applications to back off gradually before a link is dramatically congested, and also permits packet-forwarding devices to maintain enough queue capacity to handle sudden bursts of traffic. There are several different algorithms for active queue management; *Random Early Detection* (RED; Figure 8.2) is one good example (Braden 1998).

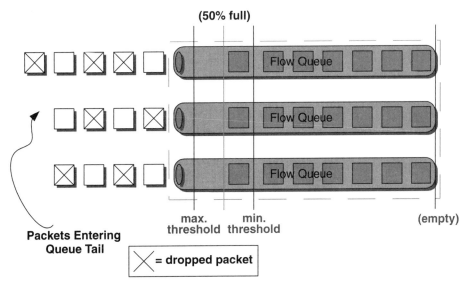

Figure 8.2   Random Early Detection operating on three data flows.

Inbound Queue Management and IPsec

Inbound queue management mechanisms do not perform any packet classification based on the source, destination, or content of a given datagram. Any queue management mechanism will therefore integrate with any instantiation of IPsec. This clean combination should not, however, inspire you to begin tweaking inbound queue sizes and queue management algorithms. Queue configuration is a tool for experts, and can have strange and surprising results if you do not know in advance exactly what you're doing. It is also designed to maintain high network throughput in general, not to prefer one or more classes of traffic in particular. What most people think of as quality of service is really an outbound scheduling or packet precedence operation.

Outbound Queue Management

Outbound queue management mechanisms operate by letting certain packets essentially cut in line in order to get out of the gateway before other, lower-priority datagrams. Such scheduling mechanisms can work to provide either *better-best-effort* delivery into a network cloud or *preemptive bandwidth access* all the way across the network.

Many QoS mechanisms remain proprietary to individual equipment vendors. In part, this exclusivity is a market tactic to force customers to build single-vendor rather than multivendor networks. QoS features also tend to take advantage of specific implementation characteristics of each router, switch, or gateway. They exploit specific quirks of queue design or packet forwarding algorithms that are highly vendor- and even platform-specific. Such mechanisms cannot reasonably be standardized, as they rely heavily on vendor-specific platform internals. The *Integrated Services* (intserv) working group's *Resource Reservation Protocol* (RSVP; Figure 8.3) and the *Differentiated Services* (diffserv) *class-of-service* (CoS) initiative in the IETF are two standards-oriented alternatives to proprietary QoS mechanisms.

Packet Precedence Mechanisms

Gateways often *color* high-priority datagrams by setting the *type of service* (ToS) portion of the IP header (now called the *Differentiated Services* or *DS byte*) to a certain preset value, so that the next hop forwarding device can identify the datagram as high priority. QoS-capable IP gateways can alter how they schedule packets into their outbound queues

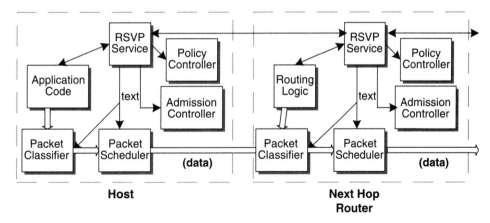

Figure 8.3 RSVP operational schema.

based on a preset policy, traffic characteristics, or existing values in the packet header.

Most QoS scheduling implementations are designed around the abstraction of a *policy domain*—a logical area (such as a campus network) where a consistent set of traffic priorities applies. For example, within a certain policy domain, Oracle database and network management traffic may be high priority, while email and Web browsing are relatively low priority. QoS mechanisms can enforce a given traffic policy either within a policy domain (intradomain) or among several domains (interdomain). Because most LANs are relatively fast and most enterprise applications are relatively tolerant of occasional congestion, the majority of initial QoS deployments are interdomain, with the domains separated by a WAN or by the Internet. Intradomain QoS is likely to become more prevalent as its technologies mature and as *voice over IP* (VoIP) and streaming video applications become viable for more environments. Like IPsec, QoS infrastructures are highly sensitive to the logical IP topology, since they must be able to provide equivalent handling for both directions of a symmetric traffic flow.

Better-Best-Effort and Preemptive Bandwidth Access

QoS scheduling technologies can operate in two basic ways. A *better-best-effort* approach is designed to give certain traffic priority access into a network, generally a WAN or the Internet. Traffic policing and shaping mechanisms on WAN or Internet gateways are better-best-effort technologies. These mechanisms are comparable to airplane boarding procedures—in which important travelers and those who need special treatment get priority—and they suffer from the same limitations. People try to sneak past the policing mechanism, and even early boarders can get stuck behind the human obstacle trying to stuff a huge suitcase into the overhead compartment. Better-best-effort technologies also lose their utility if the amount of priority traffic exceeds the available bandwidth. In that case, they function like traffic lights on a congested freeway, where cars merge politely one at a time into a creeping traffic jam, and no one gets anywhere quickly.

Preemptive bandwidth access mechanisms, in contrast, provide hop-by-hop prioritization along the entire transit path of a traffic flow. These mechanisms can be reservation-based, such as RSVP, in which the network cannot, in theory, overcommit bandwidth. Other hop-by-hop mechanisms, including most proprietary packet-precedence schemes, do not try to prevent network congestion, but simply determine what traffic gets the best shot at available bandwidth.

Differentiated Services (Diffserv)

The Differentiated Services working group of the IETF has produced a specification, currently in draft, to enable hop-by-hop CoS. Diffserv CoS operates by setting the value of the DS byte. It is valuable because it provides the first standards-based method to set a consistent hop-by-hop packet priority across a multivendor network. Figure 8.4 shows a diffserv operational schema. The term "Class of Service" is a more accurate description than "Quality of Service" for packet-go-lucky, non-reservation-based packet prioritization schemes. CoS colors packets by setting the ToS header to a specified value and then prioritizing the outbound queue schedule accordingly.

The original IPsec drafts could not support diffserv operations because they did not permit modification of the DS byte. This prohibition came about as an original intent type analysis of the IP standards; as a result, IPsec was nearly unusable for Internet VPNs, for which *service level agreements* (SLAs) guarantee certain bandwidth availability. The standards-track revision of the IPsec drafts removed the ToS restriction, and IPsec in all modes now permits application of differv CoS end-to-end. Verify that any IPsec implementation supports the full standard, rather than just an early draft, and you should have no problems with CoS.

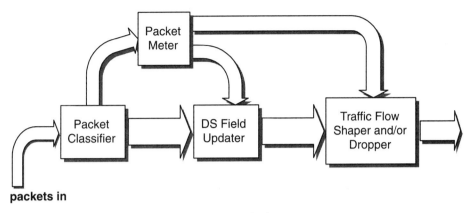

packets in

Figure 8.4 Differentiated services operational schema.

Resource Reservation Protocol (RSVP)

RSVP is a signaling protocol used to negotiate in advance a hop-by-hop bandwidth reservation for specified traffic (Braden 1997). It does not carry data, but rather negotiates on behalf of an application. To request bandwidth, an RSVP-enabled application sends a PATH request toward its destination, including a traffic specification for the application and a request for some amount of bandwidth allocation. RSVP-capable gateways reply back with RESV reservation responses. Application traffic then follows the signaling path across the network. RSVP arranges for only a unidirectional bandwidth allocation. It is designed to support applications that need significant available one-way bandwidth, such as streaming audio or video. If an application has significant bi- or multidirectional traffic requirements, each traffic originator must negotiate separately for bandwidth reservations.

RSVP does not integrate well with IPsec. Because each router along the traffic path must be able to interpret and respond to the PATH requests, these requests must be in the clear, or the end host must have an SA prenegotiated with each one (end-to-middle as opposed to simple end-to-end SAs). It is remotely possible that the end host of the requesting application could have previously negotiated an SA and IPsec connection with each device in the cloud in order to transmit RSVP over IPsec. Such a configuration would be wildly impractical, however, even if it were administratively feasible. Note that there is an IETF standard for IPsec extensions to RSVP, RFC 2207 (Berger 1997), but it does not alleviate the significant complexity of encoding an RSVP implementation of any scale in IPsec.

It's unfortunate that RSVP cannot realistically take advantage of IPsec, since it does pose significant security challenges. RSVP currently has no scalable mechanism for authenticating either PATH requests or RESV responses, making it relatively simple for a misconfigured or malign application to intercept or mimic legitimate requests in order to disrupt service or steal bandwidth.

Packet Classification

Packet classification involves interpreting link-layer, network, transport, and application headers, and in some instances, application data payload contents, as well as performing a specific function on the relevant datagram based on a set of configured rules. Some sophisticated packet classification engines can also maintain session state; that is, they can associate packets that are part of the same application session or data flow and apply rules in the context of the entire flow, rather than a packet at a time. All IP routers are designed to have, at minimum, sufficient packet-classification capability to identify the next hop destination for datagrams in flight on the network. Devices such as firewalls, address translation gateways, and Web content filters (smut blockers, for example) all rely on high-level packet classification to map traffic to a policy. Any gateway that can perform different functions on different kinds of traffic relies on some kind of packet classification engine.

Packet Classification for IPsec

IPsec gateways are required to support packet classification to determine whether and how to apply IPsec to a given packet (Atkinson 1998). This type of packet classification is also the fundamental technology for network encryptors that can claim the *doorbell* export category (see Chapter 4, "Encrypting within the Law," for more details).

Packet Classification with IPsec

Packet-classification technologies often do not integrate well with IPsec. They require a level of packet transparency that IPsec often obscures, and some packet-classification mechanisms perform functions—such as address translation—that modify the packet in such a way that it is no longer consistent with the IPsec specification and is discarded downstream.

Packet classification for network headers can work well with IPsec in transport mode. Higher-layer packet classification with IPsec ESP in any mode must occur prior to any IPsec operation, or logically after IPsec session termination. A single device such as a firewall or other security gateway can combine these operations, terminating and reinitiating IPsec connections, performing packet classification and modification operations while the packet is between IPsec sessions. However, this approach can trade an order-of-operation problem for a processing problem, and may cause latency or packet drops in high-bandwidth environments.

Packet Filtering

The IP access control list is one of the basic control mechanisms of IP networking. IP access control lists establish simple deny or permit rules that direct an IP gateway to forward or drop specific IP packets based on their network- and transport-layer headers. For example, access control lists can be configured to permit email (*Simple Mail Transport Protocol* [SMTP] TCP port 25), but block generic telnet connections (TCP port 23). Packet filtering is almost exclusively a gateway function on an edge router, firewall, or layer 3 switch. To function correctly, packet filtering gateways need access to a packet's original IP and transport headers. They can, therefore, coexist with IPsec AH in transport mode or in tunnel mode, provided the gateway can parse AH. Packet filters can operate on the IP source and destination addresses for IPsec ESP in transport mode, but any other filtering, or filtering for ESP in tunnel mode, must occur before encryption or after decryption.

Most IP devices are optimized to support simple IP packet filters. IPsec gateway implementations also rely on filtering technology in order to determine what to encrypt and to leave in the clear. Packet filters tend to be more memory-intensive than processor-intensive, so it's generally not a problem to enable full packet filtering on an IPsec gateway.

Proxy Firewalls

Proxy firewalls rely on packet classification and some filtering, but they offer significant additional functionality. A proxy firewall actually terminates and re-initiates each connection, copying the packet payload into a new datagram with new headers and (usually) the source address of the firewall's outbound interface. Most proxy firewalls function transparently: They intercept outbound and inbound traffic directly off the wire, even though it is not addressed to the firewall itself. Proxy firewalls maintain state for TCP connections and often perform network address translation (NAT). Many firewalls also provide various content-filtering capabilities. We discuss address translation and filtering in the sections that follow.

Because they perform analysis deep into the datagram, proxy firewalls require total transparency to function correctly. They do not integrate with IPsec transport-mode AH, because they generally rewrite the packet headers, destroying the integrity of the original packet and violating the IPsec specification. They also do not combine well with transport-mode ESP or AH+ESP because most of the data they need to analyze is already encrypted. Proxy firewalls can integrate with IPsec in tunnel mode, providing the firewall operations occur either prior to encryption or after decryption. Some proxy firewalls double as VPN gateways to prevent the firewalled traffic from having to cross a link in the clear. These solutions make sense, but can run into memory and performance limitations because both firewalls and IPsec are highly processor- and memory-intensive.

Content Filtering

Content filtering is first cousin to firewalling, but it operates deeper in the data payload; it maintains state across packets to identify content that may arrive in many fragments, and even out of order. Content filtering is the technology that underlies the various smut-blocker applications that screen for undesirable content in Web pages. Content filters require total packet transparency to function correctly. They do not, therefore, combine well with IPsec ESP in either tunnel or transport mode. Because content filters do not modify the packet, but only decide whether to forward or drop it, they do integrate transparently with IPsec AH in either transport or tunnel mode.

Network Address Translation

Network address translation (NAT) is a gateway technology that modifies the source and/or destination address of a datagram in transit between two end systems. It allows systems to exchange data through one or more gateways without knowing one another's addresses. NAT boxes build translation tables to ensure correct retranslation of the destination address on return traffic. Most implementations translate addresses on a one-to-one basis so that for every hidden or translated address there is a single exposed address. Some offer ways to conserve exposed addresses by multiplexing active sessions into address pools, or even into unique port numbers of a single IP address. NAT boxes are useful for concealing IP endpoints, often behind a firewall. NAT also allows network managers to connect networks with overlapping addressing schemes, such as two unregistered network 10s.

NAT and IPsec

Because NAT boxes rewrite IP packet headers, they do not integrate well with IPsec transport-mode AH, ESP, or AH+ESP. NAT can coexist with IPsec tunnel mode, provided that either the translation precedes any IPsec operation or the IPsec session terminates prior to NAT-ing in a downstream scenario. Datagrams must be NAT-ed before they are encrypted. If you require encryption both in and out of the NAT gateway, you can configure IPsec tunnels inbound and outbound, given appropriate gateway feature support. Once again, however, you may be resolving an order-of-operation conflict by swamping a gateway processor.

Network Infrastructure

The technologies described in the following sections are among those vital to network operation. If either IP routing or DNS fails, it is essentially a network down situation: The end user's experience is as dramatic as if you cut his connection with an axe. If you deploy IPsec in a gateway scenario, you will almost always need to punch explicit holes in your IPsec topology to ensure that routing information and DNS transactions do not get black holed in an encrypted tunnel.

IP Routing Protocols

This section does not discuss the design of, or differences among, various routing protocols; it only addresses the general issues related to combining routing and IPsec. IP networks rely on a variety of routing technologies to enable efficient transport of datagrams over dynamic, complex topologies. Campus networks depend on *Interior Gateway Protocols* (IGPs) such as the *Routing Information Protocol* (RIP) and *Open Shortest Path First* (OSPF) to advertise connectivity among networks and subnetworks. The Internet and other large WANs use *Exterior Gateway Protocols* (EGPs) such as *Border Gateway Protocol version 4* (BGP-4) to advertise routes among *autonomous systems* (ASs). Routing technologies are very complex. This section explains them only in a general way and without reference to their differences, in order to give you some sense of how they integrate with IPsec.

Most routing protocols are not particularly secure in their design. They generally have very weak authentication methods both for the sender of an update and for its contents. Although efforts are under-way to improve the security of next-generation routing, some network operators feel that IPsec offers a viable retrofit to improve the security of the existing protocols. Especially for TCP-based protocols such as BGP-4, IPsec could provide a feasible, if not entirely straightforward, secure transmission mechanism.

A Deployment Challenge

Unfortunately, the places where IPsec might offer the most benefit are also the places where it is most difficult to deploy—in the core of the Internet and at peering points among multiple service providers. The challenge at administrative boundaries is not IPsec, but trust. Correct authentication of the IPsec peers requires either shared secrets—which are difficult to administer and almost impossible to scale—or some form of cross-certification among PKIs, which essentially requires (today) that all PKIs come from a single vendor.

IP Routing and IPsec

The first commandment for integrating routing protocols and IPsec is "Get it right." If you decide to encrypt routing updates, you must ensure that they are decrypted for the next hop router or you will seg-ment your IP infrastructure. It is a common error not to account for routing in an initial IPsec implementation. Although the oversight is a simple one, the fix may not be; if you break routing connectivity to a remote site, you may not be able to get in-band access to your IPsec gateway in order to fix its configuration. If you don't have an alternative access method, such as a dial-up connection to its console, you might be taking a quick, unplanned trip for an onsite confabulation with your very unpopular gateway.

Domain Name System (DNS)

The *DNS* is the basic mechanism used to translate between human-comprehensible addresses (such as www.wiley.com) and IP network addresses (such as 10.235.134.17). It is a hierarchical system that allows very granular local control of *name-to-address* and *address-to-name* mappings. The two fundamental transactions conducted with the DNS are a client-to-server query to map (or *resolve*) a name to an address (or vice versa) and a server-to-server update mechanism called a *zone transfer*. Client-to-server queries can be either recursive, in which the server is responsible for locating the answer from another server if it does not have it already, or nonrecursive, in which the server simply refers the client to another server if it does not have the answer. These queries and responses are almost always UDP transactions. Server-to-server zone transfers allow a slave server to update its information from a master server. These zone transfers occur on a configurable schedule and are TCP-based.

DNS and IPsec

IPsec does not integrate particularly well with DNS client queries and responses, since SA negotiation alone may introduce an apparent delay in the network. With nonrecursive queries, IPsec is even more impractical, since it is not possible to predict in advance which clients and servers may need to communicate at any given moment.

In theory, you could use IPsec transport mode for zone transfers between a master and slave DNS server, especially with servers that participate in the same PKI and will not need cross-certification in order to authenticate one another. Fundamentally, however, IPsec does not solve many interesting problems for DNS. Since the data content of a DNS server is by definition public information, encrypting a DNS transaction does not make a lot of sense. Zone transfers and the update mechanisms for DNS servers are sensitive, but they require more specific security checks and services than are available with any mode or protocol of IPsec.

The integrity of the DNS is vital to the operation of the Internet and of any normal IP network. Accidental corruption of DNS information has caused spectacular Internet meltdowns in the past, and malicious meddling can divert email, Web traffic, and more. The IETF *DNS Security* (DNSSEC) working group has developed several standards and draft recommendations for security mechanisms specific to the DNS (see RFC 2065 and RFC 2137). Although DNSSEC does require modifications to the installed DNS, it is a more suitable technology than IPsec to secure that specific infrastructure.

Network Monitoring

All of the technologies described in this section operate in *promiscuous mode*. Promiscuous mode devices, as discussed briefly in Chapter 3, "Security Principles and Practices," eavesdrop transparently on a network segment (usually a LAN) and monitor all traffic in flight on the local wire. Network monitoring systems are most effective when deployed close to the origin or termination points of data traffic, where packets tend to be more in order, and mostly on the same path; the farther they are from these points, the less conclusive their reports will be.

Promiscuous mode devices require transparency to operate effectively. None of them operates effectively on IPsec ESP traffic. And although they can theoretically work with transport-mode AH traffic, most will require a special upgrade to do so. Even when it is in the clear, encapsulated traffic also poses a challenge for network monitoring platforms, because they aren't generally designed to look beyond the first set of packet headers.

Technologies that conceal and those that examine do not make a brilliant combination. In-depth network monitoring and traffic confidentiality are often at odds. While you may eventually be able to work around IPsec transport-mode AH, ESP will perpetually foil all attempts at promiscuous mode analysis. To the extent that you deploy end-to-end IPsec on your network, you may lose your ability to perform higher-layer network-based monitoring or traffic analysis.

Sniffers

Sniffers are monitors that expose, or *sniff* off the wire, every packet that transits their local network segments. Most recent versions have filtering capabilities that allow their operators to isolate interesting traffic and ignore the rest. For the most part, sniffers look as deep as the application headers in order to identify a packet. Some allow the network manager to create her own filters, making it possible to identify IPsec traffic without waiting for a software upgrade from a sniffer vendor.

Sniffers are network diagnostic tools. For a reasonably expert network manager, they often provide the fastest way to get direct visibility into a network connectivity problem. Of course, they aren't much use on a network with a significant amount of IPsec ESP traffic, since the important information may well be encrypted. IPsec transport-mode AH traffic ought not to be a problem for most sniffers, but tunnel-mode AH packets may pose more of a challenge, since most sniffers aren't able to work effectively on encapsulated traffic.

Network Intrusion Detection

Network intrusion detection systems generally consist of standalone or embedded promiscuous mode elements that examine traffic on a wire or an end host, scanning for certain packet patterns or *attack signatures* that characterize a known attack (such as, for example, TCP session hijacking or a SATAN scan). Network-based intrusion detection devices are specialized sniffer-type products that maintain some session state and perform rapid protocol analysis and matching against a database. Host-based systems are software packages that scan traffic coming in to a particular end host. Intrusion detection is one of the few real-time security technologies that can be configured to adapt to the actual operating characteristics of a network and can also provide rapid, specific countermeasures in the event of a possible attack.

Because intrusion detection systems often require visibility deep into each datagram in order to perform traffic analysis, they cannot operate correctly on encrypted traffic, and most cannot analyze encapsulated traffic (such as tunnel-mode AH), even when the encapsulated datagram remains in the clear. IPsec ESP in any mode will limit the usefulness of a network intrusion detection system. Transport-mode AH will probably be fine, but tunnel-mode AH will, at least in the short term, evade analysis.

Remote Monitoring (RMON and RMON2)

Remote Monitoring (RMON) is an optional component of a *Simple Network Management Protocol* (SNMP)-based network management infrastructure. We have included it in this section because an RMON probe (the data collection engine for RMON) is a promiscuous mode element similar to a sniffer. RMON is an Internet standard mechanism for collecting management information on a network segment, including errors, traffic statistics, and host-specific data (Waldbusser 1995). RMON2 is a proposed follow-up to the original standard that offers richer reporting capabilities. The standard describes the required reporting and communications mechanisms for RMON devices. RMON systems consist of agents or probes that collect statistics on one or more network segments and a management station that aggregates and interprets statistics from one or more probes.

The fundamental standards-compliant RMON probe capability is data collection at the link and network layers. For most RMON functions, packets are packets, so to speak, and IPsec in any mode does not interfere with basic monitoring. For example, an RMON probe can accurately monitor levels of good and bad (correctly and incorrectly formed) Ethernet frames, IP datagram counts, and basic traffic thresholds whether they are IPsec or regular IP datagrams. Encapsulated traffic does pose a challenge for accurate traffic identification, but ought not to be a show-stopper in the context of this particular monitoring function; RMON is generally concerned with the proper operation of the network infrastructure, rather than the specific payload of packets in transit on that infrastructure.

RMON Filter Group

RMON probes may encounter difficulties with IPsec due to an optional component of the RMON standard called the *filter group*. This part of the specification allows probes to perform real-time packet capture based on an arbitrary filter expression. The filter expressions can operate not only on the link-layer and network headers, but also within the application headers and data payload of a packet. If a filter expression requires evaluation of a packet content beyond the link-layer and network headers, IPsec (especially ESP in any mode) will obstruct the correct operation of the filter. Packets that should match a filter expression will create a false negative, since the data that would create a match is encrypted when the packet transits the RMON probe.

Some designers of network management applications have discussed IPsec in transport mode as a potentially interesting mechanism for secure configuration of RMON probes. There is no obvious reason to object to IPsec in this context, but *HTTP over SSL* (HTTPS) seems a more promising candidate, given the increasingly Web-based nature of network management.

Network Management

Commercial network management systems have always lagged discouragingly far behind network infrastructure capabilities. Good network management is not so much an intractable technical problem as a poor business proposition. A very large network may include tens of thousands of routers and switches, but will still require relatively few instantiations of a network management platform. Although the demand for good management remains high, the potential market has always been small in comparison to the rest of the networking software business. Many large networks still rely on a mix of network management tools, many of which are either public-domain or home-grown. This section focuses on a few protocols that are common to many commercial and proprietary management applications.

Security is a notoriously weak aspect of most network management mechanisms. The authentication is generally rudimentary, and the protocols provide little assurance that the configuration data will arrive intact. Some network managers are relying on IPsec as an inexpensive way to enhance their infrastructure management security without having to upgrade their installed applications. As with routing protocols, the best advice for combining IPsec and network management tools is to get it right the first time. Overlay your management transactions on your network map, and make sure that you either have enabled IPsec correctly all the way through it or have punched the appropriate holes in your topology. Configuration errors will not cause the same instantaneous disaster as black holing your routing protocols, but they can lock you out of your network devices or cause you to miss important alarms.

Simple Network Management Protocol (SNMP)

Simple Network Management Protocol (SNMP) is the Internet standard IP protocol for communication between a network management station and a network device. The SNMP management station can set configuration variables in a *Management Information Base* (MIB; see RFC 1907). There are three versions of SNMP. SNMP v2, the most broadly deployed (see RFC 1905), is a UDP-based protocol that generally uses IP addresses and plaintext passwords (*community strings*) to authenticate the management station. Since the management station may potentially need to communicate with every router or switch on the network, most IPsec networks must be configured to exclude SNMP from IPsec operations. It is possible to implement IPsec AH or AH+ESP transport mode between the management station and network devices, but even if all those devices actually support IPsec, this is generally impractical. Note that SNMP v3 includes significant security enhancements, but is not yet in common use.

Remote Monitoring (RMON) is an optional component of an SNMP-based network management infrastructure. See the earlier section entitled "Network Monitoring" for detailed coverage of RMON.

Syslog

Syslog is a UDP protocol that many network elements and hosts use to log messages and alarms dynamically to one or more central servers. Although syslog sometimes carries very sensitive information, it has no intrinsic authentication or message verification. It is easy to inject messages into (or divert messages from) a stream of syslog messages. Some proprietary syslog implementations have used Kerberos (see Chapter 6, "Cryptographic Protocols and Techniques") to secure the message packets. IPsec provides an alternative, scalable mechanism to secure syslog traffic. It should work well, as long as you are careful to maintain symmetry in your IPsec topology.

Telnet

The *Telnet* protocol enables you to open a local terminal window on a remote device. It is based on TCP, and most implementations of Telnet clients and servers rely on a plaintext username/password for authentication. Although it allows you to configure only a single device at a time, it is still a remarkably common way to configure or troubleshoot network devices. IPsec is a useful means of securing a Telnet connection. You must ensure that each client (usually an end host) and server (usually a gateway) can authenticate one another, and that no device in between each potential client and server will black hole the Telnet traffic by double-encapsulating and/or encrypting it in transit. If an intermediate gateway double-encapsulates or encrypts the connection, a different intermediate gateway must de-encapsulate and/or de-encrypt it before it arrives at the endpoint.

Trivial File Transfer Protocol (TFTP)

Many network devices use *Trivial File Transfer Protocol* (TFTP) to retrieve new versions of software from a TFTP server (usually a UNIX host) and to upload copies of their running configurations, core dumps, error messages, or other diagnostics. TFTP is a simple UDP-based protocol that provides no authentication of either the device or the configuration server, and no verification of the actual file integrity beyond optional checksum verification on the server or the device. It is a very lightweight mechanism for reading files from and writing files to a remote server (Sollins 1992). Since the mechanism is so vulnerable to exploitation, IPsec can offer significant incremental security to TFTP—as long as both the network device and the remote server support it, and you are careful not to black hole traffic by encrypting asymmetrically between them.

Voice and Video

Real-time high-quality voice and video applications are increasingly common on IP networks. Because they are extremely intolerant of even small amounts of latency, these applications generally do not integrate well with IPsec (especially IKE), even in symmetric configurations with no obvious protocol conflicts. Fortunately, many voice and video implementations take advantage of emerging security mechanisms in the higher-level protocols.

Multicast

IP protocols ordinarily enable one-to-one communications. *Multicast* enables one-to-many and many-to-many communications and is designed to support conferencing, audio, and video applications. With multicast, a single source sends a single packet to a single group address (a class D IP address). The multicast router is responsible for maintaining a current list of the individual hosts active in a multicast group. Multicast traffic relies on its own routing protocols, which are designed to optimize delivery and reduce traffic volume to common destination points (see RFC 1075 and RFC 1112).

Multicast and IPsec

Under many circumstances, latency will significantly degrade the quality of multicast content. Real-time multicast applications do not mix well, therefore, with slow links, with congestion, or with IPsec. IPsec can introduce noticeable delays during SA negotiation and cryptographic operations (key generation, bulk encryption, and decryption). IPsec also presents difficult scaling problems: Preshared secrets are impractical for large multicast installations, but a PKI will likely introduce cross-certification requirements. There are suggested multicast security mechanisms that are designed to limit overhead and not overly increase latency (see RFC 1949).

Voice over IP (VoIP)

Voice transport is among the most significant new uses of IP networks. VoIP can provide effective toll-bypass for latency-tolerant voice applications such as faxes. It can also, with sufficient network bandwidth and quality of service support, provide satisfactory real-time voice services. VoIP relies on a fairly complex set of session-layer protocols. At the network transport layer, it can use the *Real-Time Transport Protocol* (RTP) over UDP or multicast, H.323 encoding, RSVP signaling, and several gateway protocols, including H.323, the *Simple Gateway Control Protocol* (SGCP), and the *Media Gateway Control Protocol* (MGCP, poised to replace SGCP). (See RFC 1889, ITU 1998, and SGCP 1999.)

VoIP and IPsec

The relevant VoIP protocols have no overt incompatibility with IPsec. In fact, some protocol drafts refer to IPsec as an applicable security mechanism. In practice, however, early generations of IPsec products have proven to be suboptimal for many VoIP installations. They are difficult to deploy and configure correctly and very difficult to troubleshoot; in addition, they often introduce jitter. On a LAN or within a campus, IPsec will add significant complexity, and can introduce periodic latency during SA negotiation and key generation if a call persists through session rekeying. In a wide-area implementation that crosses trust domains, periodic latency will continue to be an impediment, but scalable authentication may prove to be an even greater obstacle: Pre-shared keys are impractical for spontaneous calls, especially among strangers, and cross-certification problems may torpedo a real PKI solution for the foreseeable future. Until both IPsec and VoIP technologies have a chance to mature, we recommend a conservative approach. Deploy IPsec and VoIP separately, and experiment with integration only when you have debugged both installations.

Interoperability—A Quick Summary

Table 8.2 is a quick reference to some of the information we presented earlier in this chapter. It identifies whether a given protocol or operation can usefully combine with each IPsec protocol on the same

Table 8.2 IPsec Interoperability

FUNCTIONAL CATEGORY	TRANSPORT MODE		TUNNEL MODE	
	AH	ESP	AH	ESP
Bandwidth Optimization				
Link Layer Compression	Y	N	Y	N
IPComp	Y	Y	Y	Y
Inbound Queue Management				
(like RED, and WRED)	Y	Y	Y	Y
Diffserv	Y	Y	Y	Y
RSVP	M	M	M	M
Packet Classification				
Packet Filtering	Y	Y	M	M
Proxy Firewall	N	N	M	M
Content Filtering	Y	N	M	N
Network Address Translation	N	N	M	M
Network Infrastructure				
IP Routing Protocols	M	M	N	N
DNS	N	N	N	N

Continues

Table 8.2   IPsec Interoperability *(Continued)*

FUNCTIONAL CATEGORY	TRANSPORT MODE		TUNNEL MODE	
	AH	ESP	AH	ESP
Network Monitoring				
Sniffers	M	N	M	N
Intrusion Detection	M	N	M	N
RMON (standard)	Y	Y	N	N
RMON (filter group)	M	N	M	N
Network Management				
SNMP	Y	Y	M	M
Syslog	Y	Y	M	M
Telnet	Y	Y	M	M
TFTP	Y	Y	M	M
Multicast	M	M	N	N
VoIP	M	M	M	M

traffic flow. The values are Y (Yes), N (No), and M (Maybe). Combinations that are topology-sensitive or difficult to configure, that may limit the utility of the second technology, or that may cause application problems (as with all VoIP combinations) are marked as M. Combinations that are difficult to configure, may cause application problems, and have no obvious value (as with all DNS combinations) are marked as N.

Wrap-up

It is generally unacceptable for a security technology to mangle your IP infrastructure or critical applications. IPsec in either mode, with any transform, can have a damaging effect on your network if you don't analyze your logical and applications topology precisely and in advance. Just as you would not place a teething puppy in a box of new Italian shoes, you must avoid careless installation or configuration of IPsec, especially in a gateway (tunnel-mode) configuration.

Certain types of traffic, described early in the chapter, are immediate candidates for exemption from an IPsec configuration. Applications such as email and Web applications, network management and network infrastructure technologies, and latency-sensitive protocols and applications are all candidates to be passed in the clear.

Processing Power and Order of Operations

In general, you will be able to predict and avoid IPsec integration problems by analyzing two fundamental factors: the processing power of your IPsec platforms and the order of operation of network technologies in your topology. Problems with either factor are much simpler to avoid than to diagnose or repair after the fact. An up-to-date network map is your best tool for creating a functional IPsec infrastructure that enhances security without chewing up something important.

Bear in mind that most of the specific examples we present here refer to technologies that were still under construction when this book went to press. Don't take our word for what will or will not work. Check for current drafts or standards that may ameliorate (or aggravate) the issues described herein.

Do Not Despair

You may feel by now that IPsec is too difficult to justify the effort—that it will inevitably destroy whatever it touches. We can't tell you not to worry, but we can tell you that it is a valuable tool if you use it properly. Networks are technological compost heaps, and they grow relentlessly more complex every day. You cannot avoid that complexity, but you can enhance network security. Don't despair, and good luck.

IPsec and PKI Rollout Considerations

As IP networks become more complex, the job of network manager looks increasingly like an unlucky cross between Flash Gordon and Bozo the Clown. The job description might read: "Qualified individual must juggle a thousand misshapen objects simultaneously to avert the end of the world." Although security technologies can substantially reduce an organization's exposure to risk, they do not, as a rule, make networking any easier. This chapter describes the three most common IPsec topologies and discusses the common technical problems that arise for large-scale IPsec installations.

Where Are the Case Studies?

As this book goes to press, it is impossible to provide a case study of any large IPsec installation—whether LAN-to-LAN, host-to-host, or host-to-gateway—without lengthy descriptions of vendor-specific idiosyncrasies, many of which are orthogonal to the IPsec standards. These idiosyncrasies are not, unfortunately, limited to cosmetic tweaks or interesting enhancements. In many cases, they severely restrict your ibility to deploy a multivendor infrastructure. Chapter 11, "What to Ask Your Vendors," provides a structured approach to documenting the true level of interoperability among various product offerings. Since we are explicitly uninterested in recommending one vendor over another, we have restricted this chapter to a description of generic topologies and the common technical conundrums you will face with most first- or second-generation IPsec products.

Generic IPsec Topologies

The most common IPsec designs reflect the major business concerns driving its rapid market acceptance. These concerns include the reduction of WAN and remote-access costs and the need to deploy new, secure services to customers and business partners. Topologies include (not surprisingly) gateway-to-gateway, end host-to-gateway, and end host-to-end host. The sections that follow briefly describe these three scenarios and identify some key technical issues raised by each one.

Gateway-to-Gateway

Businesses generally deploy IPsec gateway-to-gateway (or network-to-network) as a secure alternative to a private WAN or leased-line connection.

The Extranet

"Extranet" is a buzz word used to describe a network of collaborators whose principal businesses do not fall under the same organizational umbrella. This network may support one or more business-critical applications, such as supply-chain management software, databases, or specialized design software. Tunnel-mode ESP is the most common protocol for gateway-to-gateway extranets. Because of the (presumably) strong requirement for data integrity, tunnel-mode AH+ESP is also a reasonable choice.

An extranet is an instance of a *virtual private network* (VPN), described in the section that follows. Because an extranet involves a trust relationship among entities that are not part of a single trust hierarchy, either each gateway needs to participate in each organization's PKI or each organization needs to deploy a PKI capable of cross-certifying portions of its trust hierarchy. The latter alternative is more scalable and technically superior, but most commercial PKIs do not yet support standards-based cross-certification with other vendors' PKIs. If the extranet scenario is important to you, ensure that your PKI vendor supports or will soon support multivendor PKIX standard cross-certification.

The Virtual Private Network (VPN)

A VPN, in its broadest interpretation, is a private logical network that uses a shared physical medium. The privacy element can be as lightweight as a separate IP addressing scheme or as heavyweight as tunnel-mode AH+ESP with 3DES. Frame relay networks, dial-up networks, and IPsec networks are all instances of VPNs.

An increasing number of businesses are deploying IPsec tunnel-mode ESP or AH+ESP VPNs between their campuses as a lower-cost alternative to a private WAN. Critical features for such an enterprise VPN may include support for a hop-by-hop QoS mechanism such as diffserv to enforce a *service level agreement* (SLA) with the service provider and to ensure timely delivery of delay-sensitive traffic. See Chapter 8, "What Won't Work with IPsec," for a discussion of how to integrate IPsec AH or ESP with diffserv.

Many businesses require 7×24 data operations over their VPNs. To meet their needs, an IPsec infrastructure may need to support a failover mechanism to account for topology changes or problems in the physical network. Figure 9.1 depicts an IPsec VPN. Both bump-in-the-wire and integrated gateway mechanisms can usually failover correctly, albeit with some delay for SA negotiation, if all devices are configured correctly. The greater challenge is to meet a requirement for so-called *stateful failover,* in which existing connections are not disrupted by the underlying infrastructure change. In order to provide stateful failover, the IPsec gateways must share identities and an SAD. This feature can present a major security risk, since secret keys and a private key must be shared, potentially over an insecure channel. Nevertheless, if stateful failover is vital to your network, you should discuss it with your vendor before making any purchase decision.

End Host-to-Gateway: Remote-Access Scenarios

End host-to-gateway IPsec installations provide an attractive, relatively low-cost mechanism for businesses to provide their telecommuting and mobile employees with secure remote access through a local service provider.

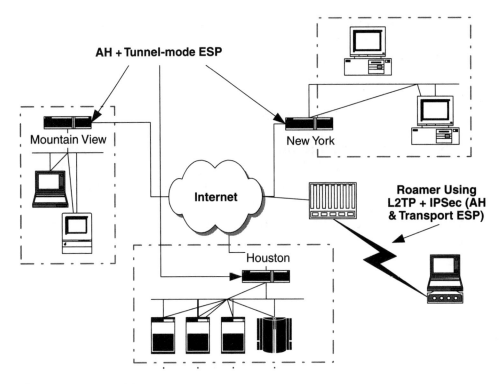

AH + Tunnel-mode ESP

Mountain View

New York

Internet

Houston

**Roamer Using
L2TP + IPSec (AH
& Transport ESP)**

Figure 9.1   IPsec VPN.

These remote-access scenarios usually rely on tunnel-mode ESP or
AH+ESP. Less common configurations allow transport-mode ESP or
AH+ESP connections from the remote user to an internal host through
a firewall or gateway.

Layer 2 Tunneling: PPTP, L2F, and L2TP

A layer 2 tunneling protocol allows a host to establish a virtual presence on a corporate network over a remote connection. Because the
tunnel is at layer 2 and terminates on a home gateway, the remote
host can receive an IP address internal to its home network. Microsoft
supports the Point to Point Tunneling Protocol (PPTP) in its 32-bit
Windows operating systems. Other vendors have implemented a protocol called the Layer Two Forwarding Protocol (L2F). To resolve interoperability problems between these two protocols, the IETF has
proposed a new protocol, called the Layer Two Tunneling Protocol
(L2TP), that supports several features of both.

Layer 2 Tunneling and IPsec

Any of the layer 2 tunneling protocols can coexist with and complement IPsec, provided that your client software supports both technologies. In fact, layer 2 tunneling protocols currently offer three major benefits to IPsec:

- They provide workarounds to many current problems that arise when using DHCP with IPsec client implementations.

- They can force an authentication sequence prior to establishing layer 3 connectivity to the home network.

- They are well integrated with existing accounting and billing mechanisms.

IPsec without a Layer 2 Tunnel

An IPsec host may establish a dial-up tunnel-mode connection to a perimeter gateway on its home network. This scenario currently presents a challenge, since it requires either that the home network preassign the *internal* or encapsulated IP address or that your vendor permit DHCP configuration of that internal address. Many first- and second-generation IPsec end-host implementations do not enable separate dynamic (or even manual) configuration of the inner address. This missing functionality may be a show-stopper for large remote-access installations. Double-check with your vendor if dynamic addressing is important to your plans.

ESP and IKE Identifiers

Using Internet Key Exchange (IKE), a host can identify itself in a number of different ways. Since the only identification a host is guaranteed to possess is its IP address, most end-host IPsec products use that address to identify themselves during a key exchange. Many key exchanges do not require the exchange of an X.509 certificate or a public key. Instead, the responding host will use the identity of the initiator to look up the relevant identity or policy information (from either an internal table or an external directory service). Such a key exchange can succeed only if the IP address of the host initiating the connection does not change.

Dynamic Host Configuration Protocol (DHCP) is a nearly ubiquitous mechanism for address management for internal and remote IP systems on large IP networks. Unfortunately, DHCP can wreak havoc if IPsec end hosts are required to have invariant addresses. One solution, if supported by your software vendor, would be to use ESP tunnel mode from the end host and assign a permanent, internal IP address to use for identification during key exchange. The external IP address could be assigned by DHCP. All IPsec secure communications would then utilize tunnel-mode ESP and wrap the internal IP packet (using the *secure* IP address) in one that is routable from the given location. This mechanism provides the desired functionality but has the very undesirable side effect of forcing static address configuration on every end host. Future standards will doubtless provide a more satisfactory alternative.

End Host-to-End Host

IPsec offers a generic mechanism for true *end-to-end* security without modification to existing IP applications on either host. End-to-end connections use transport-mode AH or ESP, as determined by the security requirements for the specific connection. Depending on the identity and location of the hosts in question, there may be a requirement for cross-certification similar to that described in the earlier section entitled "The Extranet."

Failure Modes

Any of the common IPsec scenarios is prone to fail due to configuration problems, unforeseen circumstances, or implementation bugs. Security problems can be difficult to diagnose and can add an unknown incremental level of risk to your network. IPsec failures may cause connections to drop or permit unauthenticated plaintext connections in violation of a configured policy. Your specific requirements will dictate which behavior is more desirable on your network (fail "open" or fail "shut") The following questions are worth considering as you plan your IPsec infrastructure.

Is the Failure Mode Adjustable?

Is it possible to configure the IPsec product or to redesign the network infrastructure to create the desired failure-mode behavior? For example, would you prefer your VPN to fall back to a last-resort plaintext dial-up connection or to create a hard network failure if an IPsec connection is not available?

Is the Failure Mode Predictable?

Most businesses focus their prototyping efforts on making products work correctly. Before you make a purchase decision, take the time to see how consistently the products fail. A network manager must be able to predict what will happen if a given device reloads, loses its memory or configuration, runs out of memory or CPU, or experiences a hardware failure.

What Will Cause a Failure?

Network failures are infinite in their variety. IPsec contributes certain predictable triggers (as well as many less predictable, vendor-specific ones).

IKE Failure

Probably the most common IPsec problem is an SA negotiation failure. If you are building a multivendor IPsec infrastructure, you should take into account many potential incompatibilities, including the following:

- Do all products use interoperable cryptographic algorithms?
- Do your products have compatible sets of default key lifetimes and related parameters? A product requiring a key lifetime of at least 30 minutes may not interoperate for very long with a product requiring a key lifetime of at most 29 minutes.

Authentication Failure

When X.509 certificates outlive their validity intervals, they can cause many interesting IPsec failures. If a certificate expires, it is no longer valid for use in an IKE key exchange. A more complex failure can occur if a CA's certificate expires, since IKE peers will often query their local *trust tree* for a common parent certificate. All these certificates must be valid, or the authentication will fail. It is therefore important to avoid signing a host certificate with a validity date that extends beyond the signer's own expiration date.

Some IKE implementations show a strange, related failure mode that derives from a need to verify all trust trees right up to the root CA. You might, for example, preload one such IKE node with both its own certificate and its CA's certificate. Assuming you used a self-signed root CA that had also signed certificates for all of this host's peers, everything would initially work fine. If, however, you were then to extend your PKI in such a way that the CA signing the PKI peer certificates was no longer the root, some hosts might fail until you reconfigured them with the certificates of all the CAs up the trust tree to the root. Verify a product's interaction with its PKI infrastructure before deploying in scale.

Denial-of-IKE-Service Attack

There is a specific denial-of-service attack designed to force an IKE peer to engage in guaranteed-to-fail key-exchange operations devised solely to consume resources. IKE supports a reasonably good mechanism to avoid such flooding of initiator requests. Even so, it's worth testing how a given implementation will handle a large number of successful or failed requests; it may be worthwhile to configure access lists to protect it from implausible requests.

Planning a Certificate Infrastructure

In Chapter 7, "The Basics of IPsec and Public Key Infrastructures," we described PKI infrastructures and the PKIX standards effort. In this section, we discuss two important PKI policy components—the certificate policy and the certification practices statement.

Certificate Policy and Certification Practices Statement

The *certificate policy* and the *certification practices statement* (CPS) are complementary components. A mature PKI may have many certificate policies and a single CPS.

Certificate Policy

A certificate policy assigns a security level to a particular certificate. It is a specifically profiled X.509 v3 extension in the certificate itself. Every PKI assigns a unique *object identifier* (OID) to each of its policies.

(The uniqueness does not extend outside the PKI.) The certificate policy helps an entity to assign a level of confidence to the binding of a public key to the specified subject and to adjust its level of trust accordingly. A certificate that requires three forms of photo ID and a background check should have a higher security level than one that is automatically generated.

PKIX specifies that most of its profiled certificate extensions can be marked as either critical or noncritical. In the case of a certificate policy extension, a mark of "critical" means that the certificate not only is *appropriate* for the particular application suite mentioned in the policy statement, but is *restricted* to that application suite.

Certification Practices Statement (CPS)

A CPS is a much broader document that can be globally applied to all certificates issued by a single authority. The X.509 v3 certificate policy extension may optionally reference the organization's current CPS. A CPS is based in legal documents, binding corporate contracts, and (in the United States anyway) American Bar Association (ABA) legal documents.

A CPS can include detailed documents that describe the operation of trusted systems used to issue certificates and any contract that binds the two parties (issuer and subject). The PKIX working group has written an informational RFC (RFC 2527) to provide a framework to aid in bootstrapping an organization's own CPS. A CPS usually contains both technical and legal information. The specific wording in a CPS may have legal implications, so it ought to be a joint effort between the PKI and legal staff.

Commercial PKI Products and PKIX

Not all commercial PKI products support the existing PKIX standards. They typically fall into one of the following categories, with the third being the most desirable:

- Able to produce only pre-X.509 v3 (and pre-CRL v2) certificates and CRLs
- Able to produce X.509 v3 certificates with an open-ended template for adding extensions but no specific support for the PKIX Internet profile

- Able to provide full support for the PKIX profile with rulesets to tailor request handling and creation of conformant certificates

The PKIX standards are your best defenses against a potentially dead-end PKI infrastructure. Ensure that your vendor of choice is committed to full PKIX support. The next chapter discusses some general criteria for selecting IPsec and PKI vendors.

PART

Four

Going Shopping

Part Four walks through the purchasing process for IPsec products. Chapter 10, "Evaluating Vendors," discusses general evaluation criteria for choosing a vendor, and Chapter 11, "What to Ask Your Vendors," offers a sample RFI for obtaining and comparing specific features and capabilities of actual IPsec products.

Evaluating Vendors

IPsec networks are difficult to design, hard to deploy, and wildly complex to troubleshoot. In many cases, your vendor is your best (if not your only) source of product expertise. This chapter and Chapter 11, "What to Ask Your Vendors," are designed to help you profile both vendors and products, in order to make a purchasing decision that will best meet your immediate and long-term needs. Here, we focus on how to evaluate a vendor's ability to support you through the design, licensing, rollout, and operation of your secure infrastructure.

The following sections identify some key areas to explore with all your potential vendors. These criteria will not apply equally to all networks, and there may be additional factors to consider in your specific circumstances. IPsec is an open standard, but most first- and second-generation networks will be, by necessity, single-vendor (or very-few-vendor) installations. All the complexities and problems we described in the preceding chapters only multiply in a multivendor scenario. Although simple interoperability ought to be a no-brainer even for version 1 products, any more elaborate functionality could be mind-bendingly difficult to scale, and may be impossible to manage if you combine products from more than a few vendors. This weird vendor dependency should vanish as the standards and available products mature.

The Right Products

The most obvious factor to consider first is whether a vendor can offer you the products and features that you need. Whether you are purchasing client software or a gateway, you need to plan your basic topology before you consider specific product offerings. Different vendors have different core expertise. Know your product priorities, and set your expectations accordingly. Chapter 11 provides a sample framework for identifying the features and functionality of an IPsec product line.

The Right Plans

Most vendors will initially provide only a portion of what you want. The first release of a product may implement only a small subset of all potential IPsec features, and those may not be the features you need. A good example of this problem is the case of IKE key-exchange mechanisms. The least flexible of these, and the easiest to implement, are preshared keys. A product that only implemented preshared keys for IKE would be standards-compliant, but of little value in a large network. It also would not interoperate with an IKE implementation configured to require (for example) RSA public keys in X.509 certificates.

Like it or not, you will probably end up purchasing "futures" as much as features. There is nothing wrong with accepting a roadmap for future technology, provided that it is specific and credible. Always get any vendor commitments in writing so that you and your vendors share a clear understanding of what you want and what they have offered.

Technology Integration

You will almost certainly purchase PKI software and IPsec products from different vendors. Smart cards or other authentication technologies may involve yet a third party. None of these technologies will integrate by accident, so make sure that the products you need to use together have been designed to work well together. Do not rely on vendor demos or bakeoffs, since those products are often prerelease or specially tweaked versions. Likewise, do not be overly encouraged if your potential vendors are doing joint public announcements. Industry partnerships often generate more lines of press release than lines of code. Test shipping versions of each product together in a lab, and see how they handle various configurations and error conditions.

Do not neglect to evaluate offered or planned management tools. Although most IPsec products currently have a minimal, standalone GUI, it is reasonable to hope that many of them will eventually integrate their configuration and monitoring interfaces into major enterprise management platforms.

Support Requirements

If you are building a large or complex IPsec network, you are going to get to know your vendors or suppliers much better than you might wish. Good product support begins before you ever write a purchase order and ends long afterward. Depending on your needs and available internal staff, you may want to consider your vendor's ability to provide the features listed in the following sections. Take into account the geographic scope of your network and your normal hours of operation.

Pre-Sales Design

Even if you already know how you plan to deploy IPsec, your vendor should be able to certify your design plans and vouch for their feasibility with the specified versions of the product. If, for example, you need to support failover for your VPN, your vendor should be able to provide working sample configurations that enable that capability. Make sure you provide a written design and receive a written response. Design is in the details, and every vendor's implementation will likely introduce a couple of quirks that you will want to understand in advance.

Licensing

As we discussed in Chapter 4, "Encrypting within the Law," the licensing process for IPsec products can be long and complicated. Your potential vendors should provide written lists of the countries where they can legally sell and deliver products. In some instances, a vendor may require both export and import licenses or certifications. If your vendor needs to obtain one or more licenses in order to sell you a product, get a description in writing of what applications the vendor will file, how long the process will take, and what obligations (such as reporting, or providing a local point of contact for law enforcement) you may incur as a result. An eager sales representative may well not understand the full effort and implications of any given licensing process. Insisting on a written commitment will help to ensure that both you and your vendor understand your respective licensing responsibilities.

Post-Sales Support

Some vendors provide integration assistance or can provide a list of certified professional services organizations that are trained to install a specific product line. Certainly a vendor should provide the option of 24×7 knowledgeable phone support, as well as timely access to bug fixes and maintenance upgrades.

Availability of Spares

If you have a multinational network, you need to determine whether you will have access to local spares in the event of a hardware failure. Many vendors outsource their international sparing depots to local businesses that are neither trained nor licensed to handle encryption products. The only source of a spare may be 24 hours or more away at corporate headquarters. If your vendor can't provide them, it's worth investing in your own local spares.

Follow Your Gut

Your IPsec vendor's phone number may be near the top of your speed-dial list for a long time, so make sure you select a company that you like. The technology is so immature that you are buying a relationship as much as a product offering. That being said, you will ultimately install products, not personalities. A bad product with a big smile is not going be a valuable addition to either your network or your professional career. In the following chapter, we provide a sample request for information (RFI) suitable for evaluating a potential vendor's gateway and end-host product offerings.

CHAPTER 11

What to Ask Your Vendors

Junk food manufacturers list ingredients and nutrition information on their product labels, but technology vendors generally do not. That means you'll need to ask vendors for some vital information before you make a purchasing decision. Throughout this book, we've identified technical, business, and operational issues that will impact your ability to deploy IPsec, and may also affect your purchasing plans.

In this chapter, we give you a sample *request for information* (RFI) that you can customize for an IPsec end-host or gateway vendor. If you intend to buy end-host and gateway products from the same vendor, we recommend that you gather separate data on each component of that vendor's offering. Many early-generation IPsec product lines have internal inconsistencies and asymmetries in feature support. Gateway and end-host IPsec products often come from different code bases and may evolve at different rates, even within the same company. It may eventually be safe to assume that a single vendor solution will be highly integrated, but the first several versions could well fall short of that expectation.

To address these differences, some survey sections focus just on end hosts or on gateways and are called out as such. Survey questions in sections labeled "End Host and Gateway" apply to both end-host and gateway products—bracketed text indicates you should substitute the enclosed wording to make it applicable to gateway vendors.

We encourage anyone submitting a vendor RFI to ask all of the gateway or end-host questions. Often sins of omission on the vendor's part are as telling as actual answers. We have included some commentary on the survey questions themselves and on technical details that will help to illuminate the relevance of the questions and of the vendor's responses. These notes to you, the reader, appear outside the shaded RFI sections and will help to illuminate the relevance of the questions and of the vendor's responses. Please use these comments as references when reviewing RFI responses.

We have made the RFI as complete as possible, but we may have left out something important to your specific environment. Think carefully about your particular needs, and add any additional questions you feel might be helpful. Note that in the shaded text, "you" refers to the vendor reviewing the RFI, not to you the reader. In the unshaded comment sections, "you" means you the reader.

PRICING

End Host

Describe the pricing structure for your product.

PRICE (USD)
- Per-unit
- Multi-user packs
- Site license

Gateway

Describe the pricing structure for your product(s).

PRODUCT NAME/NUMBER	PRICE (USD)

END HOST AND GATEWAY: PLATFORM SUPPORT

Describe the availability of support for the following operating systems (OSes). Note OS version(s) and whether your product is a replacement for the native (integrated) IP stack.

	SUPPORTED VERSIONS	REPLACEMENT STACK?
AIX		
HP/UX		
Linux		
MacOS		
Microsoft NT		
Microsoft		
Windows		
Solaris		
SunOS		
Other		

End Host: Bump in the Stack or Replacement Stack?

IPsec end-host implementations are highly dependent on the design and operation of the local TCP/IP stack. OS vendors invariably support IPsec as an enhancement to the original (native) IP stack. Third-party IPsec vendors must choose whether to write a complete replacement TCP/IP stack or to implement a bump-in-the-stack product, a mechanism that somehow inserts itself into the native stack and intercepts inbound and outbound traffic that requires IPsec processing. Both paths have potential problems: A replacement stack may not provide a full functional replacement, especially as the original OS vendor releases fixes and enhancements over time, and bump-in-the-stack implementations can sometimes fail to intercept all the appropriate traffic, especially if higher-layer applications attempt to bypass pieces of the local TCP/IP stack.

GATEWAY: PLATFORM AND CPU

This section identifies the basic hardware and software components of the gateway.

- What is the operating system?
- What LAN interfaces does your gateway support?
- What WAN interfaces does your gateway support?

Continues

GATEWAY: PLATFORM AND CPU *(CONTINUED)*

- Is your IPsec implementation
  - Software-only
  - Software with hardware assist for
    - Symmetric encryption
    - Public key operations
    - Exponentiation
    - Random number generation

END HOST AND GATEWAY: STANDARDS SUPPORT

Identify supported RFCs or draft standards by listing the version of your product that implements each standard. Where relevant, describe mechanisms used to maintain backward compatibility among different versions of the same standard.

Version Numbers and Shipping Products

Time-to-market is a great competitive advantage to any product vendor. It is very common for first- and second-generation IPsec products to have rudimentary, prestandard, or even proprietary components that inhibit multivendor interoperability. It is not unusual to find marketing materials that assert full standards-compliance, even though the shipping versions of a product aren't quite there yet. As you make a purchase decision, be sure to identify which features are shipping and which are associated with future planned releases.

PRODUCT VERSION

- Security Architecture for the Internet Protocol (RFC 2401)
  - RFC 2401 obsoletes RFC 1825; if you support both, describe your technical mechanism for maintaining backward compatibility between the two standards.
- IP Authentication Header (RFC 2402)
  - RFC 2402 obsoletes RFC 1826; if you support both, describe your technical mechanism for maintaining backward compatibility between the two standards.
- IP Encapsulating Security Payload (ESP; RFC 2406)
  - RFC 2406 obsoletes RFC 1827; if you support both, describe your technical mechanism for maintaining backward compatibility between the two standards.
- The Internet IP security domain of interpretation for ISAKMP (RFC 2407) Internet Security Association and Key Management Protocol (ISAKMP; RFC 2408)
- The Internet Key Exchange (IKE; RFC 2409)
- The OAKLEY Key Determination Protocol (RFC 2412)

PRODUCT VERSION *(CONTINUED)*

- IP authentication using keyed MD5 (RFC 1828)
- HMAC-MD5 IP authentication with replay prevention (RFC 2085)
- HMAC: Keyed-hashing for message authentication (RFC 2104)
- The use of HMAC-MD5-96 within ESP and AH (RFC 2403)
- The use of HMAC-SHA-1-96 within ESP and AH (RFC 2404)
- The ESP DES-CBC transform (RFC 1829)
- The NULL encryption algorithm and its use with IPsec (RFC 2410)
- The ESP CBC-mode cipher algorithms (RFC 2451)
- The ESP DES-CBC cipher algorithm with explicit IV (RFC 2405)

   Itemize additional supported RFCs, drafts, or other IPsec extensions.

How to Evaluate Claims of Standards Support

In the early development and deployment phases of a new technology, standards-compliance is a moving target. Very few vendors can afford to wait until every draft goes to a standards-track RFC before coding or even shipping a product. Many so-called standards-compliant IPsec implementations actually support early precursors to the standard. Since some standards-track IPsec protocols do not easily interoperate with earlier drafts of the same protocols, be cautious about assuming that one vendor's AH will work with another vendor's implementation of the same protocol. We address multivendor interoperability in its own section later in this chapter.

END HOST AND GATEWAY: ALGORITHMS AND KEY LENGTHS

This section requests details on symmetric encryption, hashing, and public key support.

Public/Private Key Support

KEY LENGTH(S)

- DSA
   - Provide a list of Certification Authorities that can sign and manage your DSA certificates.
   - List the other vendors whose end-host implementations can accept your certificates.
   - List the vendors whose gateway products can accept your certificates.

Continues

> **END HOST AND GATEWAY: ALGORITHMS AND KEY LENGTHS** *(CONTINUED)*
>
> **KEY LENGTH(S)**
>
> - **RSA**
>   - **Provide a list of Certification Authorities that can sign and manage your RSA certificates.**
>   - **List the other vendors whose end-host implementations can accept your certificates.**
>   - **List the vendors whose gateway products can accept your certificates.**
>   - **Describe your royalty arrangements for use of the RSA patents and/or libraries.**
>   - **Identify any royalty charges that you pass through to the customer on a per-unit basis [end-host products on a site-license basis].**

The Public Key Problem for IPsec

DSA and RSA are the most common public key algorithms. A standards-compliant implementation of IKE *must* be able to encode a DSA key pair in an IPsec certificate. In spite of this requirement, many first-generation IPsec products do not in fact support DSA, for time-to-market and other reasons. RSA is actually the de facto standard for IPsec certificates for vendors that have proceeded beyond preshared keys. Unfortunately, RSA is a patented algorithm, and it can be painful and expensive to arrange for the rights to use it. Many vendors would willingly eat broken glass rather than engage in negotiations to use RSA. Until the RSA patent expires (September 20, 2000), vendors must reach an agreement with its holder (currently Security Dynamics Technology, Inc.), rely on preshared keys (unwieldy for large operations), or use DSA.

> **PUBLIC/PRIVATE KEY PAIR GENERATION AND STORAGE**
>
> This section examines the strength and security of public/private key generation and private key storage.
>
> - **How does your product obtain its public/private key pair?**
>   - **If it receives the key pair from a third party (diskette or online CA), how does it validate the key source?**
>   - **If it generates its own key pair, how does it obtain a random seed?**
>   - **Has any third party verified your random number generation?**
>   - **How large is the random seed?**
> - **How does your product store its private key?**
> - **How does your product restrict access to its private key?**

Key Length Is Not Always Key Strength

Asking vendors exactly how their products generate public/private key pairs may seem nitpicky. The strength of the private key, however, derives only from its being difficult to guess (because it's based on a random seed and is too large to factor quickly) and difficult to steal. If the key generation process relies on a nonrandom (sometimes marketed as *near-random* or *semi-random*) number, the key is fundamentally weak. If the private key is stored in a manner that makes it easy to unlock and copy, that vulnerability too can compromise the whole system.

> **PRIVATE KEY ESCROW**
>
> - Describe your mechanism for extracting and saving a copy of the end host's [gateway's] private key.
>   - If you copy [retrieve] the private key from the end host [gateway], how do you unlock and copy it?
>   - Does the escrow mechanism allow the key to be stored in several pieces?
>   - How do you secure access to the escrowed private key?
>   - How do you prevent unauthorized use of the escrowed private key?

Bogus Answer Alert

If a vendor claims to be able to prevent unauthorized use of an escrowed private key, beware. The second copy of a private key is, by definition, as functional as the original. There is no technical way to prevent its misuse, once it's out and about. We included the question as a not-too-sneaky way to trip up unwary snake-oil sales folk.

> **ESP SYMMETRIC KEY ALGORITHMS**
>
> Describe your supported bulk encryption algorithms and key lengths.
>
> KEY LENGTHS
>
> - DES
>   - DES EBC mode
>   - DES CBC mode
> - 3DES
>   - Describe effective key length if the same key is reused for multiple rounds.
> - CAST
> - IDEA
> - Blowfish
> - Other

Algorithms Other than DES and 3DES

As this book went to print, IPsec ESP had standard encoding mechanisms (called *transforms*) for DES (EBC and CBC) and 3DES. Other transforms for other algorithms were in draft form. If a vendor claims support for a nonstandard or not-yet-standard transform, ask for interoperability data and a commitment to standardize as soon as possible.

AH AND ESP HASHING ALGORITHMS

Which hashing algorithms do you support?

- MD5
  Do you support HMAC?
- SHA-1
  Do you support HMAC?

END HOST AND GATEWAY: X.509 V3 CERTIFICATE SUPPORT

This section covers specifics of X.509 v3 certificate support. If your certificate format is not X.509 v3, please describe it later under "Additional Authentication Methods."

Enrollment Mechanisms

Indicate how your end-host implementations enroll in a CA [or gateways enroll in a CA and receive a certificate]. Specify whether the process requires manual participation from the end user or CA administrator.

	Needs Manual Intervention?	
	SUPPORTED USER/ [SUPPORTED AT THE GATEWAY]	ADMINISTRATOR/ [AT A CONSOLE]
HTML (for example, using Netscape's <keygen> tag).		
Xenroll (Xenroll is a mechanism used to generate a PKCS-10 certificate request).		
PK-INIT (Public key extensions to Kerberos RFC 1510; currently in draft).		
Certificate Enrollment Protocol (CEP is a pre-PKIX enrollment mechanism designed primarily for IPsec gateways; it also is based on PKCS 10).		
Other. Please specify.		

END HOST AND GATEWAY: X.509 V3 CERTIFICATE SUPPORT *(CONTINUED)*

Root CA Support

- How does your implementation [or gateway] identify its root CA?
- What happens if the root certificate expires?
- What happens if you revoke the root certificate?
- Does your implementation support multiple roots?
  - How many?
  - How does the end host [or gateway] acquire the names and keys of additional roots?
  - How do you expire additional root certificates?
  - How do you revoke additional root certificates?

What Is This about Roots?

A PKI is often described as an inverted tree structure, in which the trust hierarchy descends branch-wise from a single, authoritative root. Each tree, in theory, represents a real-world trust hierarchy. Sometimes an entity needs to be part of more than one trust hierarchy. For example, in an extranet scenario, an administrator for Company A may also be trusted for certain business functions at Company B. A common way to accomplish this dual role in a PKI is for the end user to hold the root certificates from both Company A's and Company B's hierarchies. The user can then establish trust relationships with members of either hierarchy.

Roots, for Gateways Only

In an extranet scenario, a gateway for Company A may need to authenticate and exchange IPsec traffic with gateways at Company B. To create this dual role in a PKI, the end user can hold the root certificates from both Company A's and Company B's hierarchies. The gateway can then establish trust relationships with entities in either hierarchy.

Many implementations do not yet support multiple roots, so it's worth asking as you shop around.

EXPIRATION/RE-ENROLLMENT

Please describe the options available for the following:

- Certificate lifetime
- Certificate expiration
- Certificate re-enrollment

ATTRIBUTE CERTIFICATES

- Describe your use, if any, of attribute certificates.
- List the vendors whose end-host [or gateway] implementations can accept your attribute certificates.

Why Insist on Certificates?

IPsec implementations are required to support X.509 certificates for standards-compliance, but preshared keys are usually the first authentication techniques implemented. Many vendors also have alternative proprietary methods. Digital certificates, however, are the most scalable of the available standards. The initial authentication step may involve manual participation from a gateway manager and/or the CA administrator, but certificates generally require little ongoing maintenance. Integration of a mainstream CA product or service is also your best opportunity to maintain the potential of a true multivendor IPsec infrastructure.

END HOST AND GATEWAY: ADDITIONAL AUTHENTICATION METHODS

Does your product support any authentication methods other than preshared keys and X.509 v3 certificates? [For gateways, does your product authenticate itself, other gateways, or end-host products using any authentication methods other than preshared keys and X.509 v3 certificates?]

End Host

- Simple passwords
- Radius
- TACACS+
- Proprietary certificates
  Please describe.
- Kerberos
- Smart cards
  - List commercial smart cards that you support.
- Biometric devices
  - List commercial biometric products that you support.
- Other

END HOST AND GATEWAY: ADDITIONAL AUTHENTICATION METHODS *(CONTINUED)*

Gateway

	ITSELF	OTHER GATEWAYS	END HOSTS
Simple passwords			
Radius			
TACACS+			
Proprietary certificates. Please describe.			
Kerberos			
Smart cards. List commercial smart cards that you support.			
Biometric devices. List commercial biometric products that you support.			
Other			

END HOST AND GATEWAY: PERFORMANCE

The following sections request specific performance metrics for discrete IPsec operations and cryptographic functions. In addition, they request metrics for platform performance for gateway products.

End-Host Memory

- What is the minimum amount of memory required to support your product?
  - List OSes and memory requirements.
- What is the recommended amount of memory for optimal performance?
  - List OSes and memory recommendations.

Gateway Memory

- What is the minimum amount of memory available on your IPsec gateway?
- What is the recommended amount of memory for optimal performance?
- What features or operations are memory-limited?

Gateway CPU

- What is the minimum amount of memory available on your IPsec gateway?
- What is the recommended amount of memory for optimal performance?
- What features or operations are memory-limited?

Continues

END HOST AND GATEWAY: PERFORMANCE *(CONTINUED)*

SA Negotiation and Termination

- How many SAs per second can your product negotiate?
  Note different rates for different platforms, where applicable.
- How many total SAs can it terminate with the minimum recommended memory?
- How many total SAs can it terminate with the maximum recommended memory?
- [For gateway products, how many total SAs can it terminate with the optimal memory configuration?]

Why Worry about SA Negotiation Speed?

Multiple (usually two or four) SA negotiations must precede any transmission of IPsec traffic. If an IPsec implementation must terminate many IPsec connections, especially in a pure software implementation, SA negotiation speed can introduce perceptible delay for real-time traffic. We discuss performance problems with SA negotiation in more detail in Chapter 8, "What Won't Work with IPsec."

End host note: It's unlikely that you would notice SA negotiation times for a desktop client, but you might observe them in the desktop implementation for a very active applications server that terminates many dynamic connections.

BULK ENCRYPTION

For each product, identify the *full duplex* performance figures in Mbs for the following IP packet sizes:

IP Packet Size (in bytes)

ALGORITHM	64	128	256	512	1024	1500	4096
DES (EBC mode)							
DES (CBC mode)							
3DES							
CAST							
IDEA							
Blowfish							
Other							

SESSION KEY GENERATION

For each algorithm and key length, describe session key generation times.

Key Generation Times

ALGORITHM	40	56	112	128	168	448	OTHER
DES (EBC mode)							
DES (CBC mode)							
3DES							
CAST							
IDEA							
Blowfish							
Other							

SESSION KEY LIFETIME AND KEY PRECALCULATION

- What is the default session key lifetime for your product?
- What is the configurable range?
- Does your product support precalculation of session keys?
  - Describe how it works.
  - Describe how it works if either IPsec peer is under load.

End Host: Why Prekey?

As we discussed in Chapter 8, session rekeying can introduce unacceptable incremental latency into IPsec for real-time application transport. Precalculating session keys is one good way to avoid this problem at the end host. Prekeying often relies on a certain amount of available CPU in both IPsec peers, which is important to consider as you plan your product deployment.

Gateway: Why Prekey?

If a gateway is terminating many IPsec tunnels and those sessions have short lifetimes, rekeying can place a substantial load on shared resources and degrade session quality. Precalculating session keys is one good way to avoid this problem, assuming the gateway has enough free cycles to precalculate. Prekeying relies on a certain spikiness in the gateway load, which is important to consider as you plan your gateway deployment.

END HOST AND GATEWAY: IPSEC POLICY CONFIGURATION

Describe how each desktop client [or gateway] does the following:

- Identifies IPsec peers and gateways [for gateway products, both dynamically and statically]
- Determines when to negotiate an IPsec connection
- Selects what IPsec protocols and encryption algorithms to use
- Chooses what traffic to transmit via IPsec
- Chooses what traffic to exclude from IPsec
- [Handles logical topology changes that impact IPsec policy (for gateway products only)]
- Instructs a gateway that certain incoming traffic from that gateway must be transmitted via IPsec
- Instructs a gateway or IPsec peer that certain incoming traffic from that peer must be transmitted via IPsec

List IPsec gateways and end-host implementations from other vendors that can interpret and act upon your policy configuration mechanism.

Vendors

Gateways (list).

End host (list).

END HOST: REMOTE CONFIGURATION AND DATA ACCESS

- Does your implementation support any mechanism or diagnostic mode to allow a local or remote entity to modify IPsec policy?
  - How is it secured?
- Does your implementation support any mechanism or diagnostic mode to allow a local or remote entity to view packet data payload?
  - How is it secured?

END HOST AND GATEWAY: INTEROPERABILITY

List the other vendors that have proven interoperability against your current products.

End Host-to-End Host [or Gateway-to-Gateway] Interoperability

	VENDOR	AUTHENTICATION MECHANISMS	AH	ESP	POLICY
1. Version: Caveats:					

END HOST AND GATEWAY: INTEROPERABILITY *(CONTINUED)*

End Host-to-End Host [or Gateway-to-Gateway] Interoperability

	VENDOR	AUTHENTICATION MECHANISMS	AH	ESP	POLICY
2. Version: Caveats:					
3. Version: Caveats:					
4. Version: Caveats:					
5. Version: Caveats:					

End Host-to-Gateway [or Gateway-to-End Host] Interoperability

	VENDOR	AUTHENTICATION MECHANISMS	AH	ESP	POLICY
1. Version: Caveats:					
2. Version: Caveats:					
3. Version: Caveats:					
4. Version: Caveats:					
5. Version: Caveats:					

END HOST AND GATEWAY: EXPORT, IMPORT, AND DOMESTIC USE LICENSING

For each product version and bulk encryption algorithm, list countries where the product is legal to use. "Legal to use" means here that an end user in that country may purchase the product at its source or from a licensed reseller, import it, operate it, and return it for repair.

- Under "version," list which product versions are covered.
- Under "license caveats," identify any use restrictions or license renewal requirements.

Continues

END HOST AND GATEWAY: EXPORT, IMPORT, AND DOMESTIC USE LICENSING *(CONTINUED)*

- Under "technical caveats," describe in detail all technical changes you made to the product in order to comply with a regulation. These changes may include, but are not limited to, restricted randomness, length, or lifetime of session keys, support for any non-IPsec key management scheme, or implementation of any plaintext data interception mechanism.

	PRODUCT	ALGORITHMS	KEY LENGTH	LICENSED COUNTRIES	LICENSED USERS

Version:
License caveats:
Technical caveats:

Version:
License caveats:
Technical caveats:

Version:
License caveats:
Technical caveats:

Version:
License caveats:
Technical caveats:

Version:
License caveats:
Technical caveats:

GATEWAY: DEVICE CONTROL AND DATA INTERCEPT POINTS

Please list all interfaces (such as console ports) and all protocols (such as Telnet or SNMP) that enable administrative access to your gateway.

INTERFACES

1.
2.
3.

PROTOCOLS

1.
2.
3.

Describe how your gateway secures access to its own configuration:

- Does any supported access mechanism enable a local or remote entity to bypass configuration security mechanisms?
- Does any supported access mechanism or diagnostic mode allow a local or remote entity to view packet data payload?
- Does any supported access mechanism or diagnostic mode allow a local or remote entity to save, copy, or redirect packet information and/or contents?

What's This about Configuration and Interception?

As we discussed in Chapter 4, "Encrypting within the Law," many government agencies use discretionary encryption licensing mechanisms to exert pressure on companies to limit the strength of their encryption products. Rumors persist of companies engineering "back doors" or data interception mechanisms into their products in exchange for favorable export treatment. Although it's not clear that a company would confess to those actions in an RFI response, it can't hurt to ask.

END HOST AND GATEWAY: PROVEN SCALABILITY

- What is the largest production installation of your end-host (or gateway) products?
- Attach a generic description of the installation, including the following:
    - IPsec end hosts
    - IPsec gateways
    - Topology [for gateway products, physical topology]
    - [For gateway products, IPsec topology. Full or partial mesh?]
    - Available bandwidth
    - Average traffic rate
    - Traffic encryption policy
    - Authentication infrastructure
    - Policy configuration infrastructure

END HOST: OTHER INTERESTING FEATURES

Indicate and describe your support for the following capabilities. Add additional differentiating features as appropriate.

- Dynamic IP Addressing
  Describe mechanism.
- Multiprotocol support
  Describe mechanism.
- Multicast support
  Describe mechanism.
- Logical IP dual-homing (one or more IPsec network, one or more trusted network)
  Describe mechanism.
- IPsec stateful failover (server software only)
  Describe mechanism.
- Other

GATEWAY: OTHER INTERESTING FEATURES

Indicate and describe your support for the following capabilities. Add additional differentiating features as appropriate.

- **Multiprotocol support**
  Describe mechanism.
- **Multicast support**
  Describe mechanism.
- **IPsec stateful failover/hot standby**
  Describe mechanism.
- **Other**

Conclusions

As mentioned earlier, examining what has been left out of an RFI is often as useful as evaluating what's been included. Taking this further, it might be valuable to evaluate vendor responses once all have been returned. This way, multiple answers to particular questions can be compared to each other. Often a formal approach for evaluating responses will reveal a clear front-runner.

- Determine which features are strictly necessary and discard responses from vendors whose products don't support this feature set.

- Determine which nonmandatory features are desirable, and sort the remaining vendor responses on their completeness of support for these features.

- Select the vendors at the top of your list and consider other positive attributes each one may possess. These can include prior positive dealings you have had, existing relationships you have already established, attractive pricing, and wide industry acceptance.

Appendix

Network Working Group   S. Kent
Request for Comments: 2401   BBN Corp
Obsoletes: 1825   R. Atkinson
Category: Standards Track   @Home Network
                                                         November 1998

              Security Architecture for the Internet Protocol

Status of this Memo

   This document specifies an Internet standards track protocol for the
   Internet community, and requests discussion and suggestions for
   improvements. Please refer to the current edition of the "Internet
   Official Protocol Standards" (STD 1) for the standardization state
   and status of this protocol. Distribution of this memo is unlimited.

Copyright Notice

Table of Contents

Kent & Atkinson   Standards Track   [Page 1]

RFC 2401   Security Architecture for IP   November 1998

1. Introduction

1.1 Summary of Contents of Document

   This memo specifies the base architecture for IPsec compliant
   systems. The goal of the architecture is to provide various security
   services for traffic at the IP layer, in both the IPv4 and IPv6
   environments. This document describes the goals of such systems,
   their components and how they fit together with each other and into
   the IP environment. It also describes the security services offered
   by the IPsec protocols, and how these services can be employed in the
   IP environment. This document does not address all aspects of IPsec
   architecture. Subsequent documents will address additional
   architectural details of a more advanced nature, e.g., use of IPsec
   in NAT environments and more complete support for IP multicast. The
   following fundamental components of the IPsec security architecture
   are discussed in terms of their underlying, required functionality.
   Additional RFCs (see Section 1.3 for pointers to other documents)
   define the protocols in (a), (c), and (d).

         a. Security Protocols -- Authentication Header (AH) and
            Encapsulating Security Payload (ESP)
         b. Security Associations -- what they are and how they work,
            how they are managed, associated processing
         c. Key Management -- manual and automatic (The Internet Key
            Exchange (IKE))
         d. Algorithms for authentication and encryption

   This document is not an overall Security Architecture for the
   Internet; it addresses security only at the IP layer, provided
   through the use of a combination of cryptographic and protocol
   security mechanisms.

   The keywords MUST, MUST NOT, REQUIRED, SHALL, SHALL NOT, SHOULD,
   SHOULD NOT, RECOMMENDED, MAY, and OPTIONAL, when they appear in this
   document, are to be interpreted as described in RFC 2119 [Bra97].

1.2 Audience

   The target audience for this document includes implementers of this
   IP security technology and others interested in gaining a general
   background understanding of this system. In particular, prospective
   users of this technology (end users or system administrators) are
   part of the target audience. A glossary is provided as an appendix

to help fill in gaps in background/vocabulary. This document assumes
that the reader is familiar with the Internet Protocol, related
networking technology, and general security terms and concepts.

1.3 Related Documents

As mentioned above, other documents provide detailed definitions of
some of the components of IPsec and of their inter-relationship.
They include RFCs on the following topics:

    a. "IP Security Document Roadmap" [TDG97] -- a document
       providing guidelines for specifications describing encryption
       and authentication algorithms used in this system.
    b. security protocols -- RFCs describing the Authentication
       Header (AH) [KA98a] and Encapsulating Security Payload (ESP)
       [KA98b] protocols.
    c. algorithms for authentication and encryption -- a separate
       RFC for each algorithm.
    d. automatic key management -- RFCs on "The Internet Key
       Exchange (IKE)" [HC98], "Internet Security Association and
       Key Management Protocol (ISAKMP)" [MSST97],"The OAKLEY Key
       Determination Protocol" [Orm97], and "The Internet IP
       Security Domain of Interpretation for ISAKMP" [Pip98].

2. Design Objectives

2.1 Goals/Objectives/Requirements/Problem Description

IPsec is designed to provide interoperable, high quality,
cryptographically-based security for IPv4 and IPv6. The set of
security services offered includes access control, connectionless
integrity, data origin authentication, protection against replays (a
form of partial sequence integrity), confidentiality (encryption),
and limited traffic flow confidentiality. These services are
provided at the IP layer, offering protection for IP and/or upper
layer protocols.

These objectives are met through the use of two traffic security
protocols, the Authentication Header (AH) and the Encapsulating
Security Payload (ESP), and through the use of cryptographic key
management procedures and protocols. The set of IPsec protocols
employed in any context, and the ways in which they are employed,
will be determined by the security and system requirements of users,
applications, and/or sites/organizations.

When these mechanisms are correctly implemented and deployed, they
ought not to adversely affect users, hosts, and other Internet
components that do not employ these security mechanisms for

protection of their traffic. These mechanisms also are designed to
be algorithm-independent. This modularity permits selection of
different sets of algorithms without affecting the other parts of the
implementation. For example, different user communities may select
different sets of algorithms (creating cliques) if required.

A standard set of default algorithms is specified to facilitate
interoperability in the global Internet. The use of these
algorithms, in conjunction with IPsec traffic protection and key
management protocols, is intended to permit system and application
developers to deploy high quality, Internet layer, cryptographic
security technology.

2.2 Caveats and Assumptions

The suite of IPsec protocols and associated default algorithms are
designed to provide high quality security for Internet traffic.
However, the security offered by use of these protocols ultimately
depends on the quality of the their implementation, which is outside
the scope of this set of standards. Moreover, the security of a
computer system or network is a function of many factors, including
personnel, physical, procedural, compromising emanations, and
computer security practices. Thus IPsec is only one part of an
overall system security architecture.

Finally, the security afforded by the use of IPsec is critically
dependent on many aspects of the operating environment in which the
IPsec implementation executes. For example, defects in OS security,
poor quality of random number sources, sloppy system management
protocols and practices, etc. can all degrade the security provided
by IPsec. As above, none of these environmental attributes are
within the scope of this or other IPsec standards.

3. System Overview

This section provides a high level description of how IPsec works,
the components of the system, and how they fit together to provide
the security services noted above. The goal of this description is
to enable the reader to "picture" the overall process/system, see how
it fits into the IP environment, and to provide context for later
sections of this document, which describe each of the components in
more detail.

An IPsec implementation operates in a host or a security gateway
environment, affording protection to IP traffic. The protection
offered is based on requirements defined by a Security Policy
Database (SPD) established and maintained by a user or system
administrator, or by an application operating within constraints

established by either of the above. In general, packets are selected
for one of three processing modes based on IP and transport layer
header information (Selectors, Section 4.4.2) matched against entries
in the database (SPD). Each packet is either afforded IPsec security
services, discarded, or allowed to bypass IPsec, based on the
applicable database policies identified by the Selectors.

3.1 What IPsec Does

IPsec provides security services at the IP layer by enabling a system
to select required security protocols, determine the algorithm(s) to
use for the service(s), and put in place any cryptographic keys
required to provide the requested services. IPsec can be used to
protect one or more "paths" between a pair of hosts, between a pair
of security gateways, or between a security gateway and a host. (The
term "security gateway" is used throughout the IPsec documents to
refer to an intermediate system that implements IPsec protocols. For
example, a router or a firewall implementing IPsec is a security
gateway.)

The set of security services that IPsec can provide includes access
control, connectionless integrity, data origin authentication,
rejection of replayed packets (a form of partial sequence integrity),
confidentiality (encryption), and limited traffic flow
confidentiality. Because these services are provided at the IP
layer, they can be used by any higher layer protocol, e.g., TCP, UDP,
ICMP, BGP, etc.

The IPsec DOI also supports negotiation of IP compression [SMPT98],
motivated in part by the observation that when encryption is employed
within IPsec, it prevents effective compression by lower protocol
layers.

3.2 How IPsec Works

IPsec uses two protocols to provide traffic security --
Authentication Header (AH) and Encapsulating Security Payload (ESP).
Both protocols are described in more detail in their respective RFCs
[KA98a, KA98b].

          o The IP Authentication Header (AH) [KA98a] provides
            connectionless integrity, data origin authentication, and an
            optional anti-replay service.
          o The Encapsulating Security Payload (ESP) protocol [KA98b] may
            provide confidentiality (encryption), and limited traffic flow
            confidentiality. It also may provide connectionless

> integrity, data origin authentication, and an anti-replay
> service. (One or the other set of these security services
> must be applied whenever ESP is invoked.)
>   o Both AH and ESP are vehicles for access control, based on the
>   distribution of cryptographic keys and the management of
>   traffic flows relative to these security protocols.

These protocols may be applied alone or in combination with each
other to provide a desired set of security services in IPv4 and IPv6.
Each protocol supports two modes of use: transport mode and tunnel
mode. In transport mode the protocols provide protection primarily
for upper layer protocols; in tunnel mode, the protocols are applied
to tunneled IP packets. The differences between the two modes are
discussed in Section 4.

IPsec allows the user (or system administrator) to control the
granularity at which a security service is offered. For example, one
can create a single encrypted tunnel to carry all the traffic between
two security gateways or a separate encrypted tunnel can be created
for each TCP connection between each pair of hosts communicating
across these gateways. IPsec management must incorporate facilities
for specifying:

>   o which security services to use and in what combinations
>   o the granularity at which a given security protection should be
>   applied
>   o the algorithms used to effect cryptographic-based security

Because these security services use shared secret values
(cryptographic keys), IPsec relies on a separate set of mechanisms
for putting these keys in place. (The keys are used for
authentication/integrity and encryption services.) This document
requires support for both manual and automatic distribution of keys.
It specifies a specific public-key based approach (IKE -- [MSST97,
Orm97, HC98]) for automatic key management, but other automated key
distribution techniques MAY be used. For example, KDC-based systems
such as Kerberos and other public-key systems such as SKIP could be
employed.

3.3 Where IPsec May Be Implemented

There are several ways in which IPsec may be implemented in a host or
in conjunction with a router or firewall (to create a security
gateway). Several common examples are provided below:

>   a. Integration of IPsec into the native IP implementation. This
>   requires access to the IP source code and is applicable to
>   both hosts and security gateways.

   b. "Bump-in-the-stack" (BITS) implementations, where IPsec is
      implemented "underneath" an existing implementation of an IP
      protocol stack, between the native IP and the local network
      drivers. Source code access for the IP stack is not required
      in this context, making this implementation approach
      appropriate for use with legacy systems. This approach, when
      it is adopted, is usually employed in hosts.

   c. The use of an outboard crypto processor is a common design
      feature of network security systems used by the military, and
      of some commercial systems as well. It is sometimes referred
      to as a "Bump-in-the-wire" (BITW) implementation. Such
      implementations may be designed to serve either a host or a
      gateway (or both). Usually the BITW device is IP
      addressable. When supporting a single host, it may be quite
      analogous to a BITS implementation, but in supporting a
      router or firewall, it must operate like a security gateway.

4. Security Associations

   This section defines Security Association management requirements for
   all IPv6 implementations and for those IPv4 implementations that
   implement AH, ESP, or both. The concept of a "Security Association"
   (SA) is fundamental to IPsec. Both AH and ESP make use of SAs and a
   major function of IKE is the establishment and maintenance of
   Security Associations. All implementations of AH or ESP MUST support
   the concept of a Security Association as described below. The
   remainder of this section describes various aspects of Security
   Association management, defining required characteristics for SA
   policy management, traffic processing, and SA management techniques.

4.1 Definition and Scope

   A Security Association (SA) is a simplex "connection" that affords
   security services to the traffic carried by it. Security services
   are afforded to an SA by the use of AH, or ESP, but not both. If
   both AH and ESP protection is applied to a traffic stream, then two
   (or more) SAs are created to afford protection to the traffic stream.
   To secure typical, bi-directional communication between two hosts, or
   between two security gateways, two Security Associations (one in each
   direction) are required.

   A security association is uniquely identified by a triple consisting
   of a Security Parameter Index (SPI), an IP Destination Address, and a
   security protocol (AH or ESP) identifier. In principle, the
   Destination Address may be a unicast address, an IP broadcast
   address, or a multicast group address. However, IPsec SA management
   mechanisms currently are defined only for unicast SAs. Hence, in the

discussions that follow, SAs will be described in the context of
point-to-point communication, even though the concept is applicable
in the point-to-multipoint case as well.

As noted above, two types of SAs are defined: transport mode and
tunnel mode. A transport mode SA is a security association between
two hosts. In IPv4, a transport mode security protocol header
appears immediately after the IP header and any options, and before
any higher layer protocols (e.g., TCP or UDP). In IPv6, the security
protocol header appears after the base IP header and extensions, but
may appear before or after destination options, and before higher
layer protocols. In the case of ESP, a transport mode SA provides
security services only for these higher layer protocols, not for the
IP header or any extension headers preceding the ESP header. In the
case of AH, the protection is also extended to selected portions of
the IP header, selected portions of extension headers, and selected
options (contained in the IPv4 header, IPv6 Hop-by-Hop extension
header, or IPv6 Destination extension headers). For more details on
the coverage afforded by AH, see the AH specification [KA98a].

A tunnel mode SA is essentially an SA applied to an IP tunnel.
Whenever either end of a security association is a security gateway,
the SA MUST be tunnel mode. Thus an SA between two security gateways
is always a tunnel mode SA, as is an SA between a host and a security
gateway. Note that for the case where traffic is destined for a
security gateway, e.g., SNMP commands, the security gateway is acting
as a host and transport mode is allowed. But in that case, the
security gateway is not acting as a gateway, i.e., not transiting
traffic. Two hosts MAY establish a tunnel mode SA between
themselves. The requirement for any (transit traffic) SA involving a
security gateway to be a tunnel SA arises due to the need to avoid
potential problems with regard to fragmentation and reassembly of
IPsec packets, and in circumstances where multiple paths (e.g., via
different security gateways) exist to the same destination behind the
security gateways.

For a tunnel mode SA, there is an "outer" IP header that specifies
the IPsec processing destination, plus an "inner" IP header that
specifies the (apparently) ultimate destination for the packet. The
security protocol header appears after the outer IP header, and
before the inner IP header. If AH is employed in tunnel mode,
portions of the outer IP header are afforded protection (as above),
as well as all of the tunneled IP packet (i.e., all of the inner IP
header is protected, as well as higher layer protocols). If ESP is
employed, the protection is afforded only to the tunneled packet, not
to the outer header.

Kent & Atkinson   Standards Track   [Page 9]

RFC 2401   Security Architecture for IP   November 1998

In summary,
        a) A host MUST support both transport and tunnel mode.
        b) A security gateway is required to support only tunnel
           mode. If it supports transport mode, that should be used
           only when the security gateway is acting as a host, e.g.,
           for network management.

4.2 Security Association Functionality

The set of security services offered by an SA depends on the security
protocol selected, the SA mode, the endpoints of the SA, and on the
election of optional services within the protocol. For example, AH
provides data origin authentication and connectionless integrity for
IP datagrams (hereafter referred to as just "authentication"). The
"precision" of the authentication service is a function of the
granularity of the security association with which AH is employed, as
discussed in Section 4.4.2, "Selectors".

AH also offers an anti-replay (partial sequence integrity) service at
the discretion of the receiver, to help counter denial of service
attacks. AH is an appropriate protocol to employ when
confidentiality is not required (or is not permitted, e.g , due to
government restrictions on use of encryption). AH also provides
authentication for selected portions of the IP header, which may be
necessary in some contexts. For example, if the integrity of an IPv4
option or IPv6 extension header must be protected en route between
sender and receiver, AH can provide this service (except for the
non-predictable but mutable parts of the IP header.)

ESP optionally provides confidentiality for traffic. (The strength
of the confidentiality service depends in part, on the encryption
algorithm employed.) ESP also may optionally provide authentication
(as defined above). If authentication is negotiated for an ESP SA,
the receiver also may elect to enforce an anti-replay service with
the same features as the AH anti-replay service. The scope of the
authentication offered by ESP is narrower than for AH, i.e., the IP
header(s) "outside" the ESP header is(are) not protected. If only
the upper layer protocols need to be authenticated, then ESP
authentication is an appropriate choice and is more space efficient
than use of AH encapsulating ESP. Note that although both
confidentiality and authentication are optional, they cannot both be
omitted. At least one of them MUST be selected.

If confidentiality service is selected, then an ESP (tunnel mode) SA
between two security gateways can offer partial traffic flow
confidentiality. The use of tunnel mode allows the inner IP headers
to be encrypted, concealing the identities of the (ultimate) traffic
source and destination. Moreover, ESP payload padding also can be

invoked to hide the size of the packets, further concealing the
external characteristics of the traffic. Similar traffic flow
confidentiality services may be offered when a mobile user is
assigned a dynamic IP address in a dialup context, and establishes a
(tunnel mode) ESP SA to a corporate firewall (acting as a security
gateway). Note that fine granularity SAs generally are more
vulnerable to traffic analysis than coarse granularity ones which are
carrying traffic from many subscribers.

4.3 Combining Security Associations

The IP datagrams transmitted over an individual SA are afforded
protection by exactly one security protocol, either AH or ESP, but
not both. Sometimes a security policy may call for a combination of
services for a particular traffic flow that is not achievable with a
single SA. In such instances it will be necessary to employ multiple
SAs to implement the required security policy. The term "security
association bundle" or "SA bundle" is applied to a sequence of SAs
through which traffic must be processed to satisfy a security policy.
The order of the sequence is defined by the policy. (Note that the
SAs that comprise a bundle may terminate at different endpoints. For
example, one SA may extend between a mobile host and a security
gateway and a second, nested SA may extend to a host behind the
gateway.)

Security associations may be combined into bundles in two ways:
transport adjacency and iterated tunneling.

        o Transport adjacency refers to applying more than one
          security protocol to the same IP datagram, without invoking
          tunneling. This approach to combining AH and ESP allows
          for only one level of combination; further nesting yields
          no added benefit (assuming use of adequately strong
          algorithms in each protocol) since the processing is
          performed at one IPsec instance at the (ultimate)
          destination.

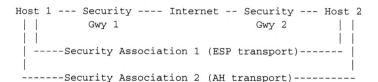

```
Host 1 --- Security ---- Internet -- Security --- Host 2
   | |        Gwy 1                    Gwy 2        | |
   | |                                              | |
   | -----Security Association 1 (ESP transport)------- |
   |                                                    |
   -------Security Association 2 (AH transport)----------
```

        o Iterated tunneling refers to the application of multiple
          layers of security protocols effected through IP tunneling.
          This approach allows for multiple levels of nesting, since
          each tunnel can originate or terminate at a different IPsec

site along the path. No special treatment is expected for
ISAKMP traffic at intermediate security gateways other than
what can be specified through appropriate SPD entries (See
Case 3 in Section 4.5)

There are 3 basic cases of iterated tunneling -- support is
required only for cases 2 and 3.:

1. both endpoints for the SAs are the same -- The inner and
   outer tunnels could each be either AH or ESP, though it
   is unlikely that Host 1 would specify both to be the
   same, i.e., AH inside of AH or ESP inside of ESP.

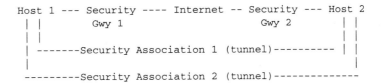

```
   Host 1 --- Security ---- Internet -- Security --- Host 2
     | |        Gwy 1                     Gwy 2        | |
     | |                                               | |
     | -------Security Association 1 (tunnel)---------- | |
     |                                                  |
     ---------Security Association 2 (tunnel)-------------
```

2. one endpoint of the SAs is the same -- The inner and
   uter tunnels could each be either AH or ESP.

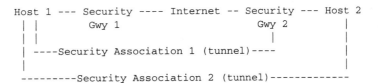

```
   Host 1 --- Security ---- Internet -- Security --- Host 2
     | |        Gwy 1                     Gwy 2        |
     | |                                   |           |
     | ----Security Association 1 (tunnel)----         |
     |                                                 |
     ---------Security Association 2 (tunnel)------------
```

3. neither endpoint is the same -- The inner and outer
   tunnels could each be either AH or ESP.

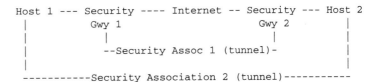

```
   Host 1 --- Security ---- Internet -- Security --- Host 2
     |          Gwy 1                     Gwy 2        |
     |            |                         |          |
     |            --Security Assoc 1 (tunnel)-         |
     |                                                 |
     -----------Security Association 2 (tunnel)-----------
```

These two approaches also can be combined, e.g., an SA bundle could
be constructed from one tunnel mode SA and one or two transport mode
SAs, applied in sequence. (See Section 4.5 "Basic Combinations of
Security Associations.") Note that nested tunnels can also occur
where neither the source nor the destination endpoints of any of the
tunnels are the same. In that case, there would be no host or
security gateway with a bundle corresponding to the nested tunnels.

For transport mode SAs, only one ordering of security protocols seems appropriate. AH is applied to both the upper layer protocols and (parts of) the IP header. Thus if AH is used in a transport mode, in conjunction with ESP, AH SHOULD appear as the first header after IP, prior to the appearance of ESP. In that context, AH is applied to the ciphertext output of ESP. In contrast, for tunnel mode SAs, one can imagine uses for various orderings of AH and ESP. The required set of SA bundle types that MUST be supported by a compliant IPsec implementation is described in Section 4.5.

4.4 Security Association Databases

Many of the details associated with processing IP traffic in an IPsec implementation are largely a local matter, not subject to standardization. However, some external aspects of the processing must be standardized, to ensure interoperability and to provide a minimum management capability that is essential for productive use of IPsec. This section describes a general model for processing IP traffic relative to security associations, in support of these interoperability and functionality goals. The model described below is nominal; compliant implementations need not match details of this model as presented, but the external behavior of such implementations must be mappable to the externally observable characteristics of this model.

There are two nominal databases in this model: the Security Policy Database and the Security Association Database. The former specifies the policies that determine the disposition of all IP traffic inbound or outbound from a host, security gateway, or BITS or BITW IPsec implementation. The latter database contains parameters that are associated with each (active) security association. This section also defines the concept of a Selector, a set of IP and upper layer protocol field values that is used by the Security Policy Database to map traffic to a policy, i.e., an SA (or SA bundle).

Each interface for which IPsec is enabled requires nominally separate inbound vs. outbound databases (SAD and SPD), because of the directionality of many of the fields that are used as selectors. Typically there is just one such interface, for a host or security gateway (SG). Note that an SG would always have at least 2 interfaces, but the "internal" one to the corporate net, usually would not have IPsec enabled and so only one pair of SADs and one pair of SPDs would be needed. On the other hand, if a host had multiple interfaces or an SG had multiple external interfaces, it might be necessary to have separate SAD and SPD pairs for each interface.

4.4.1 The Security Policy Database (SPD)

   Ultimately, a security association is a management construct used to
   enforce a security policy in the IPsec environment. Thus an
   essential element of SA processing is an underlying Security Policy
   Database (SPD) that specifies what services are to be offered to IP
   datagrams and in what fashion. The form of the database and its
   interface are outside the scope of this specification. However, this
   section does specify certain minimum management functionality that
   must be provided, to allow a user or system administrator to control
   how IPsec is applied to traffic transmitted or received by a host or
   transiting a security gateway.

   The SPD must be consulted during the processing of all traffic
   (INBOUND and OUTBOUND), including non-IPsec traffic. In order to
   support this, the SPD requires distinct entries for inbound and
   outbound traffic. One can think of this as separate SPDs (inbound
   vs. outbound). In addition, a nominally separate SPD must be
   provided for each IPsec-enabled interface.

   An SPD must discriminate among traffic that is afforded IPsec
   protection and traffic that is allowed to bypass IPsec. This applies
   to the IPsec protection to be applied by a sender and to the IPsec
   protection that must be present at the receiver. For any outbound or
   inbound datagram, three processing choices are possible: discard,
   bypass IPsec, or apply IPsec. The first choice refers to traffic
   that is not allowed to exit the host, traverse the security gateway,
   or be delivered to an application at all. The second choice refers
   to traffic that is allowed to pass without additional IPsec
   protection. The third choice refers to traffic that is afforded
   IPsec protection, and for such traffic the SPD must specify the
   security services to be provided, protocols to be employed,
   algorithms to be used, etc.

   For every IPsec implementation, there MUST be an administrative
   interface that allows a user or system administrator to manage the
   SPD. Specifically, every inbound or outbound packet is subject to
   processing by IPsec and the SPD must specify what action will be
   taken in each case. Thus the administrative interface must allow the
   user (or system administrator) to specify the security processing to
   be applied to any packet entering or exiting the system, on a packet
   by packet basis. (In a host IPsec implementation making use of a
   socket interface, the SPD may not need to be consulted on a per
   packet basis, but the effect is still the same.) The management
   interface for the SPD MUST allow creation of entries consistent with
   the selectors defined in Section 4.4.2, and MUST support (total)
   ordering of these entries. It is expected that through the use of
   wildcards in various selector fields, and because all packets on a

single UDP or TCP connection will tend to match a single SPD entry,
this requirement will not impose an unreasonably detailed level of
SPD specification. The selectors are analogous to what are found in
a stateless firewall or filtering router and which are currently
manageable this way.

In host systems, applications MAY be allowed to select what security
processing is to be applied to the traffic they generate and consume.
(Means of signalling such requests to the IPsec implementation are
outside the scope of this standard.) However, the system
administrator MUST be able to specify whether or not a user or
application can override (default) system policies. Note that
application specified policies may satisfy system requirements, so
that the system may not need to do additional IPsec processing beyond
that needed to meet an application's requirements. The form of the
management interface is not specified by this document and may differ
for hosts vs. security gateways, and within hosts the interface may
differ for socket-based vs. BITS implementations. However, this
document does specify a standard set of SPD elements that all IPsec
implementations MUST support.

The SPD contains an ordered list of policy entries. Each policy
entry is keyed by one or more selectors that define the set of IP
traffic encompassed by this policy entry. (The required selector
types are defined in Section 4.4.2.) These define the granularity of
policies or SAs. Each entry includes an indication of whether
traffic matching this policy will be bypassed, discarded, or subject
to IPsec processing. If IPsec processing is to be applied, the entry
includes an SA (or SA bundle) specification, listing the IPsec
protocols, modes, and algorithms to be employed, including any
nesting requirements. For example, an entry may call for all
matching traffic to be protected by ESP in transport mode using
3DES-CBC with an explicit IV, nested inside of AH in tunnel mode
using HMAC/SHA-1. For each selector, the policy entry specifies how
to derive the corresponding values for a new Security Association
Database (SAD, see Section 4.4.3) entry from those in the SPD and the
packet (Note that at present, ranges are only supported for IP
addresses; but wildcarding can be expressed for all selectors):

   a. use the value in the packet itself -- This will limit use
      of the SA to those packets which have this packet's value
      for the selector even if the selector for the policy entry
      has a range of allowed values or a wildcard for this
      selector.
   b. use the value associated with the policy entry -- If this
      were to be just a single value, then there would be no
      difference between (b) and (a). However, if the allowed
      values for the selector are a range (for IP addresses) or

wildcard, then in the case of a range,(b) would enable use
of the SA by any packet with a selector value within the
range not just by packets with the selector value of the
packet that triggered the creation of the SA. In the case
of a wildcard, (b) would allow use of the SA by packets
with any value for this selector.

For example, suppose there is an SPD entry where the allowed value
for source address is any of a range of hosts (192.168.2.1 to
192.168.2.10). And suppose that a packet is to be sent that has a
source address of 192.168.2.3. The value to be used for the SA could
be any of the sample values below depending on what the policy entry
for this selector says is the source of the selector value:

                source for the example of
                value to be   new SAD
                used in the SA selector value
                --------------- ------------
                a. packet   192.168.2.3 (one host)
                b. SPD entry   192.168.2.1 to 192.168.2.10 (range of hosts)

Note that if the SPD entry had an allowed value of wildcard for the
source address, then the SAD selector value could be wildcard (any
host). Case (a) can be used to prohibit sharing, even among packets
that match the same SPD entry.

As described below in Section 4.4.3, selectors may include "wildcard"
entries and hence the selectors for two entries may overlap. (This
is analogous to the overlap that arises with ACLs or filter entries
in routers or packet filtering firewalls.) Thus, to ensure
consistent, predictable processing, SPD entries MUST be ordered and
the SPD MUST always be searched in the same order, so that the first
matching entry is consistently selected. (This requirement is
necessary as the effect of processing traffic against SPD entries
must be deterministic, but there is no way to canonicalize SPD
entries given the use of wildcards for some selectors.) More detail
on matching of packets against SPD entries is provided in Section 5.

Note that if ESP is specified, either (but not both) authentication
or encryption can be omitted. So it MUST be possible to configure
the SPD value for the authentication or encryption algorithms to be
"NULL". However, at least one of these services MUST be selected,
i.e., it MUST NOT be possible to configure both of them as "NULL".

The SPD can be used to map traffic to specific SAs or SA bundles.
Thus it can function both as the reference database for security
policy and as the map to existing SAs (or SA bundles). (To
accommodate the bypass and discard policies cited above, the SPD also

MUST provide a means of mapping traffic to these functions, even
though they are not, per se, IPsec processing.) The way in which the
SPD operates is different for inbound vs. outbound traffic and it
also may differ for host vs. security gateway, BITS, and BITW
implementations. Sections 5.1 and 5.2 describe the use of the SPD
for outbound and inbound processing, respectively.

Because a security policy may require that more than one SA be
applied to a specified set of traffic, in a specific order, the
policy entry in the SPD must preserve these ordering requirements,
when present. Thus, it must be possible for an IPsec implementation
to determine that an outbound or inbound packet must be processed
thorough a sequence of SAs. Conceptually, for outbound processing,
one might imagine links (to the SAD) from an SPD entry for which
there are active SAs, and each entry would consist of either a single
SA or an ordered list of SAs that comprise an SA bundle. When a
packet is matched against an SPD entry and there is an existing SA or
SA bundle that can be used to carry the traffic, the processing of
the packet is controlled by the SA or SA bundle entry on the list.
For an inbound IPsec packet for which multiple IPsec SAs are to be
applied, the lookup based on destination address, IPsec protocol, and
SPI should identify a single SA.

The SPD is used to control the flow of ALL traffic through an IPsec
system, including security and key management traffic (e.g., ISAKMP)
from/to entities behind a security gateway. This means that ISAKMP
traffic must be explicitly accounted for in the SPD, else it will be
discarded. Note that a security gateway could prohibit traversal of
encrypted packets in various ways, e.g., having a DISCARD entry in
the SPD for ESP packets or providing proxy key exchange. In the
latter case, the traffic would be internally routed to the key
management module in the security gateway.

4.4.2 Selectors

An SA (or SA bundle) may be fine-grained or coarse-grained, depending
on the selectors used to define the set of traffic for the SA. For
example, all traffic between two hosts may be carried via a single
SA, and afforded a uniform set of security services. Alternatively,
traffic between a pair of hosts might be spread over multiple SAs,
depending on the applications being used (as defined by the Next
Protocol and Port fields), with different security services offered
by different SAs. Similarly, all traffic between a pair of security
gateways could be carried on a single SA, or one SA could be assigned
for each communicating host pair. The following selector parameters
MUST be supported for SA management to facilitate control of SA
granularity. Note that in the case of receipt of a packet with an
ESP header, e.g., at an encapsulating security gateway or BITW

implementation, the transport layer protocol, source/destination
ports, and Name (if present) may be "OPAQUE", i.e., inaccessible
because of encryption or fragmentation. Note also that both Source
and Destination addresses should either be IPv4 or IPv6.

- Destination IP Address (IPv4 or IPv6): this may be a single IP
  address (unicast, anycast, broadcast (IPv4 only), or multicast
  group), a range of addresses (high and low values (inclusive),
  address + mask, or a wildcard address. The last three are used
  to support more than one destination system sharing the same SA
  (e.g., behind a security gateway). Note that this selector is
  conceptually different from the "Destination IP Address" field
  in the <Destination IP Address, IPsec Protocol, SPI> tuple used
  to uniquely identify an SA. When a tunneled packet arrives at
  the tunnel endpoint, its SPI/Destination address/Protocol are
  used to look up the SA for this packet in the SAD. This
  destination address comes from the encapsulating IP header.
  Once the packet has been processed according to the tunnel SA
  and has come out of the tunnel, its selectors are "looked up" in
  the Inbound SPD. The Inbound SPD has a selector called
  destination address. This IP destination address is the one in
  the inner (encapsulated) IP header. In the case of a
  transport'd packet, there will be only one IP header and this
  ambiguity does not exist. [REQUIRED for all implementations]

- Source IP Address(es) (IPv4 or IPv6): this may be a single IP
  address (unicast, anycast, broadcast (IPv4 only), or multicast
  group), range of addresses (high and low values inclusive),
  address + mask, or a wildcard address. The last three are used
  to support more than one source system sharing the same SA
  (e.g., behind a security gateway or in a multihomed host).
  [REQUIRED for all implementations]

- Name: There are 2 cases (Note that these name forms are
  supported in the IPsec DOI.)
           1. User ID
              a. a fully qualified user name string (DNS), e.g.,
                 mozart@foo.bar.com
              b. X.500 distinguished name, e.g., C = US, SP = MA,
                 O = GTE Internetworking, CN = Stephen T. Kent.
           2. System name (host, security gateway, etc.)
              a. a fully qualified DNS name, e.g., foo.bar.com
              b. X.500 distinguished name
              c. X.500 general name

NOTE: One of the possible values of this selector is "OPAQUE".

[REQUIRED for the following cases. Note that support for name
forms other than addresses is not required for manually keyed
SAs.
            o User ID
                - native host implementations
                - BITW and BITS implementations acting as HOSTS
                  with only one user
                - security gateway implementations for INBOUND
                  processing.
            o System names -- all implementations]

   - Data sensitivity level: (IPSO/CIPSO labels)
     [REQUIRED for all systems providing information flow security as
     per Section 8, OPTIONAL for all other systems.]

   - Transport Layer Protocol: Obtained from the IPv4 "Protocol" or
     the IPv6 "Next Header" fields. This may be an individual
     protocol number. These packet fields may not contain the
     Transport Protocol due to the presence of IP extension headers,
     e.g., a Routing Header, AH, ESP, Fragmentation Header,
     Destination Options, Hop-by-hop options, etc. Note that the
     Transport Protocol may not be available in the case of receipt
     of a packet with an ESP header, thus a value of "OPAQUE" SHOULD
     be supported.
     [REQUIRED for all implementations]

     NOTE: To locate the transport protocol, a system has to chain
     through the packet headers checking the "Protocol" or "Next
     Header" field until it encounters either one it recognizes as a
     transport protocol, or until it reaches one that isn't on its
     list of extension headers, or until it encounters an ESP header
     that renders the transport protocol opaque.

   - Source and Destination (e.g., TCP/UDP) Ports: These may be
     individual UDP or TCP port values or a wildcard port. (The use
     of the Next Protocol field and the Source and/or Destination
     Port fields (in conjunction with the Source and/or Destination
     Address fields), as an SA selector is sometimes referred to as
     "session-oriented keying."). Note that the source and
     destination ports may not be available in the case of receipt of
     a packet with an ESP header, thus a value of "OPAQUE" SHOULD be
     supported.

     The following table summarizes the relationship between the
     "Next Header" value in the packet and SPD and the derived Port
     Selector value for the SPD and SAD.

```
        Next Hdr          Transport Layer   Derived Port Selector Field
        in Packet         Protocol in SPD   Value in SPD and SAD
        --------          ---------------   --------------------------
        ESP               ESP or ANY        ANY (i.e., don't look at it)
        -don't care-      ANY               ANY (i.e., don't look at it)
        specific value    specific value    NOT ANY (i.e., drop packet)
           fragment
        specific value    specific value    actual port selector field
           not fragment
```

   If the packet has been fragmented, then the port information may
   not be available in the current fragment. If so, discard the
   fragment. An ICMP PMTU should be sent for the first fragment,
   which will have the port information. [MAY be supported]

The IPsec implementation context determines how selectors are used.
For example, a host implementation integrated into the stack may make
use of a socket interface. When a new connection is established the
SPD can be consulted and an SA (or SA bundle) bound to the socket.
Thus traffic sent via that socket need not result in additional
lookups to the SPD/SAD. In contrast, a BITS, BITW, or security
gateway implementation needs to look at each packet and perform an
SPD/SAD lookup based on the selectors. The allowable values for the
selector fields differ between the traffic flow, the security
association, and the security policy.

The following table summarizes the kinds of entries that one needs to
be able to express in the SPD and SAD. It shows how they relate to
the fields in data traffic being subjected to IPsec screening.
(Note: the "wild" or "wildcard" entry for src and dst addresses
includes a mask, range, etc.)

```
Field          Traffic Value    SAD Entry         SPD Entry
--------       -------------    ---------------   --------------------
src addr       single IP addr   single,range,wild single,range,wildcard
dst addr       single IP addr   single,range,wild single,range,wildcard
xpt protocol*  xpt protocol     single,wildcard   single,wildcard
src port*      single src port  single,wildcard   single,wildcard
dst port*      single dst port  single,wildcard   single,wildcard
user id*       single user id   single,wildcard   single,wildcard
sec. labels    single value     single,wildcard   single,wildcard
```

      * The SAD and SPD entries for these fields could be "OPAQUE"
        because the traffic value is encrypted.

   NOTE: In principle, one could have selectors and/or selector values
   in the SPD which cannot be negotiated for an SA or SA bundle.
   Examples might include selector values used to select traffic for

discarding or enumerated lists which cause a separate SA to be
created for each item on the list. For now, this is left for future
versions of this document and the list of required selectors and
selector values is the same for the SPD and the SAD. However, it is
acceptable to have an administrative interface that supports use of
selector values which cannot be negotiated provided that it does not
mislead the user into believing it is creating an SA with these
selector values. For example, the interface may allow the user to
specify an enumerated list of values but would result in the creation
of a separate policy and SA for each item on the list. A vendor
might support such an interface to make it easier for its customers
to specify clear and concise policy specifications.

4.4.3 Security Association Database (SAD)

In each IPsec implementation there is a nominal Security Association
Database, in which each entry defines the parameters associated with
one SA. Each SA has an entry in the SAD. For outbound processing,
entries are pointed to by entries in the SPD. Note that if an SPD
entry does not currently point to an SA that is appropriate for the
packet, the implementation creates an appropriate SA (or SA Bundle)
and links the SPD entry to the SAD entry (see Section 5.1.1). For
inbound processing, each entry in the SAD is indexed by a destination
IP address, IPsec protocol type, and SPI. The following parameters
are associated with each entry in the SAD. This description does not
purport to be a MIB, but only a specification of the minimal data
items required to support an SA in an IPsec implementation.

For inbound processing: The following packet fields are used to look
up the SA in the SAD:

    o Outer Header's Destination IP address: the IPv4 or IPv6
      Destination address.
      [REQUIRED for all implementations]
    o IPsec Protocol: AH or ESP, used as an index for SA lookup
      in this database. Specifies the IPsec protocol to be
      applied to the traffic on this SA.
      [REQUIRED for all implementations]
    o SPI: the 32-bit value used to distinguish among different
      SAs terminating at the same destination and using the same
      IPsec protocol.
      [REQUIRED for all implementations]

For each of the selectors defined in Section 4.4.2, the SA entry in
the SAD MUST contain the value or values which were negotiated at the
time the SA was created. For the sender, these values are used to
decide whether a given SA is appropriate for use with an outbound
packet. This is part of checking to see if there is an existing SA

Kent & Atkinson   Standards Track   [Page 21]

RFC 2401   Security Architecture for IP   November 1998

that can be used. For the receiver, these values are used to check
that the selector values in an inbound packet match those for the SA
(and thus indirectly those for the matching policy). For the
receiver, this is part of verifying that the SA was appropriate for
this packet. (See Section 6 for rules for ICMP messages.) These
fields can have the form of specific values, ranges, wildcards, or
"OPAQUE" as described in section 4.4.2, "Selectors". Note that for
an ESP SA, the encryption algorithm or the authentication algorithm
could be "NULL". However they MUST not both be "NULL".

The following SAD fields are used in doing IPsec processing:

        o Sequence Number Counter: a 32-bit value used to generate the
          Sequence Number field in AH or ESP headers.
          [REQUIRED for all implementations, but used only for outbound
          traffic.]
        o Sequence Counter Overflow: a flag indicating whether overflow
          of the Sequence Number Counter should generate an auditable
          event and prevent transmission of additional packets on the
          SA.
          [REQUIRED for all implementations, but used only for outbound
          traffic.]
        o Anti-Replay Window: a 32-bit counter and a bit-map (or
          equivalent) used to determine whether an inbound AH or ESP
          packet is a replay.
          [REQUIRED for all implementations but used only for inbound
          traffic. NOTE: If anti-replay has been disabled by the
          receiver, e.g., in the case of a manually keyed SA, then the
          Anti-Replay Window is not used.]
        o AH Authentication algorithm, keys, etc.
          [REQUIRED for AH implementations]
        o ESP Encryption algorithm, keys, IV mode, IV, etc.
          [REQUIRED for ESP implementations]
        o ESP authentication algorithm, keys, etc. If the
          authentication service is not selected, this field will be
          null.
          [REQUIRED for ESP implementations]
        o Lifetime of this Security Association: a time interval after
          which an SA must be replaced with a new SA (and new SPI) or
          terminated, plus an indication of which of these actions
          should occur. This may be expressed as a time or byte count,
          or a simultaneous use of both, the first lifetime to expire
          taking precedence. A compliant implementation MUST support
          both types of lifetimes, and must support a simultaneous use
          of both. If time is employed, and if IKE employs X.509
          certificates for SA establishment, the SA lifetime must be
          constrained by the validity intervals of the certificates,
          and the NextIssueDate of the CRLs used in the IKE exchange

for the SA. Both initiator and responder are responsible for
constraining SA lifetime in this fashion.
[REQUIRED for all implementations]

NOTE: The details of how to handle the refreshing of keys
when SAs expire is a local matter. However, one reasonable
approach is:
  (a) If byte count is used, then the implementation
      SHOULD count the number of bytes to which the IPsec
      algorithm is applied. For ESP, this is the encryption
      algorithm (including Null encryption) and for AH,
      this is the authentication algorithm. This includes
      pad bytes, etc. Note that implementations SHOULD be
      able to handle having the counters at the ends of an
      SA get out of synch, e.g., because of packet loss or
      because the implementations at each end of the SA
      aren't doing things the same way.
  (b) There SHOULD be two kinds of lifetime -- a soft
      lifetime which warns the implementation to initiate
      action such as setting up a replacement SA and a
      hard lifetime when the current SA ends.
  (c) If the entire packet does not get delivered during
      the SAs lifetime, the packet SHOULD be discarded.

o IPsec protocol mode: tunnel, transport or wildcard.
  Indicates which mode of AH or ESP is applied to traffic on
  this SA. Note that if this field is "wildcard" at the
  sending end of the SA, then the application has to specify
  the mode to the IPsec implementation. This use of wildcard
  allows the same SA to be used for either tunnel or transport
  mode traffic on a per packet basis, e.g., by different
  sockets. The receiver does not need to know the mode in
  order to properly process the packet's IPsec headers.

  [REQUIRED as follows, unless implicitly defined by context:
            - host implementations must support all modes
            - gateway implementations must support tunnel mode]

NOTE: The use of wildcard for the protocol mode of an inbound
SA may add complexity to the situation in the receiver (host
only). Since the packets on such an SA could be delivered in
either tunnel or transport mode, the security of an incoming
packet could depend in part on which mode had been used to
deliver it. If, as a result, an application cared about the
SA mode of a given packet, then the application would need a
mechanism to obtain this mode information.

o Path MTU: any observed path MTU and aging variables. See
  Section 6.1.2.4
  [REQUIRED for all implementations but used only for outbound
  traffic]

4.5 Basic Combinations of Security Associations

This section describes four examples of combinations of security
associations that MUST be supported by compliant IPsec hosts or
security gateways. Additional combinations of AH and/or ESP in
tunnel and/or transport modes MAY be supported at the discretion of
the implementor. Compliant implementations MUST be capable of
generating these four combinations and on receipt, of processing
them, but SHOULD be able to receive and process any combination. The
diagrams and text below describe the basic cases. The legend for the
diagrams is:

        ==== = one or more security associations (AH or ESP, transport
               or tunnel)
        ---- = connectivity (or if so labelled, administrative boundary)
        Hx   = host x
        SGx = security gateway x
        X*   = X supports IPsec

NOTE: The security associations below can be either AH or ESP. The
mode (tunnel vs transport) is determined by the nature of the
endpoints. For host-to-host SAs, the mode can be either transport or
tunnel.

Case 1. The case of providing end-to-end security between 2 hosts
         across the Internet (or an Intranet).

              =====================================
              | |
              H1* ------ (Inter/Intranet) ------ H2*

Note that either transport or tunnel mode can be selected by the
hosts. So the headers in a packet between H1 and H2 could look
like any of the following:

        Transport   Tunnel
        -----------------   --------------------
        1. [IP1][AH][upper]   4. [IP2][AH][IP1][upper]
        2. [IP1][ESP][upper]   5. [IP2][ESP][IP1][upper]
        3. [IP1][AH][ESP][upper]

Note that there is no requirement to support general nesting,
but in transport mode, both AH and ESP can be applied to the
packet. In this event, the SA establishment procedure MUST
ensure that first ESP, then AH are applied to the packet.

Case 2. This case illustrates simple virtual private networks
support.

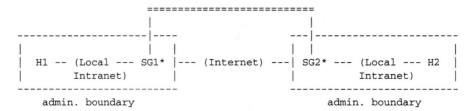

Only tunnel mode is required here. So the headers in a packet
between SG1 and SG2 could look like either of the following:

```
                    Tunnel
          --------------------
          4. [IP2][AH][IP1][upper]
          5. [IP2][ESP][IP1][upper]
```

Case 3. This case combines cases 1 and 2, adding end-to-end security
between the sending and receiving hosts. It imposes no new
requirements on the hosts or security gateways, other than a
requirement for a security gateway to be configurable to pass
IPsec traffic (including ISAKMP traffic) for hosts behind it.

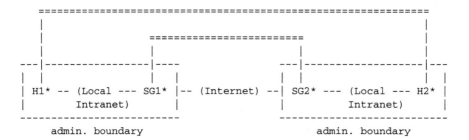

Case 4. This covers the situation where a remote host (H1) uses the
Internet to reach an organization's firewall (SG2) and to then
gain access to some server or other machine (H2). The remote
host could be a mobile host (H1) dialing up to a local PPP/ARA
server (not shown) on the Internet and then crossing the
Internet to the home organization's firewall (SG2), etc. The

Kent & Atkinson   Standards Track   [Page 25]

RFC 2401   Security Architecture for IP   November 1998

      details of support for this case, (how H1 locates SG2,
      authenticates it, and verifies its authorization to represent
      H2) are discussed in Section 4.6.3, "Locating a Security
      Gateway".

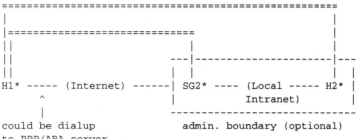

```
   ========================================================
   |                                                      |
   |==============================                        |
   ||                           |                         |
   ||                   ---|---------------------|---      |
   ||                   |  |                     |  |      |
   H1* ----- (Internet) ------| SG2* ---- (Local ----- H2* |
        ^                     |          Intranet)     |
        |                     -----------------------------
   could be dialup           admin. boundary (optional)
   to PPP/ARA server
```

      Only tunnel mode is required between H1 and SG2. So the choices
      for the SA between H1 and SG2 would be one of the ones in case
      2. The choices for the SA between H1 and H2 would be one of the
      ones in case 1.

      Note that in this case, the sender MUST apply the transport
      header before the tunnel header. Therefore the management
      interface to the IPsec implementation MUST support configuration
      of the SPD and SAD to ensure this ordering of IPsec header
      application.

   As noted above, support for additional combinations of AH and ESP is
   optional. Use of other, optional combinations may adversely affect
   interoperability.

4.6 SA and Key Management

   IPsec mandates support for both manual and automated SA and
   cryptographic key management. The IPsec protocols, AH and ESP, are
   largely independent of the associated SA management techniques,
   although the techniques involved do affect some of the security
   services offered by the protocols. For example, the optional anti-
   replay services available for AH and ESP require automated SA
   management. Moreover, the granularity of key distribution employed
   with IPsec determines the granularity of authentication provided.
   (See also a discussion of this issue in Section 4.7.) In general,
   data origin authentication in AH and ESP is limited by the extent to
   which secrets used with the authentication algorithm (or with a key
   management protocol that creates such secrets) are shared among
   multiple possible sources.

The following text describes the minimum requirements for both types of SA management.

4.6.1 Manual Techniques

The simplest form of management is manual management, in which a person manually configures each system with keying material and security association management data relevant to secure communication with other systems. Manual techniques are practical in small, static environments but they do not scale well. For example, a company could create a Virtual Private Network (VPN) using IPsec in security gateways at several sites. If the number of sites is small, and since all the sites come under the purview of a single administrative domain, this is likely to be a feasible context for manual management techniques. In this case, the security gateway might selectively protect traffic to and from other sites within the organization using a manually configured key, while not protecting traffic for other destinations. It also might be appropriate when only selected communications need to be secured. A similar argument might apply to use of IPsec entirely within an organization for a small number of hosts and/or gateways. Manual management techniques often employ statically configured, symmetric keys, though other options also exist.

4.6.2 Automated SA and Key Management

Widespread deployment and use of IPsec requires an Internet-standard, scalable, automated, SA management protocol. Such support is required to facilitate use of the anti-replay features of AH and ESP, and to accommodate on-demand creation of SAs, e.g., for user- and session-oriented keying. (Note that the notion of "rekeying" an SA actually implies creation of a new SA with a new SPI, a process that generally implies use of an automated SA/key management protocol.)

The default automated key management protocol selected for use with IPsec is IKE [MSST97, Orm97, HC98] under the IPsec domain of interpretation [Pip98]. Other automated SA management protocols MAY be employed.

When an automated SA/key management protocol is employed, the output from this protocol may be used to generate multiple keys, e.g., for a single ESP SA. This may arise because:

     o the encryption algorithm uses multiple keys (e.g., triple DES)
     o the authentication algorithm uses multiple keys
     o both encryption and authentication algorithms are employed

The Key Management System may provide a separate string of bits for
each key or it may generate one string of bits from which all of them
are extracted. If a single string of bits is provided, care needs to
be taken to ensure that the parts of the system that map the string
of bits to the required keys do so in the same fashion at both ends
of the SA. To ensure that the IPsec implementations at each end of
the SA use the same bits for the same keys, and irrespective of which
part of the system divides the string of bits into individual keys,
the encryption key(s) MUST be taken from the first (left-most, high-
order) bits and the authentication key(s) MUST be taken from the
remaining bits. The number of bits for each key is defined in the
relevant algorithm specification RFC. In the case of multiple
encryption keys or multiple authentication keys, the specification
for the algorithm must specify the order in which they are to be
selected from a single string of bits provided to the algorithm.

4.6.3 Locating a Security Gateway

This section discusses issues relating to how a host learns about the
existence of relevant security gateways and once a host has contacted
these security gateways, how it knows that these are the correct
security gateways. The details of where the required information is
stored is a local matter.

Consider a situation in which a remote host (H1) is using the
Internet to gain access to a server or other machine (H2) and there
is a security gateway (SG2), e.g., a firewall, through which H1's
traffic must pass. An example of this situation would be a mobile
host (Road Warrior) crossing the Internet to the home organization's
firewall (SG2). (See Case 4 in the section 4.5 Basic Combinations of
Security Associations.) This situation raises several issues:

    1. How does H1 know/learn about the existence of the security
       gateway SG2?
    2. How does it authenticate SG2, and once it has authenticated
       SG2, how does it confirm that SG2 has been authorized to
       represent H2?
    3. How does SG2 authenticate H1 and verify that H1 is authorized
       to contact H2?
    4. How does H1 know/learn about backup gateways which provide
       alternate paths to H2?

To address these problems, a host or security gateway MUST have an
administrative interface that allows the user/administrator to
configure the address of a security gateway for any sets of
destination addresses that require its use. This includes the ability
to configure:

    o the requisite information for locating and authenticating the
      security gateway and verifying its authorization to represent
      the destination host.
    o the requisite information for locating and authenticating any
      backup gateways and verifying their authorization to represent
      the destination host.

It is assumed that the SPD is also configured with policy information
that covers any other IPsec requirements for the path to the security
gateway and the destination host.

This document does not address the issue of how to automate the
discovery/verification of security gateways.

4.7 Security Associations and Multicast

The receiver-orientation of the Security Association implies that, in
the case of unicast traffic, the destination system will normally
select the SPI value. By having the destination select the SPI
value, there is no potential for manually configured Security
Associations to conflict with automatically configured (e.g., via a
key management protocol) Security Associations or for Security
Associations from multiple sources to conflict with each other. For
multicast traffic, there are multiple destination systems per
multicast group. So some system or person will need to coordinate
among all multicast groups to select an SPI or SPIs on behalf of each
multicast group and then communicate the group's IPsec information to
all of the legitimate members of that multicast group via mechanisms
not defined here.

Multiple senders to a multicast group SHOULD use a single Security
Association (and hence Security Parameter Index) for all traffic to
that group when a symmetric key encryption or authentication
algorithm is employed. In such circumstances, the receiver knows only
that the message came from a system possessing the key for that
multicast group. In such circumstances, a receiver generally will
not be able to authenticate which system sent the multicast traffic.
Specifications for other, more general multicast cases are deferred
to later IPsec documents.

At the time this specification was published, automated protocols for
multicast key distribution were not considered adequately mature for
standardization. For multicast groups having relatively few members,
manual key distribution or multiple use of existing unicast key
distribution algorithms such as modified Diffie-Hellman appears
feasible. For very large groups, new scalable techniques will be
needed. An example of current work in this area is the Group Key
Management Protocol (GKMP) [HM97].

5. IP Traffic Processing

   As mentioned in Section 4.4.1 "The Security Policy Database (SPD)",
   the SPD must be consulted during the processing of all traffic
   (INBOUND and OUTBOUND), including non-IPsec traffic. If no policy is
   found in the SPD that matches the packet (for either inbound or
   outbound traffic), the packet MUST be discarded.

   NOTE: All of the cryptographic algorithms used in IPsec expect their
   input in canonical network byte order (see Appendix in RFC 791) and
   generate their output in canonical network byte order. IP packets
   are also transmitted in network byte order.

5.1 Outbound IP Traffic Processing

5.1.1 Selecting and Using an SA or SA Bundle

   In a security gateway or BITW implementation (and in many BITS
   implementations), each outbound packet is compared against the SPD to
   determine what processing is required for the packet. If the packet
   is to be discarded, this is an auditable event. If the traffic is
   allowed to bypass IPsec processing, the packet continues through
   "normal" processing for the environment in which the IPsec processing
   is taking place. If IPsec processing is required, the packet is
   either mapped to an existing SA (or SA bundle), or a new SA (or SA
   bundle) is created for the packet. Since a packet's selectors might
   match multiple policies or multiple extant SAs and since the SPD is
   ordered, but the SAD is not, IPsec MUST:

            1. Match the packet's selector fields against the outbound
               policies in the SPD to locate the first appropriate
               policy, which will point to zero or more SA bundles in the
               SAD.

            2. Match the packet's selector fields against those in the SA
               bundles found in (1) to locate the first SA bundle that
               matches. If no SAs were found or none match, create an
               appropriate SA bundle and link the SPD entry to the SAD
               entry. If no key management entity is found, drop the
               packet.

            3. Use the SA bundle found/created in (2) to do the required
               IPsec processing, e.g., authenticate and encrypt.

   In a host IPsec implementation based on sockets, the SPD will be
   consulted whenever a new socket is created, to determine what, if
   any, IPsec processing will be applied to the traffic that will flow
   on that socket.

   NOTE: A compliant implementation MUST not allow instantiation of an
   ESP SA that employs both a NULL encryption and a NULL authentication
   algorithm. An attempt to negotiate such an SA is an auditable event.

5.1.2 Header Construction for Tunnel Mode

   This section describes the handling of the inner and outer IP
   headers, extension headers, and options for AH and ESP tunnels. This
   includes how to construct the encapsulating (outer) IP header, how to
   handle fields in the inner IP header, and what other actions should
   be taken. The general idea is modeled after the one used in RFC
   2003, "IP Encapsulation with IP":

      o The outer IP header Source Address and Destination Address
        identify the "endpoints" of the tunnel (the encapsulator and
        decapsulator). The inner IP header Source Address and
        Destination Addresses identify the original sender and
        recipient of the datagram, (from the perspective of this
        tunnel), respectively. (see footnote 3 after the table in
        5.1.2.1 for more details on the encapsulating source IP
        address.)
      o The inner IP header is not changed except to decrement the TTL
        as noted below, and remains unchanged during its delivery to
        the tunnel exit point.
      o No change to IP options or extension headers in the inner
        header occurs during delivery of the encapsulated datagram
        through the tunnel.
      o If need be, other protocol headers such as the IP
        Authentication header may be inserted between the outer IP
        header and the inner IP header.

   The tables in the following sub-sections show the handling for the
   different header/option fields (constructed = the value in the outer
   field is constructed independently of the value in the inner).

5.1.2.1 IPv4 -- Header Construction for Tunnel Mode

                        <-- How Outer Hdr Relates to Inner Hdr -->
                        Outer Hdr at   Inner Hdr at
        IPv4   Encapsulator   Decapsulator
          Header fields: --------------------   -----------
            version   4 (1)   no change
            header length   constructed   no change
            TOS   copied from inner hdr (5) no change
            total length   constructed   no change
            ID   constructed   no change
            flags (DF,MF)   constructed, DF (4)   no change
            fragmt offset   constructed   no change

Kent & Atkinson   Standards Track   [Page 31]

RFC 2401   Security Architecture for IP   November 1998

```
        TTL              constructed (2)          decrement (2)
        protocol         AH, ESP, routing hdr      no change
        checksum         constructed               constructed (2)
        src address      constructed (3)           no change
        dest address     constructed (3)           no change
   Options               never copied              no change
```

1. The IP version in the encapsulating header can be different from the value in the inner header.

2. The TTL in the inner header is decremented by the encapsulator prior to forwarding and by the decapsulator if it forwards the packet. (The checksum changes when the TTL changes.)

   Note: The decrementing of the TTL is one of the usual actions that takes place when forwarding a packet. Packets originating from the same node as the encapsulator do not have their TTL's decremented, as the sending node is originating the packet rather than forwarding it.

3. src and dest addresses depend on the SA, which is used to determine the dest address which in turn determines which src address (net interface) is used to forward the packet.

   NOTE: In principle, the encapsulating IP source address can be any of the encapsulator's interface addresses or even an address different from any of the encapsulator's IP addresses, (e.g., if it's acting as a NAT box) so long as the address is reachable through the encapsulator from the environment into which the packet is sent. This does not cause a problem because IPsec does not currently have any INBOUND processing requirement that involves the Source Address of the encapsulating IP header. So while the receiving tunnel endpoint looks at the Destination Address in the encapsulating IP header, it only looks at the Source Address in the inner (encapsulated) IP header.

4. configuration determines whether to copy from the inner header (IPv4 only), clear or set the DF.

5. If Inner Hdr is IPv4 (Protocol = 4), copy the TOS. If Inner Hdr is IPv6 (Protocol = 41), map the Class to TOS.

5.1.2.2 IPv6 -- Header Construction for Tunnel Mode

   See previous section 5.1.2 for notes 1-5 indicated by (footnote number).

```
                          <-- How Outer Hdr  Relates Inner Hdr --->
                          Outer Hdr at                Inner Hdr at
        IPv6              Encapsulator                Decapsulator
          Header fields:  --------------------        -----------
            version       6 (1)                       no change
            class         copied or configured (6)    no change
            flow id       copied or configured        no change
            len           constructed                 no change
            next header   AH,ESP,routing hdr          no change
            hop limit     constructed (2)             decrement (2)
            src address   constructed (3)             no change
            dest address  constructed (3)             no change
        Extension headers never copied               no change
```

        6. If Inner Hdr is IPv6 (Next Header = 41), copy the Class. If
           Inner Hdr is IPv4 (Next Header = 4), map the TOS to Class.

5.2 Processing Inbound IP Traffic

   Prior to performing AH or ESP processing, any IP fragments are
   reassembled. Each inbound IP datagram to which IPsec processing will
   be applied is identified by the appearance of the AH or ESP values in
   the IP Next Protocol field (or of AH or ESP as an extension header in
   the IPv6 context).

   Note: Appendix C contains sample code for a bitmask check for a 32
   packet window that can be used for implementing anti-replay service.

5.2.1 Selecting and Using an SA or SA Bundle

   Mapping the IP datagram to the appropriate SA is simplified because
   of the presence of the SPI in the AH or ESP header. Note that the
   selector checks are made on the inner headers not the outer (tunnel)
   headers. The steps followed are:

        1. Use the packet's destination address (outer IP header),
           IPsec protocol, and SPI to look up the SA in the SAD. If
           the SA lookup fails, drop the packet and log/report the
           error.

        2. Use the SA found in (1) to do the IPsec processing, e.g.,
           authenticate and decrypt. This step includes matching the
           packet's (Inner Header if tunneled) selectors to the
           selectors in the SA. Local policy determines the
           specificity of the SA selectors (single value, list,
           range, wildcard). In general, a packet's source address
           MUST match the SA selector value. However, an ICMP packet
           received on a tunnel mode SA may have a source address

other than that bound to the SA and thus such packets
should be permitted as exceptions to this check. For an
ICMP packet, the selectors from the enclosed problem
packet (the source and destination addresses and ports
should be swapped) should be checked against the selectors
for the SA. Note that some or all of these selectors may
be inaccessible because of limitations on how many bits of
the problem packet the ICMP packet is allowed to carry or
due to encryption. See Section 6.

Do (1) and (2) for every IPsec header until a Transport
Protocol Header or an IP header that is NOT for this
system is encountered. Keep track of what SAs have been
used and their order of application.

3. Find an incoming policy in the SPD that matches the
   packet. This could be done, for example, by use of
   backpointers from the SAs to the SPD or by matching the
   packet's selectors (Inner Header if tunneled) against
   those of the policy entries in the SPD.

4. Check whether the required IPsec processing has been
   applied, i.e., verify that the SA's found in (1) and (2)
   match the kind and order of SAs required by the policy
   found in (3).

   NOTE: The correct "matching" policy will not necessarily
   be the first inbound policy found. If the check in (4)
   fails, steps (3) and (4) are repeated until all policy
   entries have been checked or until the check succeeds.

At the end of these steps, pass the resulting packet to the Transport
Layer or forward the packet. Note that any IPsec headers processed
in these steps may have been removed, but that this information,
i.e., what SAs were used and the order of their application, may be
needed for subsequent IPsec or firewall processing.

Note that in the case of a security gateway, if forwarding causes a
packet to exit via an IPsec-enabled interface, then additional IPsec
processing may be applied.

5.2.2 Handling of AH and ESP tunnels

The handling of the inner and outer IP headers, extension headers,
and options for AH and ESP tunnels should be performed as described
in the tables in Section 5.1.

6. ICMP Processing (relevant to IPsec)

   The focus of this section is on the handling of ICMP error messages.
   Other ICMP traffic, e.g., Echo/Reply, should be treated like other
   traffic and can be protected on an end-to-end basis using SAs in the
   usual fashion.

   An ICMP error message protected by AH or ESP and generated by a
   router SHOULD be processed and forwarded in a tunnel mode SA. Local
   policy determines whether or not it is subjected to source address
   checks by the router at the destination end of the tunnel. Note that
   if the router at the originating end of the tunnel is forwarding an
   ICMP error message from another router, the source address check
   would fail. An ICMP message protected by AH or ESP and generated by
   a router MUST NOT be forwarded on a transport mode SA (unless the SA
   has been established to the router acting as a host, e.g., a Telnet
   connection used to manage a router). An ICMP message generated by a
   host SHOULD be checked against the source IP address selectors bound
   to the SA in which the message arrives. Note that even if the source
   of an ICMP error message is authenticated, the returned IP header
   could be invalid. Accordingly, the selector values in the IP header
   SHOULD also be checked to be sure that they are consistent with the
   selectors for the SA over which the ICMP message was received.

   The table in Appendix D characterize ICMP messages as being either
   host generated, router generated, both, unknown/unassigned. ICMP
   messages falling into the last two categories should be handled as
   determined by the receiver's policy.

   An ICMP message not protected by AH or ESP is unauthenticated and its
   processing and/or forwarding may result in denial of service. This
   suggests that, in general, it would be desirable to ignore such
   messages. However, it is expected that many routers (vs. security
   gateways) will not implement IPsec for transit traffic and thus
   strict adherence to this rule would cause many ICMP messages to be
   discarded. The result is that some critical IP functions would be
   lost, e.g., redirection and PMTU processing. Thus it MUST be
   possible to configure an IPsec implementation to accept or reject
   (router) ICMP traffic as per local security policy.

   The remainder of this section addresses how PMTU processing MUST be
   performed at hosts and security gateways. It addresses processing of
   both authenticated and unauthenticated ICMP PMTU messages. However,
   as noted above, unauthenticated ICMP messages MAY be discarded based
   on local policy.

6.1 PMTU/DF Processing

6.1.1 DF Bit

   In cases where a system (host or gateway) adds an encapsulating
   header (ESP tunnel or AH tunnel), it MUST support the option of
   copying the DF bit from the original packet to the encapsulating
   header (and processing ICMP PMTU messages). This means that it MUST
   be possible to configure the system's treatment of the DF bit (set,
   clear, copy from encapsulated header) for each interface. (See
   Appendix B for rationale.)

6.1.2 Path MTU Discovery (PMTU)

   This section discusses IPsec handling for Path MTU Discovery
   messages. ICMP PMTU is used here to refer to an ICMP message for:

           IPv4 (RFC 792):
                   - Type = 3 (Destination Unreachable)
                   - Code = 4 (Fragmentation needed and DF set)
                   - Next-Hop MTU in the low-order 16 bits of the second
                     word of the ICMP header (labelled "unused" in RFC
                     792), with high-order 16 bits set to zero

           IPv6 (RFC 1885):
                   - Type = 2 (Packet Too Big)
                   - Code = 0 (Fragmentation needed)
                   - Next-Hop MTU in the 32 bit MTU field of the ICMP6
                     message

6.1.2.1 Propagation of PMTU

   The amount of information returned with the ICMP PMTU message (IPv4
   or IPv6) is limited and this affects what selectors are available for
   use in further propagating the PMTU information. (See Appendix B for
   more detailed discussion of this topic.)

   o PMTU message with 64 bits of IPsec header -- If the ICMP PMTU
     message contains only 64 bits of the IPsec header (minimum for
     IPv4), then a security gateway MUST support the following options
     on a per SPI/SA basis:

         a. if the originating host can be determined (or the possible
            sources narrowed down to a manageable number), send the PM
            information to all the possible originating hosts.
         b. if the originating host cannot be determined, store the PMTU
            with the SA and wait until the next packet(s) arrive from the
            originating host for the relevant security association. If

the packet(s) are bigger than the PMTU, drop the packet(s),
and compose ICMP PMTU message(s) with the new packet(s) and
the updated PMTU, and send the ICMP message(s) about the
problem to the originating host. Retain the PMTU information
for any message that might arrive subsequently (see Section
6.1.2.4, "PMTU Aging").

o PMTU message with >64 bits of IPsec header -- If the ICMP message
   contains more information from the original packet then there may
   be enough non-opaque information to immediately determine to which
   host to propagate the ICMP/PMTU message and to provide that system
   with the 5 fields (source address, destination address, source
   port, destination port, transport protocol) needed to determine
   where to store/update the PMTU. Under such circumstances, a
   security gateway MUST generate an ICMP PMTU message immediately
   upon receipt of an ICMP PMTU from further down the path.

o Distributing the PMTU to the Transport Layer -- The host mechanism
   for getting the updated PMTU to the transport layer is unchanged,
   as specified in RFC 1191 (Path MTU Discovery).

6.1.2.2 Calculation of PMTU

The calculation of PMTU from an ICMP PMTU MUST take into account the
addition of any IPsec header -- AH transport, ESP transport, AH/ESP
transport, ESP tunnel, AH tunnel. (See Appendix B for discussion of
implementation issues.)

Note: In some situations the addition of IPsec headers could result
in an effective PMTU (as seen by the host or application) that is
unacceptably small. To avoid this problem, the implementation may
establish a threshold below which it will not report a reduced PMTU.
In such cases, the implementation would apply IPsec and then fragment
the resulting packet according to the PMTU. This would result in a
more efficient use of the available bandwidth.

6.1.2.3 Granularity of PMTU Processing

In hosts, the granularity with which ICMP PMTU processing can be done
differs depending on the implementation situation. Looking at a
host, there are 3 situations that are of interest with respect to
PMTU issues (See Appendix B for additional details on this topic.):

    a. Integration of IPsec into the native IP implementation
    b. Bump-in-the-stack implementations, where IPsec is implemented
       "underneath" an existing implementation of a TCP/IP protocol
       stack, between the native IP and the local network drivers

       c. No IPsec implementation -- This case is included because it
         is relevant in cases where a security gateway is sending PMTU
         information back to a host.

Only in case (a) can the PMTU data be maintained at the same
granularity as communication associations. In (b) and (c), the IP
layer will only be able to maintain PMTU data at the granularity of
source and destination IP addresses (and optionally TOS), as
described in RFC 1191. This is an important difference, because more
than one communication association may map to the same source and
destination IP addresses, and each communication association may have
a different amount of IPsec header overhead (e.g., due to use of
different transforms or different algorithms).

Implementation of the calculation of PMTU and support for PMTUs at
the granularity of individual communication associations is a local
matter. However, a socket-based implementation of IPsec in a host
SHOULD maintain the information on a per socket basis. Bump in the
stack systems MUST pass an ICMP PMTU to the host IP implementation,
after adjusting it for any IPsec header overhead added by these
systems. The calculation of the overhead SHOULD be determined by
analysis of the SPI and any other selector information present in a
returned ICMP PMTU message.

6.1.2.4 PMTU Aging

In all systems (host or gateway) implementing IPsec and maintaining
PMTU information, the PMTU associated with a security association
(transport or tunnel) MUST be "aged" and some mechanism put in place
for updating the PMTU in a timely manner, especially for discovering
if the PMTU is smaller than it needs to be. A given PMTU has to
remain in place long enough for a packet to get from the source end
of the security association to the system at the other end of the
security association and propagate back an ICMP error message if the
current PMTU is too big. Note that if there are nested tunnels,
multiple packets and round trip times might be required to get an
ICMP message back to an encapsulator or originating host.

Systems SHOULD use the approach described in the Path MTU Discovery
document (RFC 1191, Section 6.3), which suggests periodically
resetting the PMTU to the first-hop data-link MTU and then letting
the normal PMTU Discovery processes update the PMTU as necessary.
The period SHOULD be configurable.

Kent & Atkinson   Standards Track   [Page 38]

RFC 2401   Security Architecture for IP   November 1998

7. Auditing

   Not all systems that implement IPsec will implement auditing. For
   the most part, the granularity of auditing is a local matter.
   However, several auditable events are identified in the AH and ESP
   specifications and for each of these events a minimum set of
   information that SHOULD be included in an audit log is defined.
   Additional information also MAY be included in the audit log for each
   of these events, and additional events, not explicitly called out in
   this specification, also MAY result in audit log entries. There is
   no requirement for the receiver to transmit any message to the
   purported transmitter in response to the detection of an auditable
   event, because of the potential to induce denial of service via such
   action.

8. Use in Systems Supporting Information Flow Security

   Information of various sensitivity levels may be carried over a
   single network. Information labels (e.g., Unclassified, Company
   Proprietary, Secret) [DoD85, DoD87] are often employed to distinguish
   such information. The use of labels facilitates segregation of
   information, in support of information flow security models, e.g.,
   the Bell-LaPadula model [BL73]. Such models, and corresponding
   supporting technology, are designed to prevent the unauthorized flow
   of sensitive information, even in the face of Trojan Horse attacks.
   Conventional, discretionary access control (DAC) mechanisms, e.g.,
   based on access control lists, generally are not sufficient to
   support such policies, and thus facilities such as the SPD do not
   suffice in such environments.

   In the military context, technology that supports such models is
   often referred to as multi-level security (MLS). Computers and
   networks often are designated "multi-level secure" if they support
   the separation of labelled data in conjunction with information flow
   security policies. Although such technology is more broadly
   applicable than just military applications, this document uses the
   acronym "MLS" to designate the technology, consistent with much
   extant literature.

   IPsec mechanisms can easily support MLS networking. MLS networking
   requires the use of strong Mandatory Access Controls (MAC), which
   unprivileged users or unprivileged processes are incapable of
   controlling or violating. This section pertains only to the use of
   these IP security mechanisms in MLS (information flow security
   policy) environments. Nothing in this section applies to systems not
   claiming to provide MLS.

Kent & Atkinson   Standards Track   [Page 39]

RFC 2401   Security Architecture for IP   November 1998

As used in this section, "sensitivity information" might include
implementation-defined hierarchic levels, categories, and/or
releasability information.

AH can be used to provide strong authentication in support of
mandatory access control decisions in MLS environments. If explicit
IP sensitivity information (e.g., IPSO [Ken91]) is used and
confidentiality is not considered necessary within the particular
operational environment, AH can be used to authenticate the binding
between sensitivity labels in the IP header and the IP payload
(including user data). This is a significant improvement over
labeled IPv4 networks where the sensitivity information is trusted
even though there is no authentication or cryptographic binding of
the information to the IP header and user data. IPv4 networks might
or might not use explicit labelling. IPv6 will normally use implicit
sensitivity information that is part of the IPsec Security
Association but not transmitted with each packet instead of using
explicit sensitivity information. All explicit IP sensitivity
information MUST be authenticated using either ESP, AH, or both.

Encryption is useful and can be desirable even when all of the hosts
are within a protected environment, for example, behind a firewall or
disjoint from any external connectivity. ESP can be used, in
conjunction with appropriate key management and encryption
algorithms, in support of both DAC and MAC. (The choice of
encryption and authentication algorithms, and the assurance level of
an IPsec implementation will determine the environments in which an
implementation may be deemed sufficient to satisfy MLS requirements.)
Key management can make use of sensitivity information to provide
MAC. IPsec implementations on systems claiming to provide MLS SHOULD
be capable of using IPsec to provide MAC for IP-based communications.

8.1 Relationship Between Security Associations and Data Sensitivity

Both the Encapsulating Security Payload and the Authentication Header
can be combined with appropriate Security Association policies to
provide multi-level secure networking. In this case each SA (or SA
bundle) is normally used for only a single instance of sensitivity
information. For example, "PROPRIETARY - Internet Engineering" must
be associated with a different SA (or SA bundle) from "PROPRIETARY -
Finance".

8.2 Sensitivity Consistency Checking

An MLS implementation (both host and router) MAY associate
sensitivity information, or a range of sensitivity information with
an interface, or a configured IP address with its associated prefix
(the latter is sometimes referred to as a logical interface, or an

interface alias). If such properties exist, an implementation SHOULD
compare the sensitivity information associated with the packet
against the sensitivity information associated with the interface or
address/prefix from which the packet arrived, or through which the
packet will depart. This check will either verify that the
sensitivities match, or that the packet's sensitivity falls within
the range of the interface or address/prefix.

The checking SHOULD be done on both inbound and outbound processing.

8.3 Additional MLS Attributes for Security Association Databases

Section 4.4 discussed two Security Association databases (the
Security Policy Database (SPD) and the Security Association Database
(SAD)) and the associated policy selectors and SA attributes. MLS
networking introduces an additional selector/attribute:

        - Sensitivity information.

The Sensitivity information aids in selecting the appropriate
algorithms and key strength, so that the traffic gets a level of
protection appropriate to its importance or sensitivity as described
in section 8.1. The exact syntax of the sensitivity information is
implementation defined.

8.4 Additional Inbound Processing Steps for MLS Networking

After an inbound packet has passed through IPsec processing, an MLS
implementation SHOULD first check the packet's sensitivity (as
defined by the SA (or SA bundle) used for the packet) with the
interface or address/prefix as described in section 8.2 before
delivering the datagram to an upper-layer protocol or forwarding it.

The MLS system MUST retain the binding between the data received in
an IPsec protected packet and the sensitivity information in the SA
or SAs used for processing, so appropriate policy decisions can be
made when delivering the datagram to an application or forwarding
engine. The means for maintaining this binding are implementation
specific.

8.5 Additional Outbound Processing Steps for MLS Networking

An MLS implementation of IPsec MUST perform two additional checks
besides the normal steps detailed in section 5.1.1. When consulting
the SPD or the SAD to find an outbound security association, the MLS
implementation MUST use the sensitivity of the data to select an

appropriate outbound SA or SA bundle. The second check comes before
forwarding the packet out to its destination, and is the sensitivity
consistency checking described in section 8.2.

8.6 Additional MLS Processing for Security Gateways

An MLS security gateway MUST follow the previously mentioned inbound
and outbound processing rules as well as perform some additional
processing specific to the intermediate protection of packets in an
MLS environment.

A security gateway MAY act as an outbound proxy, creating SAs for MLS
systems that originate packets forwarded by the gateway. These MLS
systems may explicitly label the packets to be forwarded, or the
whole originating network may have sensitivity characteristics
associated with it. The security gateway MUST create and use
appropriate SAs for AH, ESP, or both, to protect such traffic it
forwards.

Similarly such a gateway SHOULD accept and process inbound AH and/or
ESP packets and forward appropriately, using explicit packet
labeling, or relying on the sensitivity characteristics of the
destination network.

9. Performance Issues

The use of IPsec imposes computational performance costs on the hosts
or security gateways that implement these protocols. These costs are
associated with the memory needed for IPsec code and data structures,
and the computation of integrity check values, encryption and
decryption, and added per-packet handling. The per-packet
computational costs will be manifested by increased latency and,
possibly, reduced throughout. Use of SA/key management protocols,
especially ones that employ public key cryptography, also adds
computational performance costs to use of IPsec. These per-
association computational costs will be manifested in terms of
increased latency in association establishment. For many hosts, it
is anticipated that software-based cryptography will not appreciably
reduce throughput, but hardware may be required for security gateways
(since they represent aggregation points), and for some hosts.

The use of IPsec also imposes bandwidth utilization costs on
transmission, switching, and routing components of the Internet
infrastructure, components not implementing IPsec. This is due to
the increase in the packet size resulting from the addition of AH
and/or ESP headers, AH and ESP tunneling (which adds a second IP
header), and the increased packet traffic associated with key
management protocols. It is anticipated that, in most instances,

this increased bandwidth demand will not noticeably affect the
Internet infrastructure. However, in some instances, the effects may
be significant, e.g., transmission of ESP encrypted traffic over a
dialup link that otherwise would have compressed the traffic.

Note: The initial SA establishment overhead will be felt in the first
packet. This delay could impact the transport layer and application.
For example, it could cause TCP to retransmit the SYN before the
ISAKMP exchange is done. The effect of the delay would be different
on UDP than TCP because TCP shouldn't transmit anything other than
the SYN until the connection is set up whereas UDP will go ahead and
transmit data beyond the first packet.

Note: As discussed earlier, compression can still be employed at
layers above IP. There is an IETF working group (IP Payload
Compression Protocol (ippcp)) working on "protocol specifications
that make it possible to perform lossless compression on individual
payloads before the payload is processed by a protocol that encrypts
it. These specifications will allow for compression operations to be
performed prior to the encryption of a payload by IPsec protocols."

10. Conformance Requirements

All IPv4 systems that claim to implement IPsec MUST comply with all
requirements of the Security Architecture document. All IPv6 systems
MUST comply with all requirements of the Security Architecture
document.

11. Security Considerations

The focus of this document is security; hence security considerations
permeate this specification.

12. Differences from RFC 1825

This architecture document differs substantially from RFC 1825 in
detail and in organization, but the fundamental notions are
unchanged. This document provides considerable additional detail in
terms of compliance specifications. It introduces the SPD and SAD,
and the notion of SA selectors. It is aligned with the new versions
of AH and ESP, which also differ from their predecessors. Specific
requirements for supported combinations of AH and ESP are newly
added, as are details of PMTU management.

Kent & Atkinson   Standards Track   [Page 43]

RFC 2401   Security Architecture for IP   November 1998

Acknowledgements

   Many of the concepts embodied in this specification were derived from
   or influenced by the US Government's SP3 security protocol, ISO/IEC's
   NLSP, the proposed swIPe security protocol [SDNS, ISO, IB93, IBK93],
   and the work done for SNMP Security and SNMPv2 Security.

   For over 3 years (although it sometimes seems *much* longer), this
   document has evolved through multiple versions and iterations.
   During this time, many people have contributed significant ideas and
   energy to the process and the documents themselves. The authors
   would like to thank Karen Seo for providing extensive help in the
   review, editing, background research, and coordination for this
   version of the specification. The authors would also like to thank
   the members of the IPsec and IPng working groups, with special
   mention of the efforts of (in alphabetic order): Steve Bellovin,
   Steve Deering, James Hughes, Phil Karn, Frank Kastenholz, Perry
   Metzger, David Mihelcic, Hilarie Orman, Norman Shulman, William
   Simpson, Harry Varnis, and Nina Yuan.

Kent & Atkinson   Standards Track   [Page 44]

RFC 2401   Security Architecture for IP   November 1998

Appendix A -- Glossary

This section provides definitions for several key terms that are
employed in this document. Other documents provide additional
definitions and background information relevant to this technology,
e.g., [VK83, HA94]. Included in this glossary are generic security
service and security mechanism terms, plus IPsec-specific terms.

  Access Control
      Access control is a security service that prevents unauthorized
      use of a resource, including the prevention of use of a resource
      in an unauthorized manner. In the IPsec context, the resource
      to which access is being controlled is often:
              o for a host, computing cycles or data
              o for a security gateway, a network behind the gateway
      or
              bandwidth on that network.

  Anti-replay
      [See "Integrity" below]

  Authentication
      This term is used informally to refer to the combination of two
      nominally distinct security services, data origin authentication
      and connectionless integrity. See the definitions below for
      each of these services.

  Availability
      Availability, when viewed as a security service, addresses the
      security concerns engendered by attacks against networks that
      deny or degrade service. For example, in the IPsec context, the
      use of anti-replay mechanisms in AH and ESP support
      availability.

  Confidentiality
      Confidentiality is the security service that protects data from
      unauthorized disclosure. The primary confidentiality concern in
      most instances is unauthorized disclosure of application level
      data, but disclosure of the external characteristics of
      communication also can be a concern in some circumstances.
      Traffic flow confidentiality is the service that addresses this
      latter concern by concealing source and destination addresses,
      message length, or frequency of communication. In the IPsec
      context, using ESP in tunnel mode, especially at a security
      gateway, can provide some level of traffic flow confidentiality.
      (See also traffic analysis, below.)

Encryption
    Encryption is a security mechanism used to transform data from
    an intelligible form (plaintext) into an unintelligible form
    (ciphertext), to provide confidentiality. The inverse
    transformation process is designated "decryption". Oftimes the
    term "encryption" is used to generically refer to both
    processes.

Data Origin Authentication
    Data origin authentication is a security service that verifies
    the identity of the claimed source of data. This service is
    usually bundled with connectionless integrity service.

Integrity
    Integrity is a security service that ensures that modifications
    to data are detectable. Integrity comes in various flavors to
    match application requirements. IPsec supports two forms of
    integrity: connectionless and a form of partial sequence
    integrity. Connectionless integrity is a service that detects
    modification of an individual IP datagram, without regard to the
    ordering of the datagram in a stream of traffic. The form of
    partial sequence integrity offered in IPsec is referred to as
    anti-replay integrity, and it detects arrival of duplicate IP
    datagrams (within a constrained window). This is in contrast to
    connection-oriented integrity, which imposes more stringent
    sequencing requirements on traffic, e.g., to be able to detect
    lost or re-ordered messages. Although authentication and
    integrity services often are cited separately, in practice they
    are intimately connected and almost always offered in tandem.

Security Association (SA)
    A simplex (uni-directional) logical connection, created for
    security purposes. All traffic traversing an SA is provided the
    same security processing. In IPsec, an SA is an internet layer
    abstraction implemented through the use of AH or ESP.

Security Gateway
    A security gateway is an intermediate system that acts as the
    communications interface between two networks. The set of hosts
    (and networks) on the external side of the security gateway is
    viewed as untrusted (or less trusted), while the networks and
    hosts and on the internal side are viewed as trusted (or more
    trusted). The internal subnets and hosts served by a security
    gateway are presumed to be trusted by virtue of sharing a
    common, local, security administration. (See "Trusted
    Subnetwork" below.) In the IPsec context, a security gateway is
    a point at which AH and/or ESP is implemented in order to serve

a set of internal hosts, providing security services for these
hosts when they communicate with external hosts also employing
IPsec (either directly or via another security gateway).

SPI

Acronym for "Security Parameters Index". The combination of a
destination address, a security protocol, and an SPI uniquely
identifies a security association (SA, see above). The SPI is
carried in AH and ESP protocols to enable the receiving system
to select the SA under which a received packet will be
processed. An SPI has only local significance, as defined by
the creator of the SA (usually the receiver of the packet
carrying the SPI); thus an SPI is generally viewed as an opaque
bit string. However, the creator of an SA may choose to
interpret the bits in an SPI to facilitate local processing.

Traffic Analysis

The analysis of network traffic flow for the purpose of deducing
information that is useful to an adversary. Examples of such
information are frequency of transmission, the identities of the
conversing parties, sizes of packets, flow identifiers, etc.
[Sch94]

Trusted Subnetwork

A subnetwork containing hosts and routers that trust each other
not to engage in active or passive attacks. There also is an
assumption that the underlying communications channel (e.g., a
LAN or CAN) isn't being attacked by other means.

Appendix B -- Analysis/Discussion of PMTU/DF/Fragmentation Issues

B.1 DF bit

    In cases where a system (host or gateway) adds an encapsulating
    header (e.g., ESP tunnel), should/must the DF bit in the original
    packet be copied to the encapsulating header?

    Fragmenting seems correct for some situations, e.g., it might be
    appropriate to fragment packets over a network with a very small MTU,
    e.g., a packet radio network, or a cellular phone hop to mobile node,
    rather than propagate back a very small PMTU for use over the rest of
    the path. In other situations, it might be appropriate to set the DF
    bit in order to get feedback from later routers about PMTU
    constraints which require fragmentation. The existence of both of
    these situations argues for enabling a system to decide whether or
    not to fragment over a particular network "link", i.e., for requiring
    an implementation to be able to copy the DF bit (and to process ICMP
    PMTU messages), but making it an option to be selected on a per
    interface basis. In other words, an administrator should be able to
    configure the router's treatment of the DF bit (set, clear, copy from
    encapsulated header) for each interface.

    Note: If a bump-in-the-stack implementation of IPsec attempts to
    apply different IPsec algorithms based on source/destination ports,
    it will be difficult to apply Path MTU adjustments.

B.2 Fragmentation

    If required, IP fragmentation occurs after IPsec processing within an
    IPsec implementation. Thus, transport mode AH or ESP is applied only
    to whole IP datagrams (not to IP fragments). An IP packet to which
    AH or ESP has been applied may itself be fragmented by routers en
    route, and such fragments MUST be reassembled prior to IPsec
    processing at a receiver. In tunnel mode, AH or ESP is applied to an
    IP packet, the payload of which may be a fragmented IP packet. For
    example, a security gateway, "bump-in-the-stack" (BITS), or "bump-
    in-the-wire" (BITW) IPsec implementation may apply tunnel mode AH to
    such fragments. Note that BITS or BITW implementations are examples
    of where a host IPsec implementation might receive fragments to which
    tunnel mode is to be applied. However, if transport mode is to be
    applied, then these implementations MUST reassemble the fragments
    prior to applying IPsec.

NOTE: IPsec always has to figure out what the encapsulating IP header
fields are. This is independent of where you insert IPsec and is
intrinsic to the definition of IPsec. Therefore any IPsec
implementation that is not integrated into an IP implementation must
include code to construct the necessary IP headers (e.g., IP2):

```
    o AH-tunnel --> IP2-AH-IP1-Transport-Data
    o ESP-tunnel -->  IP2-ESP_hdr-IP1-Transport-Data-ESP_trailer
```

****

Overall, the fragmentation/reassembly approach described above works
for all cases examined.

Implementation approach	AH Xport IPv4	AH Xport IPv6	AH Tunnel IPv4	AH Tunnel IPv6	ESP Xport IPv4	ESP Xport IPv6	ESP Tunnel IPv4	ESP Tunnel IPv6
Hosts (integr w/ IP stack)	Y	Y	Y	Y	Y	Y	Y	Y
Hosts (betw/ IP and drivers)	Y	Y	Y	Y	Y	Y	Y	Y
S. Gwy (integr w/ IP stack)			Y	Y			Y	Y
Outboard crypto processor *								

* If the crypto processor system has its own IP address, then it
  is covered by the security gateway case. This box receives
  the packet from the host and performs IPsec processing. It
  has to be able to handle the same AH, ESP, and related
  IPv4/IPv6 tunnel processing that a security gateway would have
  to handle. If it doesn't have it's own address, then it is
  similar to the bump-in-the stack implementation between IP and
  the network drivers.

The following analysis assumes that:

  1. There is only one IPsec module in a given system's stack.
     There isn't an IPsec module A (adding ESP/encryption and
     thus) hiding the transport protocol, SRC port, and DEST port
     from IPsec module B.
  2. There are several places where IPsec could be implemented (as
     shown in the table above).
         a. Hosts with integration of IPsec into the native IP
            implementation. Implementer has access to the source
            for the stack.
         b. Hosts with bump-in-the-stack implementations, where
            IPsec is implemented between IP and the local network
            drivers. Source access for stack is not available;
            but there are well-defined interfaces that allows the
            IPsec code to be incorporated into the system.

> c. Security gateways and outboard crypto processors with
>   integration of IPsec into the stack.
> 3. Not all of the above approaches are feasible in all hosts.
>   But it was assumed that for each approach, there are some
>   hosts for whom the approach is feasible.

For each of the above 3 categories, there are IPv4 and IPv6, AH
transport and tunnel modes, and ESP transport and tunnel modes -- for
a total of 24 cases (3 x 2 x 4).

Some header fields and interface fields are listed here for ease of
reference -- they're not in the header order, but instead listed to
allow comparison between the columns. (* = not covered by AH
authentication. ESP authentication doesn't cover any headers that
precede it.)

```
                                      IP/Transport Interface
         IPv4            IPv6         (RFC 1122 -- Sec 3.4)
         ----            ----         ---------------------
         Version = 4     Version = 6
         Header Len
         *TOS            Class,Flow Lbl  TOS
         Packet Len      Payload Len     Len
         ID                              ID (optional)
         *Flags                          DF
         *Offset
         *TTL            *Hop Limit      TTL
         Protocol        Next Header
         *Checksum
         Src Address     Src Address     Src Address
         Dst Address     Dst Address     Dst Address
         Options?        Options?        Opt
```

> ? = AH covers Option-Type and Option-Length, but
>   might not cover Option-Data.

The results for each of the 20 cases is shown below ("works" = will
work if system fragments after outbound IPsec processing, reassembles
before inbound IPsec processing). Notes indicate implementation
issues.

```
a. Hosts (integrated into IP stack)
     o AH-transport  --> (IP1-AH-Transport-Data)
            - IPv4 -- works
            - IPv6 -- works
     o AH-tunnel --> (IP2-AH-IP1-Transport-Data)
            - IPv4 -- works
            - IPv6 -- works
```

        o ESP-transport --> (IP1-ESP_hdr-Transport-Data-ESP_trailer)
                    - IPv4 -- works
                    - IPv6 -- works
        o ESP-tunnel --> (IP2-ESP_hdr-IP1-Transport-Data-ESP_trailer)
                    - IPv4 -- works
                    - IPv6 -- works

    b. Hosts (Bump-in-the-stack) -- put IPsec between IP layer and
       network drivers. In this case, the IPsec module would have to do
       something like one of the following for fragmentation and
       reassembly.
            - do the fragmentation/reassembly work itself and
              send/receive the packet directly to/from the network
              layer. In AH or ESP transport mode, this is fine. In AH
              or ESP tunnel mode where the tunnel end is at the ultimate
              destination, this is fine. But in AH or ESP tunnel modes
              where the tunnel end is different from the ultimate
              destination and where the source host is multi-homed, this
              approach could result in sub-optimal routing because the
              IPsec module may be unable to obtain the information
              needed (LAN interface and next-hop gateway) to direct the
              packet to the appropriate network interface. This is not
              a problem if the interface and next-hop gateway are the
              same for the ultimate destination and for the tunnel end.
              But if they are different, then IPsec would need to know
              the LAN interface and the next-hop gateway for the tunnel
              end. (Note: The tunnel end (security gateway) is highly
              likely to be on the regular path to the ultimate
              destination. But there could also be more than one path
              to the destination, e.g., the host could be at an
              organization with 2 firewalls. And the path being used
              could involve the less commonly chosen firewall.) OR
            - pass the IPsec'd packet back to the IP layer where an
              extra IP header would end up being pre-pended and the
              IPsec module would have to check and let IPsec'd fragments
              go by.
                               OR
            - pass the packet contents to the IP layer in a form such
              that the IP layer recreates an appropriate IP header

       At the network layer, the IPsec module will have access to the
       following selectors from the packet -- SRC address, DST address,
       Next Protocol, and if there's a transport layer header --> SRC
       port and DST port. One cannot assume IPsec has access to the
       Name. It is assumed that the available selector information is
       sufficient to figure out the relevant Security Policy entry and
       Security Association(s).

```
                o AH-transport  --> (IP1-AH-Transport-Data)
                        - IPv4 -- works
                        - IPv6 -- works
                o AH-tunnel --> (IP2-AH-IP1-Transport-Data)
                        - IPv4 -- works
                        - IPv6 -- works
                o ESP-transport --> (IP1-ESP_hdr-Transport-Data-ESP_trailer)
                        - IPv4 -- works
                        - IPv6 -- works
                o ESP-tunnel -->  (IP2-ESP_hdr-IP1-Transport-Data-ESP_trailer)
                        - IPv4 -- works
                        - IPv6 -- works
```

   c. Security gateways -- integrate IPsec into the IP stack

      NOTE: The IPsec module will have access to the following
      selectors from the packet -- SRC address, DST address, Next
      Protocol, and if there's a transport layer header --> SRC port
      and DST port. It won't have access to the User ID (only Hosts
      have access to User ID information.) Unlike some Bump-in-the-
      stack implementations, security gateways may be able to look up
      the Source Address in the DNS to provide a System Name, e.g., in
      situations involving use of dynamically assigned IP addresses in
      conjunction with dynamically updated DNS entries. It also won't
      have access to the transport layer information if there is an ESP
      header, or if it's not the first fragment of a fragmented
      message. It is assumed that the available selector information
      is sufficient to figure out the relevant Security Policy entry
      and Security Association(s).

```
                o AH-tunnel --> (IP2-AH-IP1-Transport-Data)
                        - IPv4 -- works
                        - IPv6 -- works
                o ESP-tunnel -->  (IP2-ESP_hdr-IP1-Transport-Data-ESP_trailer)
                        - IPv4 -- works
                        - IPv6 -- works
```

   ****

B.3 Path MTU Discovery

   As mentioned earlier, "ICMP PMTU" refers to an ICMP message used for
   Path MTU Discovery.

   The legend for the diagrams below in B.3.1 and B.3.3 (but not B.3.2)
   is:

        ==== = security association (AH or ESP, transport or tunnel)

```
            ---- = connectivity (or if so labelled, administrative boundary)
            .... = ICMP message (hereafter referred to as ICMP PMTU) for

                   IPv4:
                   - Type = 3 (Destination Unreachable)
                   - Code = 4 (Fragmentation needed and DF set)
                   - Next-Hop MTU in the low-order 16 bits of the second
                     word of the ICMP header (labelled unused in RFC 792),
                     with high-order 16 bits set to zero

                   IPv6 (RFC 1885):
                   - Type = 2 (Packet Too Big)
                   - Code = 0 (Fragmentation needed and DF set)
                   - Next-Hop MTU in the 32 bit MTU field of the ICMP6

        Hx   = host x
        Rx   = router x
        SGx  = security gateway x
        X*   = X supports IPsec
```

B.3.1 Identifying the Originating Host(s)

The amount of information returned with the ICMP message is limited and this affects what selectors are available to identify security associations, originating hosts, etc. for use in further propagating the PMTU information.

In brief... An ICMP message must contain the following information from the "offending" packet:
        - IPv4 (RFC 792) -- IP header plus a minimum of 64 bits

Accordingly, in the IPv4 context, an ICMP PMTU may identify only the first (outermost) security association. This is because the ICMP PMTU may contain only 64 bits of the "offending" packet beyond the IP header, which would capture only the first SPI from AH or ESP. In the IPv6 context, an ICMP PMTU will probably provide all the SPIs and the selectors in the IP header, but maybe not the SRC/DST ports (in the transport header) or the encapsulated (TCP, UDP, etc.) protocol. Moreover, if ESP is used, the transport ports and protocol selectors may be encrypted.

Looking at the diagram below of a security gateway tunnel (as mentioned elsewhere, security gateways do not use transport mode)...

```
   H1    ==================           H3
     \  |                   |        /
   H0 -- SG1* ---- R1 ---- SG2* ---- R2 -- H5
     /  ^          |               \
   H2  |........|                   H4
```

Suppose that the security policy for SG1 is to use a single SA to SG2
for all the traffic between hosts H0, H1, and H2 and hosts H3, H4,
and H5. And suppose H0 sends a data packet to H5 which causes R1 to
send an ICMP PMTU message to SG1. If the PMTU message has only the
SPI, SG1 will be able to look up the SA and find the list of possible
hosts (H0, H1, H2, wildcard); but SG1 will have no way to figure out
that H0 sent the traffic that triggered the ICMP PMTU message.

```
original          after IPsec      ICMP
packet            processing       packet
--------          -----------      ------
                                   IP-3 header (S = R1, D = SG1)
                                   ICMP header (includes PMTU)
                  IP-2 header      IP-2 header (S = SG1, D = SG2)
                  ESP header       minimum of 64 bits of ESP hdr (*)
IP-1 header       IP-1 header
TCP header        TCP header
TCP data          TCP data
                  ESP trailer
```

    (*) The 64 bits will include enough of the ESP (or AH) header to
        include the SPI.
              - ESP -- SPI (32 bits), Seq number (32 bits)
              - AH -- Next header (8 bits), Payload Len (8 bits),
                Reserved (16 bits), SPI (32 bits)

This limitation on the amount of information returned with an ICMP
message creates a problem in identifying the originating hosts for
the packet (so as to know where to further propagate the ICMP PMTU
information). If the ICMP message contains only 64 bits of the IPsec
header (minimum for IPv4), then the IPsec selectors (e.g., Source and
Destination addresses, Next Protocol, Source and Destination ports,
etc.) will have been lost. But the ICMP error message will still
provide SG1 with the SPI, the PMTU information and the source and
destination gateways for the relevant security association.

The destination security gateway and SPI uniquely define a security
association which in turn defines a set of possible originating
hosts. At this point, SG1 could:

    a. send the PMTU information to all the possible originating hosts.
       This would not work well if the host list is a wild card or if
       many/most of the hosts weren't sending to SG1; but it might work
       if the SPI/destination/etc mapped to just one or a small number of
       hosts.
    b. store the PMTU with the SPI/etc and wait until the next packet(s)
       arrive from the originating host(s) for the relevant security
       association. If it/they are bigger than the PMTU, drop the
       packet(s), and compose ICMP PMTU message(s) with the new packet(s)
       and the updated PMTU, and send the originating host(s) the ICMP
       message(s) about the problem. This involves a delay in notifying
       the originating host(s), but avoids the problems of (a).

Since only the latter approach is feasible in all instances, a
security gateway MUST provide such support, as an option. However,
if the ICMP message contains more information from the original
packet, then there may be enough information to immediately determine
to which host to propagate the ICMP/PMTU message and to provide that
system with the 5 fields (source address, destination address, source
port, destination port, and transport protocol) needed to determine
where to store/update the PMTU. Under such circumstances, a security
gateway MUST generate an ICMP PMTU message immediately upon receipt
of an ICMP PMTU from further down the path. NOTE: The Next Protocol
field may not be contained in the ICMP message and the use of ESP
encryption may hide the selector fields that have been encrypted.

B.3.2 Calculation of PMTU

    The calculation of PMTU from an ICMP PMTU has to take into account
    the addition of any IPsec header by H1 -- AH and/or ESP transport, or
    ESP or AH tunnel. Within a single host, multiple applications may
    share an SPI and nesting of security associations may occur. (See
    Section 4.5 Basic Combinations of Security Associations for
    description of the combinations that MUST be supported). The diagram
    below illustrates an example of security associations between a pair
    of hosts (as viewed from the perspective of one of the hosts.) (ESPx
    or AHx = transport mode)

          Socket 1 ------------------------|
                                |
          Socket 2 (ESPx/SPI-A) ---------- AHx (SPI-B) -- Internet

In order to figure out the PMTU for each socket that maps to SPI-B,
it will be necessary to have backpointers from SPI-B to each of the 2
paths that lead to it -- Socket 1 and Socket 2/SPI-A.

B.3.3 Granularity of Maintaining PMTU Data

   In hosts, the granularity with which PMTU ICMP processing can be done
   differs depending on the implementation situation. Looking at a
   host, there are three situations that are of interest with respect to
   PMTU issues:

   a. Integration of IPsec into the native IP implementation
   b. Bump-in-the-stack implementations, where IPsec is implemented
      "underneath" an existing implementation of a TCP/IP protocol
      stack, between the native IP and the local network drivers
   c. No IPsec implementation -- This case is included because it is
      relevant in cases where a security gateway is sending PMTU
      information back to a host.

   Only in case (a) can the PMTU data be maintained at the same
   granularity as communication associations. In the other cases, the
   IP layer will maintain PMTU data at the granularity of Source and
   Destination IP addresses (and optionally TOS/Class), as described in
   RFC 1191. This is an important difference, because more than one
   communication association may map to the same source and destination
   IP addresses, and each communication association may have a different
   amount of IPsec header overhead (e.g., due to use of different
   transforms or different algorithms). The examples below illustrate
   this.

   In cases (a) and (b)... Suppose you have the following situation.
   H1 is sending to H2 and the packet to be sent from R1 to R2 exceeds
   the PMTU of the network hop between them.

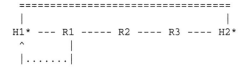

   If R1 is configured to not fragment subscriber traffic, then R1 sends
   an ICMP PMTU message with the appropriate PMTU to H1. H1's
   processing would vary with the nature of the implementation. In case
   (a) (native IP), the security services are bound to sockets or the
   equivalent. Here the IP/IPsec implementation in H1 can store/update
   the PMTU for the associated socket. In case (b), the IP layer in H1
   can store/update the PMTU but only at the granularity of Source and
   Destination addresses and possibly TOS/Class, as noted above. So the
   result may be sub-optimal, since the PMTU for a given
   SRC/DST/TOS/Class will be the subtraction of the largest amount of
   IPsec header used for any communication association between a given
   source and destination.

In case (c), there has to be a security gateway to have any IPsec
processing. So suppose you have the following situation. H1 is
sending to H2 and the packet to be sent from SG1 to R exceeds the
PMTU of the network hop between them.

```
                    =================
                    |               |
        H1 ---- SG1* --- R --- SG2* ---- H2
        ^           |
        |.......|
```

As described above for case (b), the IP layer in H1 can store/update
the PMTU but only at the granularity of Source and Destination
addresses, and possibly TOS/Class. So the result may be sub-optimal,
since the PMTU for a given SRC/DST/TOS/Class will be the subtraction
of the largest amount of IPsec header used for any communication
association between a given source and destination.

B.3.4 Per Socket Maintenance of PMTU Data

    Implementation of the calculation of PMTU (Section B.3.2) and support
    for PMTUs at the granularity of individual "communication
    associations" (Section B.3.3) is a local matter. However, a socket-
    based implementation of IPsec in a host SHOULD maintain the
    information on a per socket basis. Bump in the stack systems MUST
    pass an ICMP PMTU to the host IP implementation, after adjusting it
    for any IPsec header overhead added by these systems. The
    determination of the overhead SHOULD be determined by analysis of the
    SPI and any other selector information present in a returned ICMP
    PMTU message.

B.3.5 Delivery of PMTU Data to the Transport Layer

    The host mechanism for getting the updated PMTU to the transport
    layer is unchanged, as specified in RFC 1191 (Path MTU Discovery).

B.3.6 Aging of PMTU Data

    This topic is covered in Section 6.1.2.4.

Appendix C -- Sequence Space Window Code Example

   This appendix contains a routine that implements a bitmask check for
   a 32 packet window. It was provided by James Hughes
   (jim_hughes@stortek.com) and Harry Varnis (hgv@anubis.network.com)
   and is intended as an implementation example. Note that this code
   both checks for a replay and updates the window. Thus the algorithm,
   as shown, should only be called AFTER the packet has been
   authenticated. Implementers might wish to consider splitting the
   code to do the check for replays before computing the ICV. If the
   packet is not a replay, the code would then compute the ICV, (discard
   any bad packets), and if the packet is OK, update the window.

```
#include <stdio.h>
#include <stdlib.h>
typedef unsigned long u_long;

enum {
    ReplayWindowSize = 32
};

u_long bitmap = 0;                  /* session state - must be 32 bits */
u_long lastSeq = 0;                     /* session state */

/* Returns 0 if packet disallowed, 1 if packet permitted */
int ChkReplayWindow(u_long seq);

int ChkReplayWindow(u_long seq) {
    u_long diff;

    if (seq == 0) return 0;             /* first == 0 or wrapped */
    if (seq > lastSeq) {                /* new larger sequence number */
        diff = seq - lastSeq;
        if (diff < ReplayWindowSize) {  /* In window */
            bitmap <<= diff;
            bitmap |= 1;                /* set bit for this packet */
        } else bitmap = 1;          /* This packet has a "way larger" */
        lastSeq = seq;
        return 1;                       /* larger is good */
    }
    diff = lastSeq - seq;
    if (diff >= ReplayWindowSize) return 0; /* too old or wrapped */
    if (bitmap & ((u_long)1 << diff)) return 0; /* already seen */
    bitmap |= ((u_long)1 << diff);              /* mark as seen */
    return 1;                           /* out of order but good */
}

char string_buffer[512];
```

```
#define STRING_BUFFER_SIZE sizeof(string_buffer)

int main() {
    int result;
    u_long last, current, bits;

    printf("Input initial state (bits in hex, last msgnum):\n");
    if (!fgets(string_buffer, STRING_BUFFER_SIZE, stdin)) exit(0);
    sscanf(string_buffer, "%lx %lu", &bits, &last);
    if (last != 0)
    bits |= 1;
    bitmap = bits;
    lastSeq = last;
    printf("bits:%08lx last:%lu\n", bitmap, lastSeq);
    printf("Input value to test (current):\n");

    while (1) {
        if (!fgets(string_buffer, STRING_BUFFER_SIZE, stdin)) break;
        sscanf(string_buffer, "%lu", &current);
        result = ChkReplayWindow(current);
        printf("%-3s", result ? "OK" : "BAD");
        printf(" bits:%08lx last:%lu\n", bitmap, lastSeq);
    }
    return 0;
}
```

Kent & Atkinson   Standards Track   [Page 59]

RFC 2401   Security Architecture for IP   November 1998

Appendix D -- Categorization of ICMP messages

The tables below characterize ICMP messages as being either host
generated, router generated, both, unassigned/unknown. The first set
are IPv4. The second set are IPv6.

                            IPv4

Type   Name/Codes   Reference
==
HOST GENERATED:
    3   Destination Unreachable
        2   Protocol Unreachable   [RFC792]
        3   Port Unreachable   [RFC792]
        8   Source Host Isolated   [RFC792]
        14 Host Precedence Violation   [RFC1812]
   10   Router Selection   [RFC1256]

Type   Name/Codes   Reference
==
ROUTER GENERATED:
    3   Destination Unreachable
        0   Net Unreachable   [RFC792]
        4   Fragmentation Needed, Don't Fragment was Set   [RFC792]
        5   Source Route Failed   [RFC792]
        6   Destination Network Unknown   [RFC792]
        7   Destination Host Unknown   [RFC792]
        9   Comm. w/Dest. Net. is Administratively Prohibited [RFC792]
        11 Destination Network Unreachable for Type of Service[RFC792]
    5   Redirect
        0   Redirect Datagram for the Network (or subnet)   [RFC792]
        2   Redirect Datagram for the Type of Service & Network[RFC792]
    9   Router Advertisement   [RFC1256]
   18   Address Mask Reply   [RFC950]

Kent & Atkinson   Standards Track   [Page 60]

RFC 2401   Security Architecture for IP   November 1998

```
                              IPv4
Type    Name/Codes                                    Reference
========================================================================
BOTH ROUTER AND HOST GENERATED:
    0   Echo Reply                                    [RFC792]
    3   Destination Unreachable
        1  Host Unreachable                           [RFC792]
        10 Comm. w/Dest. Host is Administratively Prohibited [RFC792]
        12 Destination Host Unreachable for Type of Service  [RFC792]
        13 Communication Administratively Prohibited  [RFC1812]
        15 Precedence cutoff in effect                [RFC1812]
    4   Source Quench                                 [RFC792]
    5   Redirect
        1  Redirect Datagram for the Host             [RFC792]
        3  Redirect Datagram for the Type of Service and Host [RFC792]
    6   Alternate Host Address                        [JBP]
    8   Echo                                          [RFC792]
    11  Time Exceeded                                 [RFC792]
    12  Parameter Problem                    [RFC792,RFC1108]
    13  Timestamp                                     [RFC792]
    14  Timestamp Reply                               [RFC792]
    15  Information Request                           [RFC792]
    16  Information Reply                             [RFC792]
    17  Address Mask Request                          [RFC950]
    30  Traceroute                                    [RFC1393]
    31  Datagram Conversion Error                     [RFC1475]
    32  Mobile Host Redirect                          [Johnson]
    39  SKIP                                          [Markson]
    40  Photuris                                      [Simpson]


Type    Name/Codes                                    Reference
========================================================================
UNASSIGNED TYPE OR UNKNOWN GENERATOR:
    1   Unassigned                                    [JBP]
    2   Unassigned                                    [JBP]
    7   Unassigned                                    [JBP]
    19  Reserved (for Security)                       [Solo]
    20-29 Reserved (for Robustness Experiment)        [ZSu]
    33  IPv6 Where-Are-You                            [Simpson]
    34  IPv6 I-Am-Here                                [Simpson]
    35  Mobile Registration Request                   [Simpson]
    36  Mobile Registration Reply                     [Simpson]
    37  Domain Name Request                           [Simpson]
    38  Domain Name Reply                             [Simpson]
    41-255 Reserved                                   [JBP]
```

Kent & Atkinson   Standards Track   [Page 61]

RFC 2401   Security Architecture for IP   November 1998

                              IPv6

Type   Name/Codes   Reference
==
HOST GENERATED:
  1   Destination Unreachable   [RFC 1885]
        4 Port Unreachable

Type   Name/Codes   Reference
==
ROUTER GENERATED:
  1   Destination Unreachable   [RFC1885]
        0 No Route to Destination
        1 Comm. w/Destination is Administratively Prohibited
        2 Not a Neighbor
        3 Address Unreachable
  2   Packet Too Big   [RFC1885]
        0
  3   Time Exceeded   [RFC1885]
        0 Hop Limit Exceeded in Transit
        1 Fragment reassembly time exceeded

Type   Name/Codes   Reference
==
BOTH ROUTER AND HOST GENERATED:
  4   Parameter Problem   [RFC1885]
        0 Erroneous Header Field Encountered
        1 Unrecognized Next Header Type Encountered
        2 Unrecognized IPv6 Option Encountered

Kent & Atkinson   Standards Track   [Page 62]

RFC 2401   Security Architecture for IP   November 1998

References

   [BL73]   Bell, D.E. & LaPadula, L.J., "Secure Computer Systems:
            Mathematical Foundations and Model", Technical Report M74-
            244, The MITRE Corporation, Bedford, MA, May 1973.

   [Bra97]   Bradner, S., "Key words for use in RFCs to Indicate
            Requirement Level", BCP 14, RFC 2119, March 1997.

   [DoD85]   US National Computer Security Center, "Department of
            Defense Trusted Computer System Evaluation Criteria", DoD
            5200.28-STD, US Department of Defense, Ft. Meade, MD.,
            December 1985.

   [DoD87]   US National Computer Security Center, "Trusted Network
            Interpretation of the Trusted Computer System Evaluation
            Criteria", NCSC-TG-005, Version 1, US Department of
            Defense, Ft. Meade, MD., 31 July 1987.

   [HA94]   Haller, N., and R. Atkinson, "On Internet Authentication",
            RFC 1704, October 1994.

   [HC98]   Harkins, D., and D. Carrel, "The Internet Key Exchange
            (IKE)", RFC 2409, November 1998.

   [HM97]   Harney, H., and C. Muckenhirn, "Group Key Management
            Protocol (GKMP) Architecture", RFC 2094, July 1997.

   [ISO]   ISO/IEC JTC1/SC6, Network Layer Security Protocol, ISO-IEC
            DIS 11577, International Standards Organisation, Geneva,
            Switzerland, 29 November 1992.

   [IB93]   John Ioannidis and Matt Blaze, "Architecture and
            Implementation of Network-layer Security Under Unix",
            Proceedings of USENIX Security Symposium, Santa Clara, CA,
            October 1993.

   [IBK93]   John Ioannidis, Matt Blaze, & Phil Karn, "swIPe: Network-
            Layer Security for IP", presentation at the Spring 1993
            IETF Meeting, Columbus, Ohio

   [KA98a]   Kent, S., and R. Atkinson, "IP Authentication Header", RFC
            2402, November 1998.

   [KA98b]   Kent, S., and R. Atkinson, "IP Encapsulating Security
            Payload (ESP)", RFC 2406, November 1998.

Kent & Atkinson   Standards Track   [Page 63]

RFC 2401   Security Architecture for IP   November 1998

[Ken91]   Kent, S., "US DoD Security Options for the Internet
           Protocol", RFC 1108, November 1991.

[MSST97]   Maughan, D., Schertler, M., Schneider, M., and J. Turner,
           "Internet Security Association and Key Management Protocol
           (ISAKMP)", RFC 2408, November 1998.

[Orm97]   Orman, H., "The OAKLEY Key Determination Protocol", RFC
           2412, November 1998.

[Pip98]   Piper, D., "The Internet IP Security Domain of
           Interpretation for ISAKMP", RFC 2407, November 1998.

[Sch94]   Bruce Schneier, Applied Cryptography, Section 8.6, John
           Wiley & Sons, New York, NY, 1994.

[SDNS]   SDNS Secure Data Network System, Security Protocol 3, SP3,
           Document SDN.301, Revision 1.5, 15 May 1989, published in
           NIST Publication NIST-IR-90-4250, February 1990.

[SMPT98]   Shacham, A., Monsour, R., Pereira, R., and M. Thomas, "IP
           Payload Compression Protocol (IPComp)", RFC 2393, August
           1998.

[TDG97]   Thayer, R., Doraswamy, N., and R. Glenn, "IP Security
           Document Roadmap", RFC 2411, November 1998.

[VK83]   V.L. Voydock & S.T. Kent, "Security Mechanisms in High-
           level Networks", ACM Computing Surveys, Vol. 15, No. 2,
           June 1983.

Disclaimer

   The views and specification expressed in this document are those of
   the authors and are not necessarily those of their employers. The
   authors and their employers specifically disclaim responsibility for
   any problems arising from correct or incorrect implementation or use
   of this design.

Kent & Atkinson   Standards Track   [Page 64]

RFC 2401   Security Architecture for IP   November 1998

Author Information

    Stephen Kent
    BBN Corporation
    70 Fawcett Street
    Cambridge, MA 02140
    USA

    Phone: +1 (617) 873-3988
    EMail: kent@bbn.com

    Randall Atkinson
    @Home Network
    425 Broadway
    Redwood City, CA 94063
    USA

    Phone: +1 (415) 569-5000
    EMail: rja@corp.home.net

Kent & Atkinson   Standards Track   [Page 65]

RFC 2401   Security Architecture for IP   November 1998

Glossary

access control. A security service that prevents unauthorized use of a resource. In the IPsec context, the resource to which access is being controlled is often

- for a host, computing cycles or data.
- for a security gateway, a network behind the gateway or bandwidth on that network. (Kent 1998)

AH. *Authentication Header.* One of the two protocols (the other being ESP) supported as part of the IPsec mechanisms to enhance IP payload security. AH provides both data origin authentication and packet integrity.

ARP. *Address Resolution Protocol.* The discovery protocol used by host computer systems to establish the correct mapping of Internet layer addresses, also known as IP addresses, to Media Access Control (MAC) layer addresses. (Huston 1999)

authentication. A term used informally to refer to the combination of two nominally distinct security services, data origin authentication and connectionless integrity. See *data origin authentication* and *connectionless integrity*. (Kent 1998)

CA. *Certification Authority.* An entity in a PKI that vouches for (and may digitally sign) the validity of the relationship between a person or server and a public key.

CALEA. *Communications Assistance for Law Enforcement Act.* Often referred to as the digital telephony law, legislation designed to help preserve the wiretapping capabilities of law enforcement in the face of new technological developments.

CBC. *cipher block chaining.* A mechanism used in coordination with symmetric key bulk encryption algorithms (such as DES) to encrypt arbitrarily long strings of data. CBC works by using the results of previous DES operations over portions of the same message as part of the data used to encrypt future portions. This way the result of the encryption of any part of the message is dependent upon the parts that preceded it. This makes analysis of ciphertext for repeated encrypted strings much harder.

confidentiality. The security service that protects data from unauthorized disclosure. The primary confidentiality concern in most instances is unauthorized disclosure of application-level data, but disclosure of the external characteristics of communication can also be a concern in some circumstances. Traffic-flow confidentiality addresses this latter concern by concealing source and destination addresses, message length, or frequency of communication. In the IPsec context, using ESP in tunnel mode, especially at a security gateway, can provide some level of traffic-flow confidentiality. (Kent 1998)

CoS. *class of service.* A categorical method of dividing traffic into separate classes to provide differentiated service to each class within the network. (Huston 1999)

cryptography. The discipline of designing and implementing protocols and procedures that enhance the overall security of document storage, retrieval, and transmission. Cryptographic techniques are typically used to add confidentiality, integrity, and/or source attribution to messages or documents. Cryptography as a discipline significantly predates the advent of modern digital computers.

DARPA. *Defense Advanced Research Projects Agency.* The agency originally responsible for the government-sponsored program to design TCP/IP and establish it as a standard interoperable best-effort packet datagram protocol suite.

data origin authentication. A security service that verifies the identity of the claimed source of data. This service is usually bundled with connectionless integrity service. (Kent 1998)

DES. *Data Encryption Standard.* One of the oldest symmetric key bulk encryption mechanisms in current use. DES uses a 56-bit key, which is regarded by many as too short to adequately protect critical data. Today many people use triple DES (3DES) to add security to the DES algorithm by performing the operation three times with different subkeys.

DHCP. *Dynamic Host Configuration Protocol.* A protocol typically used by end-host computers to automatically obtain network configuration parameters necessary for communications. These parameters include (but are not limited to) IP address, subnet mask, broadcast address, routing information (default route), and domain name server list.

digital signature. A digital mark associated with a message or document that validates the integrity of the contents. A valid digital signature can be produced only by the subject's private key, and so by attaching a digital signature to a document, you attest to its contents.

DNS. *Domain Name Service.* The protocol used to support the hierarchical resolution of host names to IP addresses (and vice versa) in the Internet. Each organization declares a set of hosts that are responsible for resolving entries within a certain hierarchical tree (such as wiley.com) and ensures that these hosts are registered and available to querying hosts on the Internet. DNS also supports a small number of related host resolution services, such as identifying mail exchange hosts on the Internet.

DOI. *Domain of Interpretation.* A standards document describing the formal semantics of certain otherwise context-dependent components of an IKE exchange. The Internet DOI also enumerates the possible components of various pieces of information distributed during key exchange.

ECB. *electronic code book.* A simple symmetric key bulk encryption algorithm operation on a block of data. The selected encryption operation is applied over a unit of data exactly equal to the algorithm's block size. (See also *CBC.*)

encryption. A security mechanism used to transform data from an intelligible form (plaintext) into an unintelligible form (ciphertext), to provide confidentiality. The inverse transformation process is designated *decryption*. Often the term "encryption" is used generically to refer to both processes. (Kent 1998)

ESP. *Encapsulating Security Payload.* One of the two protocols (the other being AH) supported as part of the IPsec mechanisms to enhance IP payload security. ESP provides much of the functionality of AH (see AH), as well as enhanced privacy, by way of datagram payload encryption.

Ethernet. A local area network protocol specification originally developed by Xerox, Digital Equipment Corporation, and Intel. This protocol is characterized by the use of CSMA/CD (Carrier Sense Multiple Access/Collision Detection), whereby multiple host stations can share a common communications conduit and, through collision detection, negotiate communications.

firewall. A term traditionally applied to one or more specialized routers used in optional coordination with hosts supporting proxy applications. A firewall's purpose is implementing part or all of a security policy by examining the layer 3 and layer 4 protocol headers to provide selective access to some or all of a network. Typically access is controlled by source and/or destination IP address, layer 4 protocol (TCP or UDP), application (layer 4 port number), and direction of stream establishment (in the case of TCP).

HDLC. *High-level Data Link Control.* A legacy layer 2 framing protocol that has served as the basic form for many modern layer 2 protocols over synchronous and asynchronous point-to-point communications conduits.

HTTP. *Hypertext Transfer Protocol.* A connection-oriented session protocol used by hosts participating in the World Wide Web (WWW).

ICMP. *Internet Control Message Protocol.* The network-layer protocol used to provide informational and error conditions to hosts and routers participating in an IP-based network.

ICV. *integrity check value.* Typically, a hash value calculated over data and utilizing some private or secret key material. Successful recreation upon receipt of the ICV validates the integrity of the message. If the contents of a message are changed, the ICV cannot be recalculated without knowledge of the key in force.

IETF. *Internet Engineering Task Force.* An open international community of network designers, researchers, and vendors concerned with the evolution of the Internet architecture. The most visible portions of the IETF are its engineering working groups, which are organized into several dynamic areas of interest and tasked with identifying or creating interoperable standards or addressing network engineering issues.

IKE. *Internet Key Exchange.* The protocol defined by IPsec to provide secure and timely distribution of key (and related) material between participating IPsec hosts.

ISAKMP. *Internet Security Association Key Management Protocol.* The protocol encoding scheme used by IKE during the establishment of SAs. The ISAKMP protocol is an open-ended conversational protocol, and only a subset of its functionality is specified as necessary for IKE exchanges.

ISO. *International Standards Organization.* A worldwide federation of standards bodies, including groups that define international standards for data processing, data communications, and security mechanisms. ISO standards often complement and occasionally conflict with Internet standards.

integrity. A security service that ensures that modifications to data are detectable. Integrity comes in various flavors to match application requirements. IPsec supports two forms of integrity: *connectionless integrity* and a form of *partial sequence integrity*. Connectionless integrity is a service that detects modification of an individual IP datagram, without regard to the ordering of the datagram in a stream of traffic. The form of partial sequence integrity offered in IPsec is referred to as *anti-replay integrity*, and it detects the arrival of duplicate IP datagrams (within a constrained window). This is in contrast to *connection-oriented integrity*, which imposes more stringent sequencing requirements on traffic, including the ability to detect lost or re-ordered messages. Although authentication and integrity services often are cited separately, in practice they are intimately connected and almost always offered in tandem. (Kent 1998)

Internet. The worldwide network based upon the Internet Protocol (IP) that provides the infrastructure needed for global electronic mail messaging, WWW traffic, and a host of other communications services.

intranet. A local corporate or organizational network based on the Internet Protocol (IP). Typically this term is used to provide a distinction between locally managed IP hosts and hosts on the global Internet that might also be reachable.

IP. *Internet Protocol.* The network-layer protocol in the TCP/IP stack used in the Internet. IP is a connectionless protocol that provides extensibility for host and subnetwork addressing, routing, security, fragmentation, and reassembly. (Huston 1999)

IPv4. *Internet Protocol version 4.* The version of the Internet Protocol used on today's Internet and on the vast majority of IP-based private networks.

IPv6. *Internet Protocol version 6.* The successor to IPv4, also known as the *next-generation Internet protocol.* Version 6 offers the promise of improved functionality, including more address space. Transition to IPv6 is expected to be extremely gradual given the total migration cost.

ISDN. *Integrated Services Digital Network.* A protocol offered by many regional telephone companies to provide native support for both voice and data over a point-to-point connection. ISDN is available to businesses and, in some areas, private residences.

Kerberos. A third-party key distribution technology that provides security services to hosts over an insecure network. Kerberos is an example of an application- (or session-) layer security service that provides some of the basic functionality of IPsec on an application-by-application basis. Since Kerberos is used as a secure distributed authentication mechanism itself, it can dovetail nicely with IPsec in certain implementations by working in an IKE context to establish SAs.

KDC. *key distribution center.* A (typically automated) service available on a network that creates, negotiates, and distributes cryptographic key material to parties in support of one or another security protocol.

key escrow. The controversial practice of safely storing a copy of a private or secret key so that it can be used to retrieve protected data in the event that the key is lost or the key's owner is unavailable.

L2TP. *Layer 2 Tunneling Protocol.* A mechanism used to provide virtual private network service to end users. L2TP is most often employed to allow traveling users to appear to be still connected to a local corporate LAN. By tunneling the traffic over (potentially insecure) networks to an endpoint within the corporation, it causes the traffic—once extracted from the tunnel—to have addresses that appear local.

LAN. *local area network.* A local communications environment, typically managed and maintained locally. Traditionally, a LAN has been a broadcast-based multidrop network, but this interpretation must be flexible in the face of new networking infrastructure trends.

MTU. *maximum transmission unit.* The largest datagram that can be carried within a layer 2 frame. The MTU in IP networking is typically identified as the largest IP datagram (header included) that can avoid fragmentation into smaller datagrams.

multicast. A communications mode on an IP network in which multiple destination stations are addressed simultaneously. These stations may receive multicast datagrams by subscribing to a multicast service and alerting their multicast-aware router (or routers) to this fact. Multicast technology is used by certain applications—such as video conferencing—as an efficient means of contacting a large group of information receivers with a minimum amount of redundant traffic.

NAT. *network address translation.* Also *network address translator.* A function performed by certain firewalls to translate IP-layer claimed source addresses from their original form into addresses that will both obscure the actual sending host and guarantee that the response will arrive by way of the firewall. In addition to security uses, NAT devices are often used when an organization's array of externally routable IP addresses is smaller than the number of hosts potentially utilizing Internet service.

NFS. *Network File System.* A service originally developed by Sun Microsystems to provide remote access to file systems over an IP network. While NFS was originally deployed on Unix hosts, its design affords easy implementation on a wide range of IP-connected hosts.

OAKLEY protocol. A mechanism of cryptographic key exchanges that has been heavily borrowed upon by IKE to develop the specific key exchanges necessary to set up an SA.

OECD. *Organization for Economic Co-operation and Development.* A multinational agency that provides a setting in which member states can openly discuss and develop social and economic policy with an eye to establishing mutually beneficial common practices. One OECD working group established the *OECD Cryptography Policy Guidelines* as an approved document in the hopes of providing a common set of working assumptions for wider consistency in cryptographic export laws.

PBX. *public branch exchange.* A circuit switch device used in traditional (analog) telephony devices. PBX typically provides end-user access to the phone network.

PFS. *perfect forward secrecy.* A security property related to the creation and distribution of key material, whereby any given key's security is in no way dependent upon key material distributed previously. By maintaining PFS, you ensure that the disclosure of certain keys will have no security implication for keys issued later. Certain versions of IKE transactions can be configured to maintain PFS, at the cost of some additional processing overhead.

PGP. *Pretty Good Privacy.* An application originally developed by Philip Zimmerman (now a collection of products maintained and distributed by Network Associates [NAI]) that utilizes a Web approach to distributed trust in a public key security system that allows for rapid deployment in the absence of a centrally administered PKI.

PKI. *public key infrastructure.* The entire coherent collection of protocols, technologies, and written policies that define how an organization maintains, distributes, creates, and validates public keys and their associated identifying information.

PPP. *Point-to-Point Protocol.* A layer 2 framing protocol designed to carry data frames on a point-to-point (two-station) conduit. PPP is a modern variation on older point-to-point framing techniques. It is distinguished by the inclusion in its standards body of specifications for connection establishment, authentication, and the enumeration of supported network stacks. PPP is the most common protocol used for both dial-up and ISDN host connections.

QoS. *quality of service.* A very broad term covering technologies used to provide preferential treatment to certain types of traffic flowing on a network.

RAS. *remote access server.* A general term referring to the class of devices used to provide dial-up network services to computer users over traditional analog or ISDN telephony services. RAS devices are the natural extensions of the legacy terminal servers that provided character-mode access to hosts and servers by way of remote terminal emulation (or the use of genuine terminals).

RED. *Random Early Detection.* A congestion-avoidance algorithm developed by Van Jacobson and Sally Floyd at the Lawrence Berkeley National Laboratories in the early 1990s. When a queue depth on a router begins to fill to a predetermined threshold, RED begins to randomly select and discard packets from traffic flows in an effort to implicitly signal the TCP senders to throttle back their transmission rate. The success of RED is dependent upon the basic TCP behavior, in which packet loss is an implicit feedback signal to the originator of the flow to slow down its transmission rate. The ultimate mark of the success of RED is that congestion collapse is avoided. (Huston 1999)

RMON. *Remote Monitoring.* An extension to SNMP that allows hosts with promiscuous-mode interfaces to collect, collate, filter, and aggregate network traffic and make the results available to an SNMP complaint management station. RMON allows network managers the opportunity to remotely examine the traffic on a LAN segment in a manner similar to placing a sniffer on the segment directly.

RFCs. *request for comments.* Documents produced by the IETF for the purpose of documenting IETF protocols, operational procedures, and other related technologies. (Huston 1999)

RSVP. *Resource Reservation Setup Protocol.* An IP-based protocol used for communicating application QoS requirements to intermediate transit nodes in a network. RSVP uses a *soft-state* mechanism to maintain path and reservation state in each node in the reservation path.

SA. *security association.* A simplex (unidirectional) logical connection created for security purposes. All traffic traversing an SA is provided the same security processing. In IPsec, an SA is an internet-layer abstraction implemented through the use of AH or ESP. (Kent 1998)

SPA. *security posture assessment.* A comprehensive audit of one's entire network designed to characterize both internal and external (through the firewall) security-related design issues, whether implicit or arising as accidental side effects of other design decisions. An SPA is valuable as a starting point when trying to improve or redesign a network's security.

SG. *security gateway.* An intermediate system that acts as the communications interface between two networks. The set of hosts and networks on the external side of the security gateway is viewed as untrusted (or less trusted), while the networks and hosts on the internal side are viewed as trusted (or more trusted). The internal subnets and hosts served by a security gateway are presumed to be trusted by virtue of sharing a common local security administration. In the IPsec context, a security gateway is a point at which AH and/or ESP is implemented in order to provide security services for a set of internal hosts when they communicate with external hosts that also employ IPsec (either directly or via another security gateway). (Kent 1998)

SLIP. *Serial Line Internet Protocol.* A legacy mechanism designed to pass IP datagrams over a serial line. SLIP defined the absolute minimum framing support, and has largely been superseded by PPP implementations.

SMTP. *Simple Mail Transfer Protocol.* The Internet standard session-layer protocol used to transfer electronic mail from host to host.

SNA. *Systems Network Architecture.* The broad term used to describe an entire collection of networking technology invented and deployed by IBM throughout the 1970s and early 1980s. SNA is traditionally thought of as a legacy mainframe protocol.

sniffer. A general term applied to applications and devices that are able to examine all of the traffic on a LAN segment and either store it wholesale or perform some amount of interpretation of the information. Sniffers are used by network professionals to diagnose network anomalies, but they can also be used illicitly to acquire security credentials passed utilizing insecure authentication mechanisms.

SNMP. *Simple Network Management Protocol.* An interoperable IP-based protocol used to aid in the management of a large collection of network devices from a central location.

SPI. *security parameters index.* A value carried in AH and ESP protocols to enable the receiving system to select the security association (SA) under which a received packet will be processed. The combination of a destination address, a security protocol, and an SPI uniquely identifies an SA. An SPI has only local significance, as defined by the creator of the SA (usually the receiver of the packet carrying the SPI), and thus is generally viewed as an opaque bit string. However, the creator of an SA may choose to interpret the bits in an SPI to facilitate local processing. (Kent 1998)

SSL. *Secure Sockets Layer.* A security protocol designed to serve as a shim between TCP and a session-layer protocol (originally and most popularly HTTP). SSL is a flexible mechanism that allows for the selection of mutually satisfactory security protocols and modes, as well as the security identification of one or both parties utilizing a public key attached to an X.509 public key certificate.

TCP. *Transmission Control Protocol.* The layer 4 protocol that provides reliable session-oriented establishment of logical host-to-host connections of an IP substrate. TCP implements an efficient packet acknowledgment system that assures applications of an error-free, properly ordered byte stream.

Telnet. A session protocol designed to work on top of TCP/IP to provide simple terminal-to-application, terminal-to-terminal, or application-to-application data. By far the most common implementations of Telnet are designed for remote networked terminal applications where the Telnet protocol is embedded into a terminal emulator.

trusted third party. In the context of key escrow, the person, organization, or entity that is trusted with the safekeeping of the escrowed key material.

ToS. *type of service.* A field in an IP packet header with a bit pattern that can be manipulated to aid in quality of service (QoS) routing decisions.

TTL. *time to live.* A field in an IP packet header that is decremented each time the datagram is forwarded by a router. When the TTL field becomes zero, the datagram is regarded as no longer valid and is discarded. This mechanism provides protection against routing loops and ensures that datagrams don't get lost on the network looping forever.

UDP. *User Datagram Protocol.* A layer 4 protocol that provides the bare minimum in support services needed to encode application data into IP datagrams and ensure that the data's destination will be a complementary service running on a remote host. Unlike its big sister TCP, UDP supports no error checking, packet acknowledgment, or virtual session. UDP is best suited for simple request-response applications (such as DNS).

VoIP. *voice over IP.* A series of complementary technologies designed to provide telephony-style voice service on top of an IP network. VoIP is of interest to people trying to leverage their existing network infrastructure as well as those looking for a (potentially!) more cost-effective alternative to a local phone switch.

VPN. *virtual private network.* A network that can share physical resources with other VPNs but provide the convincing illusion of privacy. Often a supervisory protocol provides the privacy service. This term is also applied to the permutation in which higher-layer protocols are tunneled over the shared resources to various endpoints within a large network.

WAN. *wide area network.* A network whose components are located at substantial distances from each other. A WAN is typically composed of layer 2 networking technology that has no inherent distance limitations and is often more costly and/or slower (in very general terms) than LAN technology.

Wassenaar Arrangement. A multilateral global arrangement associated with export controls on weapons and dual-use goods and technologies such as cryptography. While it lacks the force of law, this arrangement provides for a basic set of working assumptions regarding the export of cryptographic material among the participating states.

X.509 certificate. A digital document containing key material (typically a public key) combined with fields identifying the subject (owner) and issuer of the certificate. This document is digitally signed by the issuer to ensure validity of the contents.

Bibliography

Chapter 4

Baker, S., and P. Hurst. 1998. *The Limits of Trust: Cryptography, Governments, and Electronic Commerce.* Cambridge, MA: Kluwer Law International.

Communications Assistance for Law Enforcement Act. 1994. 103d Cong., 2d sess., H.R. 4922.

IAB and IESG. August, 1996. IAB and IESG Statement on Cryptographic Technology and the Internet. *RFC 1984.* Internet Society.

Kaufman, E., and R. Thomsen. *The Export of Certain Networking Encryption Products under ELAs as an Alternative to "Key Escrow/Recovery Products" under KMI: A Networking Industry White Paper on Encryption Export Controls.* Cisco Systems, Inc. www.cisco.com/warp/public/779/govtaff/2.html

Kent, S., and R. Atkinson. November, 1998. Security Architecture for the Internet Protocol. *RFC 2401.* Internet Society.

Organisation for Economic Co-operation and Development. March, 1997. *The OECD cryptography policy guidelines and the report on background and issues of cryptography policy.* www.oecd.org/dsti/sti/it/secur/index.htm

The Technical Advisory Committee to Develop a Federal Information Processing Standard for the Federal Key Management Infrastructure, Department of Commerce. October, 1998. *TAC Report-Recommendation (11-98) with tracking,* p31. http://csrc.nist.gov/tacdfipsfkmi/

Wassenaar. December, 1998. *Dual Use List, Category 5, Part 2, Information Security.* Vienna: The Wassenaar Arrangement. www.wassenaar.org/lists/cat5p2.pdf

Chapter 5

Waitzman, D. April, 1990. Standard for the Transmission of IP Datagrams on Avian Carriers. *RFC 1149*. Internet Society.

Waitzman, D. April, 1999. IP over Avian Carriers with Quality of Service. *RFC 2549, Update to RFC 1149*. Internet Society.

Chapter 6

Kohl, J., and C. Neuman. 1993. The Kerberos Network Authentication Service (V5). *RFC 1510*. Internet Society.

Schneier, B. 1995. *Applied Cryptography: Protocols, Algorithms and Source Code in C.* 2d ed. New York: John Wiley & Sons.

Wayner, P. 1996. *Disappearing Cryptography: Being and Nothingness on the Net.* San Diego: Academic Press.

Chapter 7

Housley, R., W. Ford, W. Polk, and D. Solo. November, 1998. Internet X.509 Public Key Infrastructure Certificate and CRL Profile. *RFC 2459*. Internet Society.

Kent, S., and R. Atkinson. November, 1998a. IP Authentication Header. *RFC 2402*. Internet Society.

Kent, S., and R. Atkinson. November, 1998b. IP Encapsulating Security Payload (ESP). *RFC 2406*. Internet Society.

Kent, S., and R. Atkinson. November, 1998c. Security Architecture for the Internet Protocol. *RFC 2401*. Internet Society.

Madson, C., and N. Doraswamy. November, 1998. The ESP DES-CBC Cipher Algorithm with Explicit IV. *RFC 2405*. Internet Society.

Madson, C., and R. Glenn. November, 1998. The Use of HMAC-MD5-96 within ESP and AH. *RFC 2403*. Internet Society.

Maughan, D., M. Schertler, M. Schneider, and J. Turner. November, 1998. Internet Security Association and Key Management Protocol (ISAKMP). *RFC 2408*. Internet Society.

Orman, H. November, 1998. The OAKLEY Key Determination Protocol. *RFC 2412*. Internet Society.

Chapter 8

Ballardie, A. May, 1996. Scalable Multicast Key Distribution. *RFC 1949*. Internet Society.

Berger, L., and T. O'Malley. September, 1997. Extensions for IPSEC Data Flows. *RFC 2207*. Internet Society.

Braden, B., et al. September, 1997. Resource ReSerVation Protocol (RSVP). *RFC 2205*. Internet Society.

Braden, B., et al. April, 1998. Recommendations on Queue Management and Congestion Avoidance in the Internet. *RFC 2309*. Internet Society.

Deering, S.E. August, 1989. Host Extensions for IP Multicasting. *RFC 1112*. Internet Society.

Eastlake, D. April, 1997. Secure Domain Name System Dynamic Update. *RFC 2137*. Internet Society.

Eastlake, D., and C. Kaufman. January, 1997. Domain Name System Security Extensions. *RFC 2065*. Internet Society.

Kent, S., and R. Atkinson. November, 1998. Security Architecture for the Internet Protocol. *RFC 2401*. Internet Society.

Schulzrinne, H., S. Casner, R. Frederick, and V. Jacobson. January, 1996. RTP: A Transport Protocol for Real-Time Applications. *RFC 1889*. Audio-Video Transport Working Group, Internet Society.

Sollins, K. July, 1992. The TFTP Protocol (Revision 2). *RFC 1350*. Internet Society.

Stevens, W. January, 1997. TCP Slow Start, Congestion Avoidance, Fast Retransmit, and Fast Recovery Algorithms. *RFC 2001*. Internet Society.

Waitzman, D., C. Partridge, and S.E. Deering. November, 1988. Distance Vector Multicast Routing Protocol. *RFC 1075*. Internet Society.

Waldbusser, S. February, 1995. Remote Network Monitoring Management Information Base. *RFC 1757*. Internet Society.

Chapter 9

Chokhani, S., and W. Ford. March, 1999. Internet X.509 Public Key Infrastructure Certificate Policy and Certification Practices Framework. *RFC 2527*. Internet Society.

Chapter 11

Glenn, R., and S. Kent. November, 1998. The NULL Encryption Algorithm and Its Use with IPsec. *RFC 2410*. Internet Society.

Harkins, D., and D. Carrel. November, 1998. The Internet Key Exchange (IKE). *RFC 2409*. Internet Society.

Karn, P., P. Metzger, and W. Simpson. August, 1995. The ESP DES-CBC Transform. *RFC 1829*. Internet Society.

Kent, S., and R. Atkinson. November, 1998a. IP Authentication Header. *RFC 2402*. Internet Society.

Kent, S., and R. Atkinson. November, 1998b. IP Encapsulating Security Payload (ESP). *RFC 2406*. Internet Society.

Kent, S., and R. Atkinson. November, 1998c. Security Architecture for the Internet Protocol. *RFC 2401*. Internet Society.

Kohl, J., and C. Neuman. 1993. The Kerberos Network Authentication Service (V5). *RFC 1510*. Internet Society.

Madson, C., and N. Doraswamy. November, 1998. The ESP DES-CBC Cipher Algorithm with Explicit IV. *RFC 2405*. Internet Society.

Madson, C., and R. Glenn. November, 1998a. The Use of HMAC-MD5-96 within ESP and AH. *RFC 2403*. Internet Society.

Madson, C., and R. Glenn. November, 1998b. The Use of HMAC-SHA-1-96 within ESP and AH. *RFC 2404*. Internet Society.

Maughan, D., M. Schertler, M. Schneider, and J. Turner. November, 1998. Internet Security Association and Key Management Protocol (ISAKMP). *RFC 2408*. Internet Society.

Metzger, P., and W. Simpson. August, 1995. IP Authentication using Keyed MD5. *RFC 1828*. Internet Society.

Oehler, M., and R. Glenn. February, 1997. HMAC-MD5 IP Authentication with Replay Prevention. *RFC 2085*. Internet Society.

Orman, H. November, 1998. The OAKLEY Key Determination Protocol. *RFC 2412*. Internet Society.

Pereira, R., and R. Adams. November, 1998. The ESP CBC-Mode Cipher Algorithms. *RFC 2451*. Internet Society.

Piper, D. November, 1998. The Internet IP Security Domain of Interpretation for ISAKMP. *RFC 2407*. Internet Society.

Glossary

Huston, G. 1999. *ISP Survival Guide*. New York: John Wiley & Sons.

Kent, S., and R. Atkinson. November, 1998. Security Architecture for the Internet Protocol. *RFC 2401*. Internet Society.

Index